Environmental Anthropology

Environmental Anthropology

Edited by

Madhu Bala Sharma
Vinod Kaul
Jagadish Chandra Das

Anthropological Survey of India, Ministry of Culture, Department of Culture, Government of India

SERIALS PUBLICATIONS
NEW DELHI (INDIA)

First Published - 2011

ISBN: 978-81-8387-450-2

Published by

SERIALS PUBLICATIONS
4830/24, Prahlad Street, Ansari Road
Darya Ganj, New Delhi-110002 (India)
Phone : 23245225 Fax : 91-11-23272135
E-mail: serials@sify.com

Contents

Part-2
Survival Strategies in the Himalayas

Part-3
Biological Aspects of Adaptation

Part-4
Ecological Variation and Changing Lifeways

Part-5
Ecology, Economy and Population

Part-6
Environmental Perspectives: Multi-disciplinary Approach

Preface

Madhu Bala Sharma & Vinod Kaul

The environment plays a vital role in shaping the culture of people wherever he lives. His safety and security is dictated by the eco-niche. The influence of local environment is clearly apparent in material culture and economic life of the people, which has been successfully brought out in two papers presented by Dr. Ramesh Chandra and M K Raha separately in case of Kinnaurese of Himachal Pradesh, who face harsh and varied environment in different parts of the district: Wet in lower kinnaur, dry in middle kinnaur and arid in upper kinnaur. Likewise Jitendra Singh who studied Garhwal Himalayas clearly brought out that people of different zones have shaped their economy and material culture to counteract and adapt to adverse conditions of Himalayas.

Dipali G. Danda, while analyzing the eco-cultural adaptations of semsa of North Cachar hills emphasizes the role of environment, history and culture in shaping the adaptive strategies of a community.

J. Parthasarathy, while studying the life ways of Yerukula tribe of Andhra Pradesh, shows the adoption of skills for optimum utilization of locally available resources in different habitats. Likewise D. K. Samantha has also shown in case of Korku of Amaravati district (Maharashtra) that change in environment results in change of economy and thereby their culture.

N. K. Ghatak presents a cognized model of beliefs about malevolent and benevolent spirits which exist in the Boksa tribe, who were earlier forest dwellers, of Nainital district to elicit behavior contributing to the well being of the tribe, and in turn maintenance of eco-system. The supernatural veil, according to author, provide some protection to the eco-system against human parochialism and destructiveness.

P. N. Lal attempts to show the influences of altitude, topography, rainfall, soil and slope of the land on the land use and economic life of the people living at low and mid altitudes in the Kashmir Himalayas.

V. Sarkar and R.Sarkar explain the reasons of increased participation of women in productive economy in the inhospitable central & western Himalayas as compared to other regions of the country. In another paper they demonstrate the transhumance mode of adaptation among Gaddi in the Bharmour sub tehsil of the Chamba district of Himachal Pradesh due to the environmental conditions.

R. Gupta and T. Lal describe in detail upper Sutlej valley in Himachal Pradesh. Large scale deforestation in the Sutlej valley has created ecological imbalance. They have suggested a conservational approach to stop forest degradation and to protect the interest of people and forest. In another paper the authors discuss ecology and land use in Thachwa village of Nirmand sub-tehsil of Kullu district (Himachal Pradesh) which is situated in the Middle sutlej valley.

Skin tanning is partly determined by environmental factor like altitude and incidence of ultraviolet radiation, besides genetic endowment. I J S Jaswal discusses the skin tanning variations in six north Indian populations.

M.B. Sharma and D. Chowdhury have discussed the differences in variables such as menarche, reproductive wastage, sex ratio, total numbers of conceptions etc. between sicklers and non sicklers of Gonds of Nagpur to test the hypothesis of selective advantage of sicklers (AS) in a particular environment.

Sanjit K. Chakraborty and S. H. Ahmad studied 14 somatometric measurements among Galongs inhabiting the iodine deficient area of Siang district (Arunachal Pradesh) to find out its effect on health.

A. K. Bhatia is of the opinion that the delayed osseous development in wild monkeys than those in captivity can be due to various stresses and strains of the natural environment.

G. R.Laxmi discusses the effects of parity and socio-economic environment on birth weight.

S. S. Bandopadhyay has brought to focus the nutritional stresses in spite of better economic conditions in migrating Gujjar as compared to settled Gujjar.

In another paper on Gujjar's demographic structure, A.C. Srivastava and R.S.Balgir compare the demographic studies of the settled Hindu Gujjar with the pastoral and nomadic Muslim Gujjar. Though nomadic life has decreased their life span but Muslim Gujjar maintains higher fertility rate and lesser reproductive wastage than the Hindu counterparts.

Dr. Rizvi cites three case studies from Kashmir, Madhya Pradesh and Andhra Pradesh to illustrate how developmental activities, without consideration of local human element, have adversely affected the local populations by disturbing the eco-cultural homeostasis and running their traditional economy.

R. S. Raypa describes the different stages of ecological succession through which Onge of Little Andaman, who were basically hunters, gatherers and fishers have been exposed and the impact there upon which has resulted in the population gradually dwindling:

Subal Chatterjee has analysed the demographic profile of the population of western Himalayas and the bordering districts keeping in mind the physiographic and geomorphic conditions of the area.

Shibani Roy opines that the high frequency of consanguineous marriages among the Asna Ashariya Muslims as an adaptive strategy to prevent gradual disintegration of the family land holdings.

Jayanta Sarkar highlights the role of ecology in shaping the economy, village type and size, and political organization in Arunachal Pradesh, which has narrow valleys, broad valleys and plateau and foot hills.

R. K. Saha has attempted to explain the evolution of social hierarchy in Manipur due to physical, socio-political and human environment.

Sanchita Ghatak analysed adaptations, due to the micro topographic variations of physical environment, of the Semsa and Langia saora, who primarily undertake shifting cultivation. While Langia Saora solely practice shifting cultivation, Semsa due to limitations of shifting cultivation have tried to diversify their economy to the household industry which in turn has affected demographic profile of the two populations.

S. C. Panchbhai has presented a brief appraisal of the various developments in environmental perspectives through different historical phases of modern psychology.

T. K. Ghosh and A. K. Das in their papers have highlighted the role of museums and display pattern for better appreciation of different cultures which are a product of different eco systems.

Pasupati Prasad Mahato has analyzed the structural contents of chow dance of Purulia (West Bengal) and Mayurbhanj (Orissa) in relation to environment.

A. R. Sankhyan has presented a broad spectrum of palaeo-environment during middle Miocene to Middle Pleistocene of shivaliks on basis of fossil faunal evidence.

Welcome Address
Seminar on
Environmental Anthropology

A. K. Danda

I, on behalf of the Anthropological Survey of India, and on my personal behalf welcome you all to this three-day seminar on 'Environmental Anthropology' organized by the North-Western Regional Office of the Anthropological Survey of India at Dehradun. As you are aware, initially the Survey proposed to organize a seminar on Environmental Adaptations to the Himalayas. Of late, discussions on environment evoke so much interest that we felt quite convincingly though, rather compelled to extend the scope of this seminar from the exclusive heights of the Himalayas to the plateaus, valleys, plains, and even to the island territories. As it would be evident from the papers to be presented during the following six academic sessions: various issues pertaining to the relationship of man and environment have been highlighted from almost all over the country. It pleases me most to put on record that besides those from the North-Western region of India in this gathering, we have representatives from North-Eastern, southern, central, and western regions of the country as well as from the island territories of the Andaman & Nicobar.

It is truism that men in their present form are largely the product of environment both external and internal. At the same time, it is also a fact that environment as the governing force has been perceived only by men among all animals and perhaps civilized men alone consciously tried to manipulate the environment to its advantage, particularly in order to have an edge over its controlling forces. As concomitant to this endeavor, men had to change themselves, the process of which in broad but technical sense may be described as one of the mechanisms of adaptation. The ultimate outcome of this seems to be the transformation of an apparent harmonic relationship to a spirit of unhealthy competition.

Environment as a topic for discussion earned general popularity only recently. Anthropologists among academicians however were one among the pioneers to study the effect of environment on man, society, and culture. It needs no evidence to add that anthropologists themselves have travelled a long way from the point they had started in this respect. Today, to an anthropologist environment is not the determining agency for the development of culture and society as it was presumed by some several decades back. What I propose to emphasize here is that environmental determinism as an anthropological argument has lost its weight. Instead, emphasis on a relationship of feedback between man and environment, according to its own merit, has gained eminence.

There are multiple ways of perceiving environment. Even in a gathering like this, when various participants would refer to environment during the next three days, I would not wonder if they do not always mean one and the same thing. Usually more often they do not than they do. It is very important, therefore, that some such discussions of scholars are arranged so that they can have the opportunity to discuss, define and assign specific meaning to it and review the concept and the major associated issues to arrive at a consensus.

Interest in environment in the contemporary world grew out rather of a negative perspective. Civilized man's greed for power and authority led to wanton damage and destruction of environment and disturbance of the nature's balance to such an extent that has brought the humanity on the threshold of disastrous consequences. The present interest in the affairs of the environment is an outcome of the awareness of this fact. What surprises me most in this respect is that in spite of this awareness there has been no perceptible difference in the civilized man's approach to and, nature of exploitation of the environment yet. Even the mad race for having greater control over superior nuclear capability with blatant disregard to the spirit of nature has shown no decline.

Nature took millions of years to develop the human race. The history of modern man: Homo sapiens, is recent, about 40,000 years old. The antiquity of the civilized man is too recent: only a couple of thousand years; a small fraction of the total history of even the modern man. During this short span of existence, the so called civilized creatures have so boastfully exploited their environment that this has led the entire living world to the brink of extinction. It is high time, therefore, that some serious thoughts are given to the issues. It is true that only a seminar of this kind would be no match to the magnitude of the problem in this respect. But I feel fairly assured that this would help spreading the message of wisdom, the nature of adoption of which would in the long run decide the future course of humanity. With these few words and expressing my deep appreciation for the fine job done by the conveners of the seminar I welcome you all again to these three days seminar on 'Environmental Anthropology' and hope that you will enjoy it.

A. K. Danda
Director,
Anthropological Survey of India, Kolkata

Key-note Address
Seminar on Environmental Anthropology

D. P. Mukherjee

Anthropology has to play a unique role in the current world wide movement of environmental awareness, conservation and planning, prevention of environmental degradation, ridiculous utilization of resources and search for an ever brightening future. Environmental consideration is not in itself a new phenomenon in the dialogue between anthropologists themselves. But, this has to be focused in the context of increasing attention to environmental problems and emergence of multidisciplinary endeavors that link up physical, biological and social sciences.

The concept of environment can be meaningful only with reference to the life that emerges within it and the specific organism that it is surrounded by it. It is in this sense that anthropology is a relevant discipline to deal with man's environment. Human environment can be divided into biotic, abiotic and cultural components. Man interact with not only the natural environment in which he finds himself or to which he places his demands but also with the structures built by him and his own developmental activities.

The environmental study in Anthropology can be organized into three major fields of investigation, namely:

(1) Processes of Human origin and ongoing of human evolution – the adaptive radiation of biological and cultural variations;

(2) The awareness and utilization of resources and strategies of their life-support management and

(3) Environmental stresses and limitations of Man's capacity to exploit nature and the need for rationing and maintaining balance between components of the ecosystem.

The story of human evolution is a story of how men responded to the diversities and changes of environment. In the beginning, they survived by subsisting on what environment had to offer. Later, they specialized with skillful hands and visual activity, in hunting and collecting games, fishes and fruits. With the experience and climatic change that favored man, he practiced subsistence cultivation. This was the beginning of a change of environment by men.

Cultural and social changes in response to ecological niches are now known to affect the demographical structures and the genetical make up of human populations. Economic pursuits of isolated populations are inseparable from the environmental settings. But as Dobhzansky puts it "*An idea has gained credence that biological evolution of man has come to a halt when our species developed culture. Confronted with this assertion, a biologist is in an embarrassing position*". True enough, Man became adapted to environmental changes principally by means of Culture. But cultural and genetical changes are continued to be connected by a feed back relationship. The agricultural castes of Southern India for example, form part of the tallest segment of the local population. I have also observed earlier how the subsistence economy of the tribal populations of India are associated with their demographic features nutritional levels, body size, physiological adaptations, incidence of diseases such as colour blindness, abnormal hemoglobin and even such common genetical variations as frequencies of blood groups. Among the poor people, as population of Kurnool district the shorter boy display a smaller risk of offspring mortality than the tall Boy. A senior fellow of Anthropological Survey has recently demonstrated how different sections of Yanadi who have taken to settled agriculture display a marked increase the stature over that observed in other isolated sections of the tribe who are in transition from hunting gathering economy. We are well aware about the trend of declining stature in some tribal populations of India, caught up in adverse socio economic environment as reported by Dr. P. Ganguly of this Survey.

Anthropologists generally agreed about the genetical adaptations that have accompanied the change of natural and cultural environment from nomadism to agriculture - the balanced polymorphism of deleterious genes causing sickle cell or G6PD deficiency and the relaxation of selection against impairment of colour vision, are examples. The natural ecosystem has been further modified by production, agriculture and exploitation of forests for fuel, house and other purposes. This has brought in water-logging and hence the vectors of malaria. Epidemic diseases can not survive in a small and dispersed population as are the hunting gathering groups. Infectious diseases have thrived on increasing population density. Population movements and acculturation have led initially to successive epidemic waves. The isolated virgin populations have no genetical or acquired immunity for new environments. As the population ages it becomes resistant to the changed environment as I communicated to an A.A.A.S. seminar in Anthropology on population age held in Philadelphia in 1971. This was further confirmed by another fellow of the Anthropological Survey of India among the Nulia fishermen of the Puri coast. The endemic diseases have also played an important role in the history of human populations- the gastroenteritis, the respiratory problems and parasitic loads. Dunn has pointed out that biotic variation holds also for the pathogens and the complex environment of the rain forest of Africa carries seven times the species number than those carried in the deserts.

Mourant suggested that selective screening by infections must have favored certain immunological characters which relate to specific blood groups. Vogel & Chakravarthi and others think that the bacillus of bubonic plague is characterized by a H. antigen and the virus of small pox carries a reactive antigen. Plague ravaged areas of eastern Asia and Turkey demonstrate high 'A' or 'B' frequencies at the expense of 'O' and similarly, the small pox epidemics in Northern India in the past are supposed to explain the stretch of high 'B' frequency in the Indo-Gangetic plain. The role of environment in cultural evolution has been considered from early period of theoretical Anthropology not only by those who thought that environment dictated cultural forms but by culture historians and others. More recently a theory of cultural ecology has developed independently of the general ecological framework that applies to biological evolution. Julian Steward separates man the organism from man the super organism.

The technology and productive level which utilize the environment for the organic man, forms the core of culture. Marvin Harris extends this idea to calculate the food-calorie out put per calorie of human labour.

The alternative model of general ecology which includes population ecology combined with the system theory and has a great power of unifying the biological and cultural aspects of human life and as such is truly anthropological. It considers such important biological factors as epidemiology of diseases, the matter of medical Anthropology, the environmental changes and diversities that affect our distribution, development, longevity, survival and reproduction. We examine the belief and ideologies within this frame work – the phenomenon of Indian sacred cattle for example. Culture is considered as a solution to environmental problems and as man's tools of biological adaptation.

Environmental Anthropology should analyze the strategy of resource utilization from the point of view of ecological balance and also ethno-ecology-the knowledge and experience of the people concerned. The best strategy of nutrition, agricultural production or industrial complex must come from people themselves and it is a task of anthropologists to mediate between the people and outside agencies of change. It is often futile to ask the people on the steep slopes of the eastern Himalayas to do away with shifting cultivation or to adopt a new method of sowing seeds replacing the traditional methods they learnt through experience. A colleague in this survey has told me how in the Western fringe of M.P. the peasants grow their crops from east to west in winter to suit with the wind currents. It is again not possibly appropriate to introduce now nutrients without consideration of the traditional diets which may be best suited to the genetic code and cultural make up of the population. Anthropologists know very well how the utilization of resources may jeopardize the life ways of local populations. The poorest tribes live on the richest mines. Can't Anthropologists come forward to mediate between these people's traditional life and the demands of modern developments?

Much of the recent knowledge about human adaptability to the changing condition of life, the adaptive mechanism of human population living under some form of environmental stress have resulted from the studies on Blood pressure. The enormous adaptability of human life has also got its limits and attempts to exceed their limits to reduce functions and produce diseases and death. There are also cultural means to buffer low oxygen pressure for about 25 million people that live at an elevation of about 2000 meters or for 12 million people who suffer from hypoxia at an altitude of above 3000 meters, with corresponding respiratory changes and increase in Hb content in theses populations. The high altitude populations are however immune to the condition of hypoxia. We have recently observed a clear trend of declining perception of Salt and Sugar tastes but children of high altitude populations seem to retain high taste ability. This corroborates with our earlier suggestion of a selective elimination of non taster gene for PTC in Himalayan populations. The special needs of iodine and other nutritional deficiencies, the stress of malnutrition and diseases may alter the living tissues and jeopardize the survival in extreme environments. It is in these areas that biological factors and potentialities may directly influence culture as suggested by Socio-biologists.

The rapid development of industry which is super imposed on our traditional agricultural way of life has gradually led to environmental problems. Intensive drives for production have lead to the threat of depletion of resources. We killed the other species; we burnt and cut down forests, depleted our resources and had created pollution. These gross perspectives of human survival appear to be rather gloomy. Deforestation is said to be progressing at a rate of 20% per year, desertification increasing by 15% petroleum resources to be depleted in about 70 years leading to a drastic change of our elitist life style, irregular explosions of nuclear blast both over ground and underground are said to be causing drought and earthquakes. Chemical fertilizers diffusing from advance countries are contaminating food and causing soil erosion. Demographers estimate that the three fourths of the population of the developed world will live in urban centres and about a half of the third world will huddle together in the cities by the mid 21st century. The long deprived but unaware majority of the population now wanting more and more of the share of the luxury. Time, which is the most precious wealth and was used for aesthetic and creative and educational pursuits have become elusive.

Anthropologist has a task of not only measuring the present and analyzing the negative aspects environmental change; they must come forward with positive solutions, for a prosperous and happy future and to caution against a luxuriant over growth. There are already signs of positive efforts to replace fuel energy by Solar, Chemical fertilizer by organic; recycling of wastage and rediversification of wealth. Anthropologists can find out suitable strategies in the light of their experience of comparative studies and evolutionary out look. Along with the conservation of wild life we have at least an equally important task of saving human population we are in danger. If humans are not the measure of all things they are at least the chief concern of anthropologists. We must utilize our talents to develop the natural environment which is essential for human life. Other wise we shall loose our nutrients, the perception and appreciation that make us what we now consider as human. By studying simple groups anthropologists have gained important insight of human interaction - how people response to perturbations and stresses, diseases, energy flow and food availability, climate and activity requirements. We have only a few integrated studies of human ecology that have been conducted successfully. But the potential returns of such studies will provide us with the information useful for maintaining the delicate balance of the bio-sphere. For these hopes to materialize, both biological and cultural anthropologists must work together to make a place that is due to them in the centres for environmental activities. I believe that the Anthropological Survey of India could contribute significantly. University departments should also come forward to share the responsibility of the environmental research at all levels.

I therefore, look forward to a successful outcome of this important seminar.

D. P. Mukherjee
Professor of Anthropology, Calcutta University

Part-1

Tribal Cultures in Diverse Eco-systems

1 Quest for Environmental Adaptation Among the Kinners of North Western Himalayas

RAMESH CHANDRA

Environment posses challenge to the existence, survival and perpetuity of human societies no matter wherever they have dared to settle – in islands, coastal regions, plains or high mountains. Geology, topography, climatic conditions have their say in moulding the way of life for any society living in particular conditions. The environmental phenomena are responsible to some extent for the origin or development of the cultural behaviour of the society. In other words, how a society will live and what code of conduct, in terms of physical context and social set up will it adopt, has a direct bearing on the environment that envelops it; cultural behaviour of a society can easily be viewed as leaning heavily on its environment. Immediate surroundings (in physical sense) determine to a great extent the material culture of the society and also plays its role in framing the norms and rules for various social systems. The relation of environment and cultural treasures of any society could be understood in two distinct ways, one, culture itself works as 'environment' within the larger frame work of environment that surrounds the people or culture functions as part of the whole environmental system and two, environment has its deterministic value in shaping cultural behaviour (cf Vayda, 1978 : xi). It is the latter view point that gets due attention here. Human beings, both as individuals as well as a group, suitably respond to environmental conditions as countervail to the situation in the interest of their survival, thus perpetuating their lot. For environmental adaptation of the man while the physical anthropologists may provide a charter illustrating the phenomenon in the best possible way (Montagu, 1962; Cohen, 1969; Stott, 1962), a social/cultural anthropologist would perhaps restrict at the doings of man within the framework of 'culture' to define all those actions of man in the light of environmental determinism. More so, man as a member of a corporate group - society - has also evolved certain mechanisms, ethos and social systems to face the challenges of the environment.

Though not many studies on environmental anthropology exist as such, yet a fresh look at some of the existing researches done among different societies coupled with fresh attempts to interpret or reinterpret various cultural practices in the light of man's quest for coping with the environment have revealed some significant findings in terms of strategies adopted by them which have culture as basis and survival/perpetuity as the genesis. 'Ecologic relationship of three ethnic groups - Pathan, Kohistani and Gujar - in Swat area of Pakistan' (Barth, 1956), 'Potlatch system of kwakiutl' reinterpreted by Piddoke (1965), 'Rituals regulations of environmental relations' dealing with pig surplus among the Tsembaga of New Guinea (Rappaport, 1967) and 'Territorial expansion and aspect of Warfare' among the Maoris of New Zealand (Vayda, 1961) are some such illustrations. Similarly in Indian scene also not many attempts have been made to understand role of environment in the make up of social systems and life style of the people. Vidyarthi (1963) viewed ecology giving it a bearing on religion - that too of 'local order' - and this was followed by other anthropologists who studied environment within the framework of religious complexity and ecological interdependence with economy and other institutions (Varma, 1977; Prasad, 1978; Sandhwar, 1978; Morab, 1980; Chandra, 1981). Nevertheless these studies provide some understanding of the role of environment in shaping the 'religious world' and fulfilling some needs of the people living in particular environments. Adaptation forms the nucleus of understanding the relationship of society with its environment. It is true that adaptation itself is dynamic and keeps pace with its variables - the organism and environment which do not remain constant for long. The relationship and interplay between behaviour pattern and productive technology enables us to understand environmental adaptation. A close view of this phenomenon or process of interplay between environment and responding behaviour patterns yields a balanced plane - the adaptation for society to exist, survive and perpetuate.

"It is the functional relationship of relevant environmental factors that cause organizational relationships. Anderson viewed that "creative cultural core-enviornmental nexus is little affected by historical factors and inter-societal relationships. The equilibrium of socio-cultural environmental systems is long lasting. "The hypothesis of adaptation of man to environmental conditions through socio-cultural institutions and behaviour has been widely employed" (Mann, 1981 xi). In this paper such an illustration has been attempted to explain the quest for environmental adaptation of a people - the Kinners - living in high mountainous region in the north-western Himalayas. The north-western Himalayas present in general an environment peculiar of its own which is considered to be harsh, tough and challenging to the people who have taken shelter in this mountainous region. However in the case of Kinners, I would try to demonstrate as how best these people have stood by and faced the challenge of tough and harsh environment by way of adaptation.

This paper is based on a field research conducted in Kinnaur, Himachal Pradesh, among the people known as Kinners, during 1970-72 with some further substantive research in the similar environmental area in Himachal Pradesh until 1974. To demonstrate the quest for adaptation in the mountainous environment, the Kinners have shown a great deal of their efforts many of which are consciously done suiting to the requirements of 'maintenance of equilibrium of socio-cultural-environmental system' (Physical context) and quite a few are followed just intently in the interest of the same (social context). I would take up all such adaptations presented by the Kinners as model and key remedy for survival in the tough and challenging mountainous environment at a latter stage after I give a glimpse of environment of Kinnaur.

To clarify the position I would consider all process and products of adaptations of material culture as adaptations of physical context since they are visible in concrete terms as a 'saving device' or countervail to the posed situation; whereas all such adaptations which have taken form in the social systems and are not concretely visible but add to a great deal to make the survival easy for these people and have indirect rewards for the quest for environmental adaptation would be deemed as adaptations of social context. More so all adaptations of physical context could be regarded as adaptations at individual level and those of social context would give a clue for adaptations at a corporate group level as they concern and involve all the members of their society as a whole for the benefit of all the members of the society.

Environment

Kinnaur is considerably secluded and rugged area nearly 250 kms. away from Simla – the state capital – in deep north-western Himalayan range. The whole district comprises of rugged and lofty terrains of the Himalayan range. Altitude of the district ranges between 2000 metres to 4500 metres. The face of the region presents high mountains and low dales and is marked by precipitious sky high mountains with their peaks covered with perpetual snow (District handbook 1961). The Kinner Kailash Mountain of great Himalayan range lies between the eastern and north eastern faces of the area and western Tibet. The district is divided into 3 sub-divisions namely Nichar, Kalpa and Pooh. Incidentally these administratively divided sub-divisions also correspond to natural divisions based on ecological conditions. Geologically mountains present a varied picture. 'Rocks varying in age from pre-cambrian to permocarboniferous are exposed in Kinnaur. The district can be sub-divided in three main sectors viz. (1) Between the border of Kinnaur and Mahasu district (presently Simla) and Jangi;

(2) Between Jangi and Shipki la comprising slates, graphytes, phyllites etc. and (3) Area north and West of Shipki la.

In general, Kinnaur has shown a variety in geological formations and that has some bearing on environment too. At places mountains are quite hard, solid and stony whereas at other places they are composed of loose rocks to the extent that with the rise of temperature during day and gales, the rocks start loosing their base and boulders fall; and it becomes quite dusty all around. This kind of geological formation is more evident in Pooh sub-division where Khatra dhang needs a special mention. In Kalpa and Nichar sub-divisions rocks are more stony and stable in nature. How geological formations determine the life style of the Kinners will be discussed a little later after I describe the climatic conditions and other ecological factors.

Kinnaur, though a cold place by its location in Himalayan range, gives a varied picture from the climatic conditions view point. One may feel the marked difference from the heat of tropics to freezing temperature of snow bound area. This varied climate is conditioned by the intensity of rainfall, temperature, snowfall and nature of vegetation. Rainfall in this area is from ordinary to scanty with the advancement in its territory. Monsoons have easy access upto Nichar, have some way to Kalpa and do not have access to Pooh region and beyond. As a consequence, it rains sufficiently well in Nichar, to some extent in Kalpa and almost nil in Pooh region and beyond. The annual rainfall, as per District handbook 1961, varies from 46.51 cms. to 90.72 cms. with an average of 21.51 cms. At the subdivision level, average rainfall in Pooh is approximately 40.00 cms., Kalpa 51.5 cms. and Nichar 70.5 cms. respectively. This variation in rainfall has contributed to a great deal in determining the environment at the local level and the Kinners have borne this in mind for adaptation as well; from the rainfall point of view the entire district could be divided into three zones namely (1) moist zone - comprising of the area of Nichar sub-division, or western part; (2) moderate zone - Kalpa area or central Kinnaur; (3) dry zone - Pooh area or the north and north-eastern part of the district including Hangarang valley.

During November to March Kinnaur experiences heavy snow fall and remains covered with thick snow. Average snowfall recorded is 2.16 metres per year. There are several surrounding mountains covered with perpetual snow as well. In general climate is cold. The temperature varies from place to place in the district depending upon the extent of forests; altitude, rainfall and snow fall. The mean maximum temperature in dry zone or Pooh area varies from 58°F in October to 78°F in July and the mean minimum temperature varies from 50°F in April to 67°F in August (District Handbook, 1961).

Flora is an inherent part of environment and plays an important role in adaptation for the Kinners, for they base heavily on flora for their material culture as well as dietary habits. Moist zone and extension of it, the moderate zone, are considerably rich in forests. The dry zone comprising of north and north eastern parts does not have much greenery. This area presents almost a bare look of their mountains which are loose in their formation and are quite dusty in nature and as such no thick forests are seen. This is mainly because of variation in soil type and climatic conditions. Whatsoever greenery is seen is in the form of agricultural land and some perrineal trees of Cederous etc. In general Pinus, Cederous and Abies are some commonly found genus in the forests of Kinnaur. *Pinus Gerardiana, Longifolia* and *Willichiana, Cederous devadara, Picea smithi* and *Abies Pindro* form the major bulk of Kinnaur forests. Depending upon the variation in rock type, altitude and rainfall these forests are divisible into two zones:

The moist zone forests in western Kinnaur: They comprise Taranda range forests. On the left side of the valley with northern exposure, forests come much lower down towards the river than they do on the right bank, while isolation of direct sun light restricts the spread of vegetation. On the left side, the forests are particularly continuous from the (Sutlej) river side at about 1000 metres to alpine pasture at 4000 metres, the right base consists of grass lands and higher up are the forest belt.

Dry zone forests of Kalpa and Kilba Kailash villages: In this zone low level pine is neoza which forms a very open forest. Above this are deodara forming pure forest belt with light mixture of neoza. Still above these there are blue pine and spruce followed by silver fir between 3000 metres to 4000 metres. Timber of these forest trees is used in many ways in the material life of the Kinners and flowers are used in decoration and offering to deities (Chandra, 1981: 274).

Mention about agricultural crops and horticultural produce would also show their distribution pattern depending upon the ecological conditions with whatever little variation there may be Maize. *China, Kodo, Ogla, Phaphra, Kungni, tulai,* in Kharif and wheat, barley, buckwheat, cheston (black pea) in Rabi crops are the main serials grown in moist zone areas whereas in dry zone only Maize, *Ogla, Phaphra* and *Bathu* are grown. Potato is grown as a cash crop in moist zone area quite profitably. Apple, Peer, Grapes and some plums are the fruits of horticultural produce in moist zone which do not grow in dry zone area. Likewise Neoza (chilgoza) walnuts and to some extent Almonds are the main dry fruits grown in dry zone area. Wild apricot (*chulli*) is widely grown throughout the district and edible oil is extracted from its seeds. Cultivation is the main occupation besides sheep rearing, domestication of *dzo, dzomo* and Muleteering etc., for Kinners. The distribution of cultivable land with irrigation facilities is given in the following Table 1.

Table 1
Distribution of Cultivable Land with Irrigation

	Cultivable land (in acres)		
Land Area	*Total cultivable land*	*Irrigated*	*Non-Irrigated*
Kinnaur	23075.50 (100%)	12226 (52.98%)	10849.50 (47.07%)
Dry zone	6370.50 (27.60%)	6370 (100%)	-
Moderate Zone	8605 (37.29%)	5323 (60.70%)	3382 (39.30%)
Moist Zone	8100 (35.10%)	632.50 (7.8%)	7467.50 (92.13%)

Source: Census of India 1971 (provisional tables)

The dry zone has total irrigated cultivable land whereas the moist zone has almost non-irrigated land with moderate zone having 60% irrigated land. This has an impact on the total adaptation process of the Kinners.

As mentioned, agriculture forms the basis of livelihood. Land in general is not much fertile and landholdings at the 'household level' are usually small. Situation is still worse in the dry zone area where cultivation could be done only with the help of irrigation. "Agricultural lands are spread over from high mountain to low levels and are distinctly divided into three types:

1. *Kanda:* Agricultural land in the higher reaches usually at a height ranging from 3000 metres to 45000 metres. Such land yields only one crop in a year and remains covered with snow over a considerable period.
2. *Gaonang or Kimsaring* : Agricultural land situated at the village level. Two crops may be realized with some pressure.
3. *Neole Land* : Agricultural land is at the lower level than the village. Usually it is stretched upto considerably low height. It is fertile and produces two crops in a year. In some moist zone areas people realize even three crops.

Agricultural fields are on the slope of hills in form of terraces and Kinners do practise terrace cultivation (Chandra 1981: 278). Generally each Kinner household has its agricultural land spread over in all the three levels no matter how small or big and as such has to cover a vast distance either on steep ascents or descents to work on the land. Thus the situation of unconsolidated land spread in vast area of harsh environment has itself posed problems as how best the people can manage various agricultural operations to realize the yields.

Adaptation–Physical context

The harsh environment and inaccessibility have made an impact on population size among the Kinners. The entire district having an area of 6520 sq. kms. has a population of 49673 only with a density of eight persons per square kilometer. This is considerably a thin concentration thus leaving more space to nature in the form of mountains, forests, pasture lands etc. According to climatic conditions, Kinners have shown adjustment with regard to their settlements, village size, households and population distribution. An attempt is made in table 2 in this regard. It is revealed from the table that usually villages in mountainous environment are small in size (less than 100 households and population less than 500 persons). Other Himalayan areas also present similar picture in this regard (Chandra, 1974). Studies done by various anthropoloigists in U.P. Hills, Ladakh and Sirmur areas clearly support this view. Further in moist zone villages, average household size is more as compared to dry zone villages (6.00 persons per household and 5.40 persons respectively). Pressure on land is more in moist zone, but land is also more fertile as compared to dry zone land and yield two or even three crops and as such an intent adjustment is accomplished by the people in this regard.

The Kinners irrespective of variation in topography at intra-regional level, face intense cold climate throughout the year. More so area being mountainous it is often difficult to get relatively bigger even lands to construct the dwellings.

To face the cold climate, Kinners construct their houses in such a manner that it saves them from cold to a great extent. Normal pattern of house construction is that they face some hill to check the icy cool breeze. Entrance doors are usually small. Rooms have a very small ventilator round in shape in the wall at a height of nearly one and a half metre or so from the floor through which one can see outside as well; or, a hole of considerable size is made in the ceiling itself to let the smoke of hearth go out and natural light to fall in the room to make it a bit bright and things kept inside visible. In some cases even ventilators are not thought of as necessary and the room is made quite compact and cozy to avoid cold. Another adaptation to the cold environment is that the Kinners build a winter dwelling called Gunsa. The winter dwelling – Gunsa is usually made either underground or in the inner portions of the first floor. Gunsa is used for living purpose during the months of snowfall. Necessity of Gunsa is felt more in eastern parts of dry zone villages where snowfall is relatively more than the moist zone area and as such Gunsa is not, therefore, seen in Nichar area at all.

Table 2
Census of Kinnaur Village

	Rainfall (cms)	*No. of villages*	*Villages with households*			*Villages according to population distribution*				*Average size of household*
			Less than 50	*50-99*	*100-199*	*Less than 200 persons*	*200-400 persons*	*500-999 persons*	*1000+ persons*	
Dry zone	40.00	32	12	13	7	10	15	5	2	5.40
Moderate Zone	51.50	24	4	12	8	1	10	8	5	6.26
Moist Zone	70.50	21	8	5	8	2	9	7	3	6.00
Kinnaur	54.00	77	24	30	23	13	34	20	10	-

Source: Adapted from Census of India 1961 District Handbook and Census of India (Provisional).

House constructions in Kinnaur reflect the environmental accordance in their structure and material used as well. For instance in moist zone where it rains sufficiently well and thick vegetation is found, besides slate stones found in abundance, houses are built in stories - in a smaller patch of land, as big even patch of land is rare and the construction material used is wood and stone mainly. House walls are erected by alternate layers of wooden beams and stone pieces, floor is made of wood, ceiling is supported by a wooden structure and slate-stones and the shape of roof is kept sloppy. This helps in avoiding the rain water which rolls down in no time. Even snowfall will also not effect it because of the roof being sloppy in nature. In Kalpa region, representing moderate zone, houses are usually built on the same pattern as has just been described for the similar reasons; however in some areas houses more akin to dry zone villages are also seen. In the dry zone area houses are built of some wood, stone, Bhojpatra (*Betula utilis*) and/or Burtse grass. Mud is used for plastering the floor, cementing wall, and for construction of roof material. Here roofs are made flat, for, it doesn't rain much here and then the roof works as space of utility, for drying chulli seeds (wild apricots) and other things as and when required. Lesser use of wood, stone and no use of gabled slates for roofs which are flat and not sloppy, these all are based on the environmental conditions prevailing at the local level.

In the name of furniture, Kinners keep woolen mats called Khercha prepared from goat hair; some wooden furniture is also used now with the advancement of technical know-how in the area of crafts. In some well-to-do houses woolen carpets are also used. The idea of this is just to avoid cold, of course, besides reflecting the socio-economic condition of the house. Until recently wooden wares were much in use like Dongbo (to prepare saltish tea) and traditional water container etc. Some skin sacks are also used to store the items like flour, spices and butter etc. The skin is easily available from the sheep and goat herds owned by the Kinners.

The climate being cold Kinners use woolen garments throughout the year. These dresses are heavy and warm to provide sufficient protection. Pure wool available locally from sheep, owned by each household, is used for the purpose. From head to toe body is covered with woolen dresses. A set of dress for women consists of a *Thepang* (cap), *Choli* (blouse), *Dhoru* (woolen 5 meters long sari tied in style of Lungi), *Gachchang, Bunkub* (socks) and *Spona* (shoes made of leather and wool). Male dress consists of *Thepang, Kameez* (cotton shirt), *Chhuba* (long woolen coat), *Sutan* (woollen trousers), *Bunksub* and *Spona*. It is obvious that only a heavy woolen robe can save the people from intense cold and hence this is used. Procurement of wool is also based on environmental conditions as in such climatic conditions rearing of sheep and goat is but obvious for they are not merely used for wool production but in many other ways which will be alluded during discussion.

Some variation in climatic conditions at local level is evident in dress types also. In moist zone where woolens are worn round the year, it remains cold even during day time but in dry zone area due to bare mountains it becomes somewhat hot with the rise of sun. More so atmosphere becomes dusty due to loose soil of mountains. Under such circumstances Kinners of dry zone villages also wear cotton dresses which are easy to wash. Women wear *Kurta* and *Salwar* (cotton Punjabi style ladies dress) and a woolen jacket instead of full woolen dress. They use *pattu* (woolen shawl) when it is cold. Men also use cotton shirts in abundance and instead of *Chhuba* they wear short coats. Cotton clothes used by women are generally of dark shades which absorb dirt to some extent and also the natural heat. This could be understood as an intent effort to countervail the situation of dusty and cold climate. Another adaptation observed from the local variation point of view is of women's hair do. In moist zone area Kinner women do one pleat of hair whereas dry zone Kinner women tie number of pleats and tie their hair tightly and preferably keep them inside the Thepang. This hair style is commonly practised in all such environmental areas viz. Lahaula, Spiti, Ladakhi and in parts of Tibet. This is so because of dusty atmosphere; as it is not possible to bath and wash hair every day. Women wash and clean their hair usually after a fortnight or even after a month.

This, though minor yet significant adaptation at personal hygiene level on the part of Kinner women, cannot be ignored while talking of their quest of adaptation.

Food habit and intake of food items is significantly important in the quest for adaptation of these people. We have listed the items of agricultural produce and horticultural rewards. A hypothesis that in cold climate such things are required which provide sufficient amount of heat and energy comes true in case of Kinners. Kinners intake is largely in forms of protein rich diet in terms of mutton, maize flour and pulses; oil and fats in terms of locally extracted chulli oil ghee and butter prepared from the milk of cow (whatsoever they have) and goat and sheep and carbohydrates in form of rice and potato etc. For warmth, drink, locally called *Ghanti*, and beer (*Chhang*), are taken on regular basis; besides, some dry fruits like neoza, walnut etc., are also consumed. *Ghanti* is prepared from Barley or some fruits like apple, chulli and grapes etc. Its use is so essential in Kinners' life (to save them from biting cold) that Ghanti got sanctified by the religion and attained so much importance in Kinner's socio-religious life that no ceremony or ritual can take place without offering *Ghanti* to the deity (*op. cit,* 279). *Chhang* prepared from rice also gives good amount of warmth to the people. Besides all these even the corns of Ogla and Phaphra generate lot of heat in the body, when consumed. As mutton is a rich protein diet, it is used in regular life and like ghanti it also got its importance and prominence by the element of sacrifice in religious pursuits of the Kinners. Purpose of sacrificing goat or sheep, besides venerating or propitiating the deity, is obvious, and that is consumption of mutton which is so essential for survival in such cold places. As described elsewhere in Kinnaur where Hinduism does not prevail but Buddhism dominates the area and as a tenet of it sacrifice of animal is prohibited, religion of local level has given these people a remedy in form of morphism of some deity of lesser order like yulsa in shape of goat/sheep horns. Then there are several evil spirits like Zimbo, Digyt and Lande who need be appeased with the offering of goat/sheep; and the purpose is served i.e., Prasad is distributed in form of mutton of the sacrificed animal. Keeping Yulsa at each house on roofs is rather a must and for its morphism one has to have goat/sheep sacrificed; this goes without saying. Thus Kinners have sought solution to their requirement to cope up with the cold environmental conditions (Op. cit., 289).

Cattles have played some role in the quest of environmental adaptation of the Kinners that is vital for them. Type of domestic animals, their availability and distribution etc. clearly show the effect of environment as Kinners keep and use these animals in accordance with the environmental factors. For milch cattles it is significant to note that buffaloes, which are domesticated at lower heights and almost in plains, are not domesticated by the Kinners in general. This may be due to the climatic conditions and high altitude that Buffaloes can't survive in such area. The Table 3 given below about the domesticated animals (as per Census of 1971) revealed that altogether only nine buffaloes were there in Nichar area. Cows as found in abundance in the plains are also not seen in herds there. The intense cold climate is best suited for Yak a prominent cattle of Tibet. Some mixed breed of yak and cow called *choru* or *dzo* (male) in moist and dry zones respectively, and *dzomo* (females) are the common drought and milk cattles. Ploughing is done by *dzo* in moist and moderate zones. However in dry zone villages, mules and even donkeys are used for different agricultural activities viz., ploughing, thrashing and husking etc., for there are not many dzo owned by the people. More so, mules and donkeys are owned by the Kinners as transport and pack animals. Muleteering is an occupation of some Kinners in the dry zone villages. This has been so under special circumstances that the Kinners had trade links with far off places in and out side the country until recently and as such needed pack animals. These animals are best suited for ride and transporting the goods on briddle narrow mule paths in the mountainous tracks.

Big number of sheep and goat in Kinnaur is nothing but a response to the prevailing environmental conditions. As mentioned earlier the sheep and goat are used for wool, milk and milk products, protein diet and religious purposes thus

Table 3
Domesticated Animals and their Distribution

	Moist Zone	*Moderate Zone*	*Dry Zone*	*Total*
Cattle (dzo and dzomo)	8976	7890	5236	22102
Buffaloes	9	-	-	9
Horses/Ponies	99	385	463	947
Donkey	110	603	902	1615
Mules	8	5	264	277
Sheep	17999	27004	19620	64623
Goat	6841	19616	11928	33385

Source: Census of India, 1971.

fulfilling the requirement of adaptation from different view points. As a quest for adaptation it is seen that the Kinners maintain and domesticate animals in accordance with the varying local environmental conditions. To illustrate the point, it is observed that as fodder and pasture lands are in abundance in moist zone area, people domesticate rather hefty animals (e.g. *dzo, dzomo* and cows), whereas with the decrease in the availability of such facilities in dry zone villages Kinners keep light animals which suit more to the local environment (e.g. sheep, goat, mules etc.)

Adaptation–Social context

Cultural adaptation, understood in terms of appropriate organization of social relations and value system, comes out after engendering the need by relationship of society with its surroundings. The social system of the Kinners shows a great amount of potential for environmental adaptation. In order to maintain the well balanced equilibrium between socio-cultural-environmental systems and to substantiate various adaptations to meet the challenges relating to physical context, social systems have extended scope for complimentary-supplementary situation. It is already mentioned that in Kinnaur lands are less fertile and scattered; landholdings are small and need joint venture to realize production. There is need for the people to live united at the production. There is need for the people to live united at the domestic unit level to work in joint venture on their lands, look after different economic pursuits viz., agriculture, horticulture, sheep-rearing and muleteering etc. which all put together, no individual can attend and look after well. Notion of jointness and mutual cooperation are must in the interest of the easy survival in such environments. More so, under circumstances of limited resources available in nature, a check on population growth to avoid further pressure on land and the resources is very necessary. It is evident from Stott's views on this issue, "the most evident devices for limiting human population are cultural in character. In case of infanticide it is a self conscious one. In many cultures the taboo upon sexual intercourse during lactation and long nursing period would have the effect of spacing out births. The institutions of marriage and the customs and sexual morality that go with it, must have the effect of limiting the number of children" Stott (1962 in Vayda, 1978, 102). The Kinners observe some of these practices for similar reasons; what is most significant is marriage form in which fraternal polyandry practised by these people. It is with the practice of fraternal polyandry that the Kinners have horizontal or vertical extended household based on the idea of jointness, mutual cooperation and division of labour. Due to their following polyandry the Kinners could maintain the plurality of economic pursuits, meet the call for intent check on population growth and could "keep the members of 'domestic unit' united ..... ratio of working hands or adults to children high ....." (cf. Chandra, 1981).

The concept of extended households of either type horizontally or vertically based on polyandry further strengthen the position of these people by cementing kinship ties among the members, as all brothers remain united through the common wife. The whole unit works as a 'domestic unit' for all practical purposes. Gangun-Nangma kind of households based on Tibetan family system, followed in dry zone or north-eastern Kinnaur are also based on the practice of polyandry where significance is attached to horizontally extended joint households. In such cases all property, both movable and immovable, remain intact and is transferred to the next generation like that as children are also owned jointly (Chandra,

1972). Fragmentation of property would make the situation Chaotic and unviable for the people in this environment, and the Kinners dare not challenge the environment on this account unless they feel confident of managing their lives by some other sources. In polyandry a good reward is seen in terms of adaptation and perhaps on this assumption it could be noted that fraternal polyandry is practised, atleast in India, by the people living in hills at a height more than 2000 metres approximately, viz., the Khasas, Lahulians, Spitians, Sirmurese or even the Toda of the Nilgiri hills.

Pattern of kinship ties are greatly influenced by the factors of socio-cultural importance keeping pace with environment. However this could be perhaps best understood as adaptation to the relationship of the society and its productive system and need for social security (ultimate goal being survival and perpetuity). As evident from my study as well as the one done by Raha et al., 1975, the Kinners have shown some specific trends in this regard i.e., kinship. They have a close knit kinship structure based on ethnic hierarchy, idea of jointness and concern for 'domestic units' and 'corporate group'. "As in polyandry brothers marry a common wife and a child born of this union, considers all the brothers as his father .... So, the term for the father and all his brothers become same" (Raha *et al.* 1975). Similarly in case of households based on allied forms of polyandry as described elsewhere there is a common term for father, his brothers and their wives equal to the term for father and mother respectively (Chandra, 1972). Some more significant adjustments keeping pace with the environment are also seen among the Kinners for a strong quest for maintaining jointness and group solidarity. These are based on marriage net work, distance and identity etc. Terms Shakpo and Baisa commonly used through out the area referring to wife's brothers and sister's husbands respectively, and Ajang and Ane which stand for father's sister's husband and wife's father and for father's sister and wife's mother respectively, do reveal their importance in the light of above discussion.

In brief, to put forward support for significance of environmental adaptation, as reflected through kinship system of the Kinners, it could be added that "a bilateral system such as ours (followed by the Westerners) is closely related to people's freedom to choose their own spouses rather than have their marriages arranged; they establish their own households regardless of where their parents live, and men and women inherit wealth equally from both parents. On the other hand, the choice of spouse, rules governing where people will reside after they have married, and modes of inheritance are very different when people reckon their kinship affiliations patrilineally (Cohen, 1969: 285-6). Following the quest of adaptation the Kinners are patrilineal by descent, patriarchal by rule of property inheritance (again emphasis is laid on joint treasure) and patrilocal by residence, i.e., they reside in the inherited house of their fathers. To sum up the kinship patterns are closely tied to the society's strategy of adaptation for betterment in their condition from the point of view of their quest for deriving easy existence.

Summing Up

From the discussion and material provided here, it can be noted that the Kinners' quest for environmental adaptation has been a success to a great extent. The environmental conditions of this mountainous region are conspicuously tough and pose much challenge for human survival. The Kinners who took this region as their home since ages have shown a tremendous amount of patience, sharpness and mental ability in accepting these challenges; and have moulded themselves in terms of their physical, socio-cultural requirements in such a way that the adjustment seems to provide ready answers to any question that relates to their environmental conditions or factor. It has been clearly demonstrated by their material culture and social systems that the Kinners as a 'people' have a well adjusted plan of balanced 'environment -- socio-cultural framework' for survival and perpetuity of their society.

Acknowledgement

I express my indebtedness to the Director, Anthropological Survey of India for his awarding me two research fellowships during the years 1970-74, which enabled me to conduct this research in Northwestern Himalayas. I am also thankful to Dr. P.K. Misra, Regional Officer, Southern Region, Anthropological Survey of India, for providing necessary facilities in the preparation of this paper.

References

Anderson, J. W. (1973), 'Ecological Anthropology and Anthropological Ecology'. In *Hand Book of Social and Cultural Anthropology*, J. J. Honigmann, ed. Chicago.

Ashley Montagu, M. F. (Ed.) (1962), *Culture and Evolution of Man*. New York.

Bonghey, A. S. (1971), *Man and the Environment*, New York.

Census of India 1961. District Hand Book of Kinnaur (Pt. 6).

Census of India: Provisional tables for Himachal Pradesh, Shimla.

Chandra, Ramesh 1972. Socio-economic Study of Kinnaurese of Himachal Pradesh. Report. *Anthropological Survey of India* (Unpublished).

Chandra, Ramesh (1972), Notion of Paternity Among the Polyandrous Kanet of Kinnaur. *Bulletin of Anthropological Survey of India*, Calcutta. Vol. XXI, No. 1 and 2.

Chandra, Ramesh (1974), Polyandry in a Himalayan village, Report. *Bulletin of Anthropological Survey of India*, Vol. XXIV, Nos. 3-4 (in press).

Chandra, Ramesh (1978), *The Kinner : A Study in their Society and Religion*. Ph.D. Thesis, Lucknow Univerity, Lucknow.

Chandra, Ramesh (1981), 'Sex Role Arrangement to Achieve Economic Security in Northwestern Himalayas'. In *Asian Highland Societies in Anthropological Perspective*. C. Von Furer Haimendorf (ed), New Delhi, Sterling Pub.

Chandra, Ramesh (1981), Ecology and Religion of Kinners : Mountain Dwellers of Northwestern Himalayas'. In *Nature Man Spirit Complex in Tribal India*. R.S. Mann., (Ed.), New Delhi: Concept Pub.

Cohen, Y.A. (1969), *Man in Adaptation: The Bio-social background*. Chicago.

Fredrik Barth (1956), Ecologic Relationship of Ethnic Groups in Swat, North Pakistan. *American Anthropologist*, Vol. 58.

Mann, R. S. (1981), *Nature Man Spirit Complex in Tribal India*. Delhi.

Morab, S.G. (1980), *The Soliga: A Study in Ecology, Economy, Society and Religion of a Hill Tribe*. Ph.D. Thesis. Ranchi, Ranchi University.

Piddoke Stuartat (1965), 'The Potlatch System of the Southern Kwakiutl. A New Approach in Environment and Cultural Behaviour, A.P. Vayda (ed.), Texas 1978.

Prasad, R. K. (1978), The Paruhiyas: A Study in Cultural Ecology and Tribal Dynamics. Series Indica 8 Wien.

Raha, M. K., S.N. Mahato and R. S. Negi (1976), Kinnaurese Kinship System: A Terminological System, *Bulletin of Anthropological Survey of India*. Vol. XXV, No. 3-4. Calcutta.

Sandhwar, A. N. (1978), The Korwa of Palamu: A Study in their Society and Economy. Series Indica 9. Wien.

Stott, D. H. (1962), Cultural and Natural Checks on Population Growth. In, *Culture and the Evolution of Man*. M.F. Ashley-Montagu (ed.), New York.

Varma, K.K. (1977), *Cultural Ecology and Population*. New Delhi, National Pub. House.

Vayda, A.P. (ed.) (1978), *Environment and Cultural Behaviour* (First Published 1969).

Vidyarthi, J. P. (1963), *The Maler : A Study in Nature-Man-Spirit Complex*. Calcutta: Book Land Pvt. Ltd.

Wiesenfeld, S. L. (1967), Sickle-Cell Trait in Human Biological and Cultural Evolution In *Environment and Cultural Behaviour*, A.P. Vayda (ed.) Texas, 1978.

2

Eco-Cultural Adaptation of the Semsa

DIPALI G. DANDA

In earlier ethnography, a particular culture was generally studied as a self-perpetuating unit, independent of other neighbouring cultures. Of late, it has been realized that no culture can operate by itself. It is considered as an integral part of a given eco-system. One culture not only interacts with other cultures, it interacts with various elements of the environment as well for sustenance of life of its members. Daryll Forde (1934) is one of the pioneers among anthropologists to emphasize the study of relationship between man and his environment, resources, technology and social organisation. He introduced the concept of socio-cultural ecology that connotes the interrelationship between organized human behaviour and material world. Julian Steward (1955) also laid emphasis on the relationship between man and his environment, of course, with an evolutionary inclination.

In the later researches, various concepts like equilibrium model, cybernetic model etc. emerged to emphasize the interrelationship between ecological system and the concerned community. Eco-system theorists consider various populations and other animal beings as equal partners of this system and do not take into account the history of individual social groups and its inter-relationship within the system. They view a community in a state of equilibrium among the species. The population of each species is regulated by relations among species in a given environment. This may be true for the species that are primarily governed by natural instincts without having intervention of culture working as an adaptive mechanism. On the other hand, every single human community living in a common environment has its distinctive culture. Though their material base of life is acquired from the same environment, and resources are utilized in almost the same way, the communities may show a wide range of variation in other spheres of culture which may be due to their respective cultural history and the consequent cultural capability. A close examination of the situation where, in a similar environment, a number of communities live side by side may provide a deeper understanding of the phenomenon.

In the North Cachar hills of Assam a number of ethno linguistic communities share a common ecological niche. The majority of the population there are sylvan, largely dependent on the forest for their subsistence. The only urban center in the district is Haflong which is also the district headquarters. The population of the district is composed of different tribal groups; the Naga-primarily the Zemi, the Kuki-primarily the Hmar, and the Dimasa (Kachari) are important among them. There are also some Khasis in the area. As these people share the same physical environment and then show considerable similarities in the material aspects of their life. Shifting cultivation is the basic means of subsistence of all these communities; bamboo and elephant grass are the major housing materials for all of them. None of the groups knows the use of pottery. Technological attainments of all these groups are nearly at the same level. Though the sharing of material traits is common, diversities in other spheres of culture like settlement pattern, social organization and political system are conspicuous.

Among these communities of the North Cachar hills, the Dimasa are the most numerous. The three groups of tribal people prefer to live in different elevations of the hills. The Naga like to live on the hill tops and the Dimasa on the valley. The Kuki occupy an area in between. The Dimasa of the valley are primarily rice growers of both *jhum* and wet fields. The

Kuki and the upland Naga also grow paddy but they have no wet land. All of them, however, grow paddy for self-consumption. The Khasi and to some extent the Kuki, maintain orchards of orange and banana and sell their produce in the market. The Dimasa also sell the surplus vegetables grown in their *jhum* fields. None of these tribes sell rice in the market. A few exchange paddy with their own people for some selected commodities and/or labour.

Preference for different elevations and land use pattern of the people may be explained in terms of their respective adaptive strategy for survival of the peoples themselves in an apparently common ecological niche. Their choice of elevation seems to be culturally circumscribed too. In earlier days, the tradition of inter-village feuds was very common among the Nagas. So they chose to set up their villages on the hill-tops to have some security. The land use pattern adopted by them, therefore, becomes to some extent subservient to the settlement pattern of the people. The Dimasa, on the other hand, is basically a river loving folk. Wherever they live, they always prefer a flowing river by the side of their habitation. Their villages also are mostly named after rivers. Even the Semsa, the primordial isolated section of the Dimasa, who could not live in the valley, have their village at a site between two rivers.

The adaptive strategies thus, are not governed by the environmental factors alone; rather the distinctive characteristics of different ethno linguistic groups also play their role with regard to their adjustment in a given ecological setting. So the various groups of people live in the North Cachar in demarcated areas according to their choice, convenience and cultural capability. They are, however, well aware of their physical boundary which they consider as the spatial expression of their cultural boundary. They restrict their movement for the purpose of subsistence as well as marriage within this boundary. In other words, these limitations ascribed by environment help them to maintain their respective ethnic boundary as well as to maintain a harmonious balance in a particular ecological niche. Thus environment plays a great role in moulding the material base of life of the people, specially the economy. But habitat and economy cannot explain the finer nuances of culture in a geographical area as Forde rightly observes: "The study of the relations between cultural patterns and physical conditions is of the greatest importance for an understanding of human society, but it cannot be undertaken in terms of simple geographical control alleged to be identifiable on sight. The culture must, in the first place be studied as an entity as an historical development; there can be no other effective approach to interrelations of such complexity" (Forde, 1970: 464-465). Every single community in a multi-community cultural setting has its own distinctive history - which roots of differentiation among the cultures. How history effects the community life may be examined in a micro situation from the North Cachar hills of Assam.

The Semsa is a small community who live in the dense forest of North Cachar hills. They once formed part of the Dimasa tribe. When the Kachari kings were at constant war with the Ahoms and shifted their capital from Dimapur to Maibong, a section of them took shelter in a place somewhat far away from Maibong and settled there and ultimately became isolated. The place they inhabit has got a special characteristic of having a number of natural saline pits. The village Semkhor where the Semsa live derived its name from these saline pits. In Dimasa dialect '*sem*' means salt and '*khor*' means source i.e., the place is the source of natural salt. The section of the Dimasa who settled in this village got associated themselves with their environment and instead of identifying themselves as *Dimasa* (son of the river) they took the name *Semsa* i.e. 'son of salt'. It signifies that their immediate environment contributed to their cultural identity and became an integral part of their physical existence. They attained a new ethnic identity forsaking the old one. Though they speak Dimasa dialect, the feeling of ethnicity derived from their Semsa identity is distinctly conspicuous in every sphere of their life. Their environment helped them to raise a boundary between them and the Dimasa of the area. Their relationship with the immediate ecology have gone so deep that the people cannot think of moving out of this village in spite of high population pressure on land. The density of population in Semkhor is 170 per sq km whereas in the whole of North Cachar it is 16 per sq. km. They believe that as they are Semsa, they cannot survive outside the village Semkhor. This idea got reinforced by an incident as narrated below:

Once in remote past a few Semsa families shifted to a new place and set up a new area of habitation. Within a short while of their shifting, an epidemic broke out and most of the migrants died. The surviving few got so much frightened at this that they returned to their original village forthwith. This is a century old incident but still very fresh in the minds of the people. A deserted village site is pointed out as the proof of this fact.

The saline pits have become object of veneration by the Semsa. Thus a natural object has become part and parcel of the life and living of the people there. Now Semkhor and Semsa of the North Cachar are independent units in the strict sense of ethnic composition.

It is evident that the Semsa emerged as an ethnic group as the effect of multiple factors like historical, ecological, and cultural. They still bear their relationship with the Dimasa by sharing in common certain salient characteristics of the social structure like double bilineal system of descent and dialect. But at the same time, the Semsa has developed certain special characteristics of their own which make them a discrete identity amidst other cultures of North Cacher. Their dialect, though belongs to the Dimasa tongue, has grown characeristic Semsa vocabulary of its own. Their typical dress and hair style, especially of the males helped them to be distinct and thus created an identity independent of the Dimasa culture. Besides they maintain their social boundary by resorting to village endogamy. As they are surrounded by non-Dimasa people like Naga and Kuki, they observe the clause of tribal endogamy rather strictly for perpetuation of their continuity. On the other hand, the Dimasa consider the Semsa backward and avoid any marriage relationship with them. As a result, the latter had to develop certain mechanisms for survival of the group with self-respect. Village endogamy emerged as a mechanism of getting a mate which in turn strengthened the sense of group solidarity among the people and helped them creating an independent Semsa culture. Incidentally, the Semsa live only in Semkhor.

The Semsa depend on forest for their survival. Utilisation of forest for different purpose is given in the following chart:

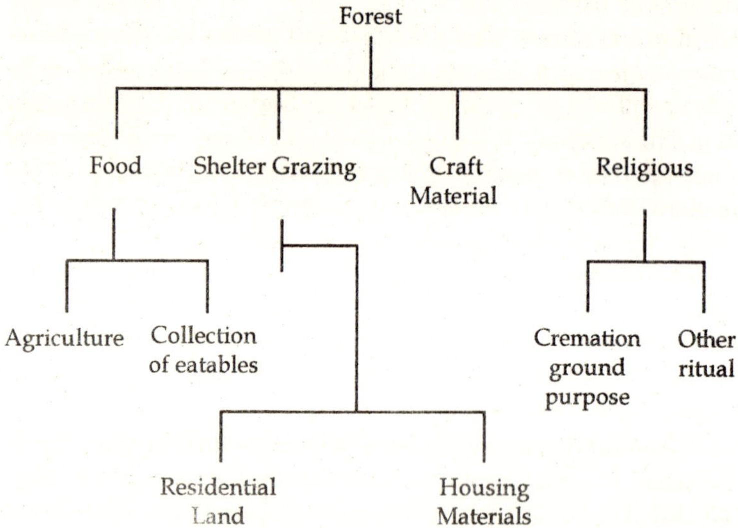

As the Semsa do not shift from their natal village Semkhor, with the growth of population, they had to make various kinds of adjustments with their environment. Forest is primarily the source of food through cultivation and collection of eatables. There is no individual ownership of the land. The whole area is owned by the members of the community. The areas of forest meant for shifting cultivation are, however, divided among the five patriclans.

One can cultivate any amount of land he likes with the formal permission of the head of the respective patriclan. Once a plot of land is cultivated, the same is kept fallow for four to five years, and it goes back to the clan. Previously *jhum* cycle had about nine years. Now-a-days, due to growth of population and consequent pressure on land, the same is recultivated after about five years.

They grow paddy and other vegetables simultaneously in the *jhum* field. The Semsa collect eatables in the form of roots, fruits, tubers and leafy vegetables throughout the year. Residential land is also part of the forest on the hill slopes. There is acute crisis of residential land in Semkhor, as the pressure on homestead land increases with every new marriage in the community where neolocal is the residence rule. Considerable adjustment is also made in order to accommodate all families within the boundary of the village.

A portion of the forest is marked and fenced for grazing purpose. This land is communally owned and all owners of cattle of the village fence this part of the forest during the cultivation season. All the villagers have equal right for collection of firewood, banana leaves, and housing materials from the forest.

The Semsa men are reputed for basket making and their baskets have good demand in the neighbouring areas. Some Semsa men supplement their income by selling of baskets. Canes and bamboos are collected from the neighbouring forests. There is, however, no clanwise demarcation of the forest. Cremation grounds are located within the settlement area itself. Five particlans have their respective cremation grounds. Similarly space for the worship of clan gods are specified within the settlement area. As the Semsa live in a single village, the territory of the area gods of different particlans is also within the boundary of the village itself. They made this sort of adjustment to confine themselves within their habitat.

As already stated, the Semsa marry among themselves within the boundary of the village. Marriage relations are restricted among seven particlans and seventeen matriclans. Continuous marriage for the last two hundred years within the boundary of the village among the same set of population has some effect on the Semsa as a mating group. As Steward observes, "Social group as determined by marriage customs as well as economic activities in particular environment have undoubtedly been crucial in the differentiations of local populations and may even have contributed to the emergence of varieties and sub races of men". (Steward: 1955: 31).This phenomenon has already made this small, isolated population a distinct bio-cultural entity.

The Semsa are numerically small, (population less than a thousand), relatively isolated, and non-literate. Forest is the main resource to the people. Their economic system is almost self-sufficient and confined to their village. Their socio-cultural life rotates within the limit of their village. Their meager relationship with other surrounding people is limited to their economic transactions mainly through barter. The Semsa entirely depend on their environment for their subsistence and survival.

It may however, be pointed out that the emergence of the Semsa from the Dimasa was not a motivated effort on the part of the people. This happened as a natural process due to multiple reasons: historical, ecological, and cultural. At the same time there was not any intentional maneuver to sever their relationship with their parental stock. The Semsa emerged as discrete cultural group as a result of the eco-cultural adaptation to their typical environmental condition and historical antecedents.

From the above presentation of the micro situation of the North Cachar and specially the Semsa case it can be stated that environment plays a role in the life and culture of the people. But environment alone cannot explain all the facts of adaptation in a particular culture. A number of other factors are discernible in the process of adaptation. History of the group is one such factor, responsible to a great extent, for a particular mode of adaptation in a given environment. Third dimension is added to the sphere of adaptation by the specific culture of a group. Culture itself is often viewed as adaptive mechanism of the people that manifests itself in multiple forms among the different populations in the apparently identical environmental situation. Impact of a particular culture in this respect is very significant.

References

Ford, C. Daryll (1970), *Habitat Economy and Society*. London : Methuen and Co. Ltd.

Steward, Julian H. (1955), *Theory of Culture Change*. Urbana : University of Illinois Press.

Danda, Dipali (1981), The Semsa Economy. *Journal of the Indian Anthropological Society*, Vol. 16, No. 2.

3 Environment And Adaptation – A Case Study of Two Yerukula Villages in Andhra Pradesh

JAKKA PARTHASARATHY

Theorists who advocated an ecological point of view usually observe environmental circumstances in combination with a community's technology and even determining forms of social organisation. As Kroeber (1969 : 350) rightly opines "that on the one hand culture can be understood primarily only in terms of cultural factors, but that on the other hand no culture is wholly intelligible without reference to the non-cultural or so-called environmental factors with which it is in relation and which condition it", is incontrovertible. In Levine's (1975 : 213) words, "culture is composed of the energy systems of a population and its methods of exploiting them, of the organization of social, political, and economic relations of language, customs, beliefs, rules and arts – of everything that is learned from other people or their works". This view emphasizes the functional importance of culture as an adaptive mechanism, as a generic term for the sum total of the ways; a society organizes its relations to its environment and the way it is internally organized. Thus culture can be conceptualized a strategy of adaptation.

Cohen (1968 : 3) defines a population's adaptation as "its relationship to its habitat" and states that "the adaptation of man is accomplished by cultural means, through the harnessing of new sources of energy for productive ends and through the organisation of social relations that make it possible to use these energy systems effectively" (op. cit. p. 4). Elesewhere (1968: 4) he says, "Adaptation in man is the process by which he makes effective use for productive ends of the energy potential in his habitat". Thus adaptation refers to a particular aspect of ecological relationship. That is, how people in a particular environment characteristically extract and use the resources of that environment. This paper seeks to explain the life of the Yerukula, a scheduled tribe in Andhra Pradesh and to understand them in two different locations in terms of environment and adaptation.

The Yerukula

The Yerukula are one of the largest tribes of Andhra Pradesh numbering 1,62,560 (1971 Census). They are also found sparsely in Karnataka and Tamil Nadu states. According to 1971 census, the Yerukula who are classified as a scheduled tribe in eleven districts of Andhra Pradesh form 0.31% of the total population of Andhra Pradesh and 9.81% of the total scheduled tribe population of the state. It is noticed that 86.53 per cent of the Yerukula population live in rural areas, while 13.46% are in urban areas.

The Yerukula are known by several names like Korcha, Korava, Kaikadi etc. They were once a nomadic population and like many other nomadic groups they are also gradually settling down. The Yerukula derive their name from 'Yeruka' which means 'knowledge or acquaintance'. The females of the tribe profess to be experts in fortune telling. They speak a dialect called '*Yerkali basha*', which appears to be a mixture of several Dravidian speeches. The common belief is that the Yerukula are congenital thieves. I have discussed this issue elsewhere (Parthasarathy: 1979). Generally, even now police keep a watch on them. The Yerukula are divided into three large endogamous groups on the basis of their traditional occupations. They are *Bidari* Yerukula (collectors of forest produce) *Dabba* Yerukula (Basket making) and *Kunche* Yerukula (fortune telling). The present study is mainly concerned with Bidari Yerukula whose primary occupation is collecting the curry leaf (*Murraya Kolnigii*), tamarind, pulses, rock salt and other minor forest produce from their immediate ecological setting and selling it in the nearby villages on barter basis, which still continues. Besides the above activity, they also make mats, ropes, twines, slings etc.

Area of Study and its Topography

The present paper is based on the data collected from two villages namely Epilapalli and Kalagalla of Anantapur District in Andhra Pradesh during 1979 and 1981. Anantapur district is the western most of the 'ceded districts' and is surrounded on the east and north by Cuddapah and Kurnool districts respectively and its south and west sides are flanked by Chittoor district and the state of Karnataka.

The Villages

Epilapalli

The village Epilappalli is situated in Kadiri east division of Kadiri taluk of Anatapur district, Andhra Pradesh. It lies at a distance of 33.5 kilometers to east of Kadiri town and 8 kilometers from B.Kothapalli, a village which is situated on Kadiri-Pullivendla road. Also the village is located amidst huge hills, surrounded on the cast and south by Palakonda hills. Its north and west sides are touched by Durgamkonda hills and Donnalakonda hills respectively. The Palakonda hills are the most extensive of the ranges lying in Cuddapah district. This range runs in a south-easterly direction along the borders of Pulivendla and Kadiri taluks and soon rises over 1,750 feet. From its initial course, it presents a ridge towards the uplands and a scarp along the higher slopes, improving in vegetation around a few villages including Epilapalli.

The forest around the village is situated on the principle hill range of Palakonda and Durgam hills. The forest is of a dry deciduous type and fall under *Torai* or fuel forest. The climatic and geographical conditions of the village have a direct bearing on its flora. A few common trees and shrubs that are found in this area are: *Maha buxifolia* (Utti), *Erythroxylon monogynum* (Devadasi), *Diosphyros chloroxylon* (Ullinda),

Mimusops potatorum (Chilla), *Vitex altissima* (Nemali adagu), *Murrya konigii* (Karepaku), *Webera corymboga* (Kommi), *Cochlospermum gossypisum* (Konda gogu),*Ixora parviflora* (Kurivi), *Carissa carandas* (Kalivi), *Zizyphus jujuba* (Ganga renu), *Pergularia daemia* (Dussaru Teega) etc. In this area most of the vertebrate fauna among wild life is present. A few are suscristatus (wild boar), *Melussus Ursinus* (Boar), *Hystria lincura* (Porcupine), *Hespestese dwardsii* (Mongoose) etc.

The average annual rainfall in this area is 685.5 mm (26.99 inches). The rainfall is mostly confined to the months of May to November. The highest temperature is 42.2°C (108°F) and minimum is 12.2°C (54.0°F). In the summer season the relative humidity is generally 50 to 60 per cent in the mornings and 35 to 40 per cent in the afternoons. Winds are generally light to moderate with some what strong during the south-east monsoon season.

The village Epilapalli is inhabited by the Bidari Yerukula only. There are no other castes or tribes in this village. The Yorukula population in the village is 290 with (141 males and 149 females) 55 households. Except two Pucca houses, others are huts. Only a foot path connects Epilapalli with the surrounding villages. For 290 Yerukulas, only one small well and a small pond provide drinking water. There is no electricity in this village.

Kalagalla

The village Kalagalla is situated in the north-east corner of Anantapur taluk. It lies at a distance of 27 kilometers north-east of Anantapur town on the Kuderu (Kudair) - Penakacherla metal road. Kuderu, the Panchayat, and the revenue firka head quarters is at a distance of 8 kilometers from this village.

The habitation area is encircled by isolated peaks and rocky clusters which is characteristic of the Deccan plateau. The forest is of scrub jungles with trees of average height. A few patches of dense growth can be noticed only in low lying portions. At present, the flora of the area reflects some of the representative general on a modest scale in a very small proportion. Date palm (eethaku) is grown in larger extent in this area. A few of the vertebrate fauna among wild life is present. The average annual rainfall in this area is 544.1 mm (21.42"). The highest temperature is 43.2°C and minimum is 14.2°C. The period from February to May is the driest part of the year when the relative humidities are 50-60 per cent in the mornings and 20-30 per cent in the afternoons. Humidities are higher in the south-west monsoon. Winds are generally light to moderate to acquiring some strength in the south-west monsoon season.

The total area of Kalagalla village is 14.30 square miles. It is a multicaste village. Most of the households of the Kapu (Reddy) and the Kuruba castes occupy the center of the habitat. The households of the Ekila, Ediga, Boya and Vodda castes are on the northern side of the main street. Surrounding the Boya and Vodda households are the households of Sale, Marati and Chakali. The households of Madiga (Harijans) are situated separately in the western corner of the habitat. The households of the Bidari Yorukula occupy the complete northern side of the main street opposite to Kapu and a Brahmin household and their locality is known as 'Koracha geri'. Adjacent to the Yerukula are 3 households of Sugalis (Lambadi tribe). The Bidari Yerukula population of the village is 277 (142 males and 146 females). There is a bus from Anantapur town to Kalagalla village which passes via Kuderu. The Yerukula have a separate well in their locality for drinking water. The Yerukula are not allowed to fetch water from the other three wells of the village. There is no electricity in this village. For irrigation purposes, some of the cultivators have diesel pump sets in their wells.

Occupation and Environment

The recognition of a close relation between occupational structure and settlement should be taken to imply that the habitation will depend on the resources of the natural environment. In his analysis of primitive economics, Forde (1960: 331) mentioned: "men by his skill and labour produces a kind of secondary environment, which is a function of techniques as well as of resources. This ecological framework, product of man's skill and his environment, varies widely from one people and region to the next, according to the different materials at hand and the individual bent of their interest and skills". While discussing about ethnic segmentation and economic interdependence, Barth (1968; 324) stated "Thus the 'environment' of any one ethnic group is not only defined by natural conditions, but also by the presence and activities of the other ethnic groups on which it depends". Keeping the above views in mind, let me described the occupational structure of the Yerukula of two villages with reference to different environments.

As stated earlier, the primary occupation of the Bidari Yerukula is collection of minor forest produce and selling it in the nearby villages. In olden days the Bidari Yerukula moved from place to place with their commodities carried on the back of asses and bullocks. As they possessed a large number of domestic animals like asses, bullocks and cows, they were also engaged as carrier of goods. About this Ramesan (960: 8) writes: "Before the advent of British in India ..... this tribe viz., 'Kabadi' or 'Uppu', or 'Bidar Korawar' owned hundreds of asses, bullocks and barren cows and utilized them in the transport of salt, grain ....". After settling down, at present many of the Bidari Yerukula in the studied areas, besides their traditional occupation, have adapted to some other occupation due to the impact of surrounding environment. Table 1 gives the distribution of occupational activities of the Bidari Yerukula in Epilapalli and Kalagalla villages.

In Epilapalli village 16 households of the Yerukula are completely depending upon their traditional trade of 'Karepaku' leaves. 'Karepaku chettu' (Murraya Konigii tree) is a small tree available in large extent in the Palakonda and Durgam hills. The dry as well as fresh leaves of the tree are useful to flavour curries. Two or three Yerukula families as a group go to forest along with their assess, gunny bags to pick up the leaves of 'Karepaku'. They spend about 10 to 15 days in the forest and each family will collect as much as 20 to 30 bags of it. After returning to Epilapalli village, they get it dried on the wide surfaced rocks.

Later on, husband and wife along with their small kids carry the dried 'Karepaku' which is packed in gunny bags on the back of asses, and sell them in the neighbouring villages and towns. Throughout the distance they go by feet along with their asses. They prefer to sell the 'Karepaku' for grains than for cash. They do not spend the earnings during the period of selling, instead the female folk go from house to house begging for food. It takes about 20 days of sojourn to dispose of the commodity which they possess. The amount of grain and cash which they collect is sufficient enough for their family until they go out for another trip after a period of two months. This occupational activity of 'Karepaku' selling is completely absent in Kalagalla village, because of non-availability of 'Karepaku' trees. The Yerukula of Kalagalla village do not possess asses as they do not require afforesaid service by these animals.

Table 1
Distribution of Occupational Activity of the Bidari Yerukula Households in Epilapalli and Kalagalla Villages

	Epilapalli		*Kalagalla*	
Activity	*No. of house holds*	*Per cent*	*No. of house holds*	*Per cent*
Karepaku (Murraya Kenigii) selling	16	29.09	-	-
Household industry – broomsticks, ropes, twines and slings	9	16.36	-	-
Household industry – mats and bags	-	-	11	24.44
Agriculture	5	9.09	8	17.78
Agriculture + household industry	4	7.27	7	15.56
Firewood and forest fruits selling	6	10.91	-	-
Sheep and goat selling	7	12.73	2	4.44
Sheep, goat selling and agriculture	3	5.45	1	2.22
Milk selling + Agriculture	-	-	9	20.00
Bonded labour	-	-	4	8.89
Carpentry	-	-	1	2.22
Thievery	5	9.09	2	4.44
TOTAL	55	99.99	45	99.99

Besides trade, the Yerukula are experts in making mats, ropes, broomsticks, twines, slings, bags etc. This household industry is also dependent on the availability of the raw materials in their surrounding environment. In Epilapalli village, the Yerukula household industry produces only broomsticks, ropes, twines and slings but whereas the Kalagalla village Yerukula produces only mats and bags of date palm. In Epilapalli, the Yerukula, for their household industry, depend upon the shrubs of *Cochlospormum gossypium* (Konda gogu), *Pergularia daomia* (Dussaru teega) etc. which are grown in large extent in Palakonda hills. The Yerukula after collecting them, prepare various types of broomsticks, ropes, twines and slings and sell those in Pulivendla weekly market. The Yerukula generally go on foot to weekly market which is at a distance of 16 kilometers through forest track. Again they use the ass as a mode of transport. In Kalagalla village the Yerukula prepare only mats and bags in their household industry because, in large quantity the date palm trees are grown in the surrounding area. The Yerukula males carry the mats and bags to Anantapur by bus and sell them for cash, quite frequently, because of the convenience of communication.

The soil of Epilapalli and surrounding areas is predominantly of the black clay type. Epilapalli records average rainfall of 26.99 inches and with lowest net irrigated area can not boast of any important irrigation sources. The Yerukula of this region are completely depending upon rain for the agriculture. Only five households of them are doing agriculture and other seven household industries. The crops grown in this village are Jonna (Jowar), various pulses of Ulava (horse gram), Kandi (red gram), Pesara (green gram), Senaga (Bengal gram) and verusenaga (ground nut). They use compost manure only. After storing the required grain and pulses for domestic consumption, they sell the remaining pulses at Pulivendla market. The soil of the Kalagalla village is predominantly of the black type. Due to the flow of river channels from the Pennuru river which is at a distance of 40 kilometers the high level underground water belt of the Kalagalla area can provide sufficient water in the wells to irrigate the lands. In Kalagalla village 25 households of the Yerukula are involved in agricultural activity besides other subsidiary occupations. For irrigation purposes, some of the cultivators have diesel pump sets in their wells. With the popularization of well-subsidy scheme by government, the digging of the wells is steadily going up in recent years. The more important of the crops grown in this village are paddy, Jowar, Pulses, onions, chillies, gingelly, castor etc. The crops are normally rotated so that the natural soiled content is considered. They use modern fertilizers for high yields.

Selling of fire-wood and forest produce like fruits etc., are one of the most important occupational activity in Epilapalli village. Six households of the Yerukula are completely depending upon this activity. They collect firewood from the trees of *Diospyros chloroxylen* (Ullinda), *Maba buxifolia* (Utti), *Erythroxylon monogynum* (Devedasi), *Pterospermu, Vitex altissima* (Nemaliadugu), *Zizyphus cenoplia* (Pariki) etc., and sell them regularly in Pulivendla town. Ass is a good transport of fire wood for them. In Kalagella, this activity is completely absent because the firewood which they extract from the shrubs are not even sufficient for self consumption. They often purchase fire wood from outside.

Livestock always had a prominent place in the Yerukula economy of Epilapalli. In Epilapalli the Yerukula are good traders of sheep, goat and pigs whereas in Kalagalla they are expert in selling calves, bullocks and cows. In Epilapalli the Yerukula have large number of sheep and goats than cows and bullocks. The rearing of these ovine is practically monopolized by the Yerukula in Epilapalli region. During day time, the herds are allowed grazing but during nights they are securely penned in an enclosure just adjacent to their house. Seven households of the Yerukula are completely depending upon this trade of sheep and goat and other three households are indirectly dependent on this trade. They sell animals at Pulivendla weekly market, which is claimed to be one of the best cattle market in the Cuddapah district. Pigs are largely reared in Epilapalli. They sell pig manure which is of great demand for garden cultivation. In Kalagalla village, the Yerukula trade in calves and bullocks to a large extent. They sell them in the surrounding villages. Poor soil, sparse vegetation and susceptibility to seasonal uncertainties are the main reasons contributing villages. Poor soil, sparse vegetation and susceptibility to seasonal uncertainties are the main reasons contributing to the scarcity of grazing facilities in Kalagalla village. Paddy and ragi hay constitute the chief fodder in this area. Groundnut haulm and horse gram chaff are also used as fodder for animals.

Dairying is a necessary concomitant of livestock economy and is undertaken in a fairly substantial scale in Kalagalla village. Along with other castes, most of the Yerukula own a cow or a buffalo to provide milk and milk products for sale. Many Yerukulas of this village supply milk to hotels of Anantapur town. Bus is a good transport for them. However, in Epilapalli village, the Yerukula think that selling milk is a sin.

In Kalagalla village, four Yerukula households earn their livelihood as bonded labourers of neighbouring Hindu peasantry. Under this system, a written contract is made between the employer and the labourer stating that the latter will serve the former for one year, or for an indefinite period. The *Jeetagadu* or labourer of this type works in the field and attends to other work given by the Reddy or master from morning till night. In return, he is provided food two times a day, clothes twice a year. This system is completely absent in Epilapalli village because of the absence of other castes within the settlement and the existence of the mode of independent economic activity.

In village Kalagalla, one household of the Yerukula has taken up the occupation of carpentry due to the close interaction with carpenter caste. This Yerukula family prepares agricultural implements of the Yerukula cultivators. In Epilapalli, the Yerukula are depending on a carpenter of neighbouring village for agricultural implements.

Though the Yerukula engage themselves in several occupations, they are frequently suspected of committing thefts. In Epilapalli, five households and, in Kalagalla, two households, depend on thieving to a large extent. Their female folk help them in giving clues about those houses where they have a good possibility to commit thefts. In Epilapalli, the thieves mainly concentrate on sheep, goat and other cattles whereas in Kalagalla they go for ornaments and utensils. When the male persons are caught in thieving and kept in jail, their women folk do labour work until the return of their men.

Social System, Environment and Adaptation

As Nicholas (1963) noted in his comparative study of two villages, a kind of ecological influence affects the intensity and flow of social relations. The social system of any community, whether relatively complex or simple, rests on surrounding environmental and natural systems. Let us discuss some of the aspects of the adaptation on the social systems of the Yerukula living in two different environments.

We already know that the village Epilapalli is situated in forest terrains where the Yerukula population is sparse and communication difficult. The principal links among them are based on kinship. Individual equality as Kinsman is assumed; dependency and subordination among men are minimized. Their primary organization is concerned with preserving the natural resources, maintaining social harmony and building proper sentiment for the ongoing functioning of the society. They are liberal in maintaining their social organization according to their community wishes, without interference of other castes and tribes who are living far away from their settlement. Social co-operation among them is extended for beyond the family unit and even the families are very cohesive. Consciousness of caste hierarchy with reference to other castes never arises because they are minimizing their activities with dominant caste groups.

But in contrast to this, an extreme instance of individual autonomy is found among the Yerukula in Kalagalla village. Social co-operation among them is limited to nuclear families and even the families are not very cohesive. In Kalagalla, the Yerukula are living along with other castes. As Misra (1979: 11) in his study of the Indian nomads notes, "In the highly structured, hierarchical caste society the lowest castes though numerically large in number ordinarily should not have any stake in the system ..... the system provided some scope so that they can also feel superior to some groups and thereby develop some vested interest in the system". In Kalagalla village also, the Yerukula without having any alternative developed in the system, are extreme, consciousness of their own as superior to the scheduled caste like Mala and Madiga. The dominant castes like the Kapu, the Kuruba, and the Ekila also placed the Bidari Yerukula above the Mala and Madiga in local caste hierarchy, the Yerukula accepted the procedure and are following the same along with other castes within the settlement.

Bride price, known as *'sulla ponnu'* in Yerakali tongue, is a common custom among the Yerukula during the marriage ceremony. After fixing the date for marriage the father of the bridegroom pays a fixed amount of Rs. 48/- as bridge price to the father of the bride. This system is very strictly followed by the Yerukula of Epilapalli village. But in Kalagalla village due to the surrounding environment of other dominant caste groups, and the dependence of Yerukula on advanced cash economy, the Yerukula adapted the system of dowry, by which the father of the bride has to pay some amount to the father of the bridegroom as a dowry before starting marriage ceremony.

The dominant feature of the Yerukula political organization is its *'kula panchayat'*. In both Epilapalli and Kalagalla villages they have their own 'kula panchayat'. The members of the 'kula panchayat' are usually elders who are called 'pedda monushulu' and the head of the Yerukula settlement is called *'Berumonusha'*. Cases related to sex, property, loans, land and quarrels between families are taken up for arbitration in the 'kula panchayat'. When the 'kula panchayat' is unable to identify the guilty person in spite of several adjournments in a particular case, they try to determine the guilty through ordeals like both the parties dipping their fingers in boiling oil or lifting a red hot crow-bar in the presence of the 'Berumonusha' and the elders gathered for the purpose. The proceedings in the 'kula panchayat' of Epilapalli are based on the decisions of 'Berumonusha'. But in Kalagalla, due to the interference of the village elders of dominant castes, the Yerukula are following two types of political decisions, one is of their 'Berumonusha' and another one of the other caste elders. At present the Yerukula of Kalagalla village need not have to face the ordeals because of the interference of the police through the local caste village elders.

As for religion, the Yerukula of Epilapalli is typically polytheistic. Each sphere of nature or activity is governed by its own deity. Thus, for instance the Yerukula of this village worship 'Patrabhanda deity' to get good rains. According to the Yerukula, without rain, the forest remains bares and unfruitful, their people suffer, animals get in poor condition and their young are ill-nourish and susceptible to disease. Rain has therefore come to be directly associated not only with sufficiency of food but with the welfare and fertility of the people, forest and their livestock. Rituals for getting rain are consequently of the first importance to the Yerukula of Epilapalli village. They worship 'Nadeedi Gangamma' for crop's good fertility and availability of forest produce and they worship 'Karunoothala gangamma' deity for proper passage of individuals through the life cycle from birth to departure of the soul. In Epilapalli the relationship with supernatural is maintained primarily on an individual basis. That is, there are no priests; each Yerukula has his own religious functionary. Though group rituals, do occur, mainly in reference to 'life cycle' ceremonies. Their religion tends to be less systematized, less specialized and less elaborated than is the religion of the Yerukula of Kalagalla village. In Kalagalla village, among the Yerukula, Hindu religious practices appear to be useful ways for invoking supernatural help. Their beliefs and practices are more directly influenced by scriptural Hinduism. Though they are polytheistic in religious aspects, but in the course of adaptation of the elements of other castes the Yerukula started worshipping the Sanskritic deities like Lord Anjaneya, Lord Shiva etc. for them agricultural rituals are of the first importance than rituals for getting rain. In Kalagalla, among the Yerukula, the relationship with the supernatural is maintained through a priest. The Yerukula invite a Brahmin priest to do rituals of life cycle.

Concluding Observations

The data on the whole, lend support to the assumption that the people in a particular environment characteristically extract and use the resources of that environment. New adaptations should be developed if effective relationship with altered habitational conditions is to be maintained. The people continue their primary activity if their habitational conditions are not at all altered. This paper does not attempt to explain everything about the Bidari Yerukula but it has been oriented towards a specific set of conditions and problems in different environments. However, the interpretation herein presented has been that there are important differences among the socio-economic systems of the Bidari Yerukula who live in different ecological situations.

Here two villages namely Epilapalli and Kalagalla, situated in two different ecological environments with the inhabitants of the same community, the Bidari Yerukula are studied. Epilapalli is located amidst thick forest whereas Kalagalla is situated on a plain area. The present study is mainly concerned with Bidari Yerukula whose primary occupation is collecting the minor forest produce and selling it in the nearby villages.

It is found that a close relation between occupational structure and the settlement exists, and the product of Yerukula's skill and their environment varies widely from one habitation to another basing on the evidence of material available at hand. For instance selling of 'Karepaku', firewood, forest fruits and the household industry of broomsticks, ropes, twines and slings are the primary occupation of the Yerukula of Epilapalli. Whereas in Kalagalla, the Yerukula have adapted to agriculture, milk selling, bonded labour, carpentry etc., as their primary occupation.

It has been noticed that in both the villages, a kind of environmental influence affected the social system of the Yerukula. In Epilapalli the Yerukula are liberal in maintaining their social organization according to their community wishes, whereas in Kalagalla, it is found that an individual autonomy and the changes in social organization is interefered by the other castes that are living along with them. The development of the vested interests in the caste hierarchy and the adaptation of the practice of dowry system instead of bride price by the Yerukula of Kalagalla village show that they are relatively based on surrounding environment. As for religion, the Yerukula of Epilapalli is typically polytheistic. Here the relationship with the supernatural is maintained primarily on an individual basis without religious functionary or priest whereas in Kalagalla, the Yerukula have the system of inviting a Brahmin priest to perform their rituals. In Kalagalla the religious practices tend to be more systematized and too elaborated. This shows how the same community in different ecological situations adapts to the variations of its environment.

Acknowledgement

I am grateful to the Director and Dr. P.K. Misra, Ex-Deputy Director, Anthropological Survey of India, Mysore for extending necessary facilities. I am also greatly indebted to Dr. N.V.K. Rao and Shri V.S. Nailk, for their valuable comments and encouragement in preparing this paper.

References

Barth, Fredrik (1968), "Ecologic Relationships of Ethnic Groups in Swat, North Pakistan" in 'Man in Adaptation: The Cultural Present, Ed by Cohen, A. Yehudi, Chicago Aldine Publishing Company.

Cenus of India 1971. Scheduled Castes and Scheduled Tribes", Seires 1.

Cohen, A. Yehudi (Ed.) (1968), 'Introduction' in 'Man in Adaptation: The Cultural Present ed. by Coher A. Yehudi, Chicage : Aldine PublishingCo.

Cohen, A. Yehudi (Ed.) (1968), "Culture as Adaptation", in'Man in Adaptation : The Cultural Present, ed by Cohen A. Yehudi, Chicago, Aldine Publishing Company.

Forde, Daryll (1960), "Primitive Economics", in Man, Culture and Society, Ed by Harry L. Shapiro, New York, Oxford University Press.

Kroeber, L. Alfred (1969), "Relations of Environmental and Cultural Factors" in Environment and Cultural Behaviour Ed by Andrew P. Vayada, London, University of Texas Press.

Levine, N. D. (1975), "Human Ecology", North Scituate, Mass: Duxbury Press.

Misra, P. K. (1979), "Indian Nomads" (Unpublished), Anthropological Survey of India, Calcutta.

Nicholas, W. Ralph (1963), "Ecology and Village Structure in Deltaic West Bengal", *The Economic Weekly,* 15: 1185-1196.

Parthasarathy, J. (1979), "Yerukula and their Customary Law", (Unpublished), Anthropological Survey of India, Calcutta.

Ramesan (1960), "A Tribe in Andhra", in *The Hindu,* Newspaper dated 31.1.1960.

4 The Bhoksas and their Environment: A Study in the Light of Cognized Model

N. K. Ghatak

A culture is the way of life of a people; it refers to that part of the total setting that includes the material objects of human manufacture, techniques, social orientation, points of view and sanctioned ends, which are the immediate conditioning factors underlying behaviour; environment is the total setting of human life encompassing both culture or what is learned, and habitat or natural setting (Herskovits, 1955). From the above definition of the culture and the environment, it may be said that culture and the environment are interdependent on each other. But it is the culture that acts as a design for society's continuity, stipulates its environment, and its regularities permit it to be analyzed, and it is the means by which a person adjusts to his environment. The nature is seen by men through a screen composed of beliefs, knowledge and purposes and it is in terms of their cultural image of nature, rather than in terms of the actual structure of nature that men act. "To understand the environmental relations of men, one needs to take into account their knowledge and beliefs concerning the world around them, and their culturally defined motives for acting as they do" (Rappaport 1971: 216). Thus it may be said that configuration of environment is the configuration of culture.

Rappaport (1971) has proposed two models to study Man and Environmental relationship, the first is cognized model and the second is the operational model. According to him the cognized model is a description of knowledge and beliefs concerning their environment entertained by people. And the operational model is description of the same ecological system (including the people). The operational model includes the knowledge that one would require for the biological well-being of the organisms, population and ecosystems under consideration. But on the other hand, the cognized model includes components such as supernatural whose existence cannot be demonstrated by empirical procedure but whose existence moves the actors to behave in a particular way. A cognized model may be regarded as a part of a population's distinctive means for maintaining itself in its environment.

In this paper an attempt has been made to highlight the "cognized model" as described by Rappaport, as it operates among the Bhoksas of U.P. The paper is based on the data collected during the field work in the year 1979 in the Tarai regions of Nainital district.

The Bhoksa

The Bhoksa, a scheduled tribe of Uttar Pradesh are mainly found in the four districts of U.P., i.e., Nainital, Dehradun, Bijnor and Pauri-Garhwal. They have acquired the Scheduled tribe status in 1967. Before 1967, they were considered as Bhoksa Rajput. According to the 1971 Census, the Bhoksa population in U.P. was 23,217, forming 11.14% of the total scheduled tribes of the state. Majority i.e. 70% of the total Bhoksa population live in rural areas and the rest inhabit urban and semi-urban centers.

The meaning of the term, Bhoksa, is still unknown. But the term '*Bhuxsar*' was given to a pargana of Rudrapur and Kilpuri of present Nainital district and it was mentioned in *Ain-I-Akbari*. In fact, at Rudrapur, there is a dense forest which is called by the local people as Bhuksar, i.e., a Jungle which is full of wild animals. According to the Bhoksas, they were the indigenous inhabitants of the area of the forest. So, the term Bhoksa may have been derived from the name of the place of their original inhabitation. Bhoksas are a patrilineal tribe. The rules governing both the inheritance of property, descent and residence after marriage are patrilineal. They identify themselves as thakurs, claiming Rajput origin. Although Bhoksa society is an admixture of some social groups and these groups are also segmented into a number of subgroups, yet their interactional pattern does not suggest any kind of social hierarchy existing among them. The subgroup names among the Bhoksas are perhaps derived from their different places of original habitat of the remote past. Many sub-groups however, do not even know as to how they have come to own the subgroup names.

The Bhoksa and Their Immediate Environment: A Few Empirical Observations

The Bhoksas are an immigrant group. They cannot give the exact period of their migration from their original habitat. They know only this much that they have been in this part of the country at least for the last 1,200 or 1,400 years (Turner 1933: 588). Their settlements are mainly found in the Bhabar and Tarai regions of Nainital district. The *Bhabar* is a narrow strip lying immediately below the foothill, largely covered with forest. The *Tarai* is a damp marshy strip. It is covered for the most part with dense jungle and tall grass. The Bhabar and the Tarai regions are famous for their malarious weather. Most of the Bhoksas are found at the proximity of the forest. For the present study the village Pipal-sanna of Nainital district, located in the Tarai region of Kumaon Himalaya had been selected. This village forms a part of the Ramnagar Block and is close to another Block town Kashipur. Ramnagar and Kashipur are 23 kms and 18 kms respectively from the village. This village may be called a uniethnic village, except for a few pahari and only one harijan family in the village. All the houses are constructed in such a way that they form a straight line. The forest is only one km from the village. Villagers have regular interaction with the forest.

Forest in Connection With the Bhoksa Economy

The Bhoksas are an agricultural community. They are the landowners and cultivators. The agricultural products of their lands are the main source of their income. The land-based economy among them has actually been started after the independence of the country. Before the independence, the area inhabited by the Bhoksas remained comparatively isolated for the following two reasons (i) lack of communication-accessibility road transport and town facilities were not there and (ii) the area was highly malarious. The Bhoksa, in those days were practicing swidden cultivation. At present, cultivation of their personal holding, on one hand and working in agricultural fields of others as agricultural labourers, on the other hand are the main economic activities performed by the Bhoksas. The landowners are engaged in their fields for the better products, and those who are landless or have a little land, work on daily wages for agricultural activities. Although, most of the time, they are engaged in agricultural activities, yet, influence of the forest in their life cannot be ruled out. In the past, they lived in the forest as a forest dwelling community. They made their living by food gathering, pasturing cattle and a little hunting that they could do. They were accustomed with the forest life. The forest provides them all the required materials for the settlements and supplied fruits, roots; barks etc. for their subsistence and also provide them grazing ground for their cattle or domestic animals.

After the independence, the situation of the Bhoksa community has changed. Forest is not free to them as it was in the past when they practiced swidden cultivation. Further encroachment into the forest is not possible. But for their living in the proximity of the forest, they get some special privileges from the forest department. They are:

1. Allowed to collect dry wood from the forest for their personal use.
2. Permitted to get the wooden poles from the forest, free or at a concessional rate, from the forest after obtaining the permission of the forest department.
3. Allowed to graze their domestic animals in the forest.

As described by them, the forest is not that rich in edible roots and fruits or other forest products as used to be. Even then, they are the regular visitors of the forest and also exploit the forest products for various purposes for their day to day life. At present, they utilize the forest for the following purposes:

1. Collect dry wood for fuel.
2. Collect wooden poles for repairing old houses or for construction of new houses.
3. Collect *bind* - a kind of grass which they use for making rope for *Charpai*.
4. Collect *Munch* – a kind of thick grass which is used for preparing basket *Daliaiya, Sufa* etc.
5. Collect *Chalta* – a kind of herb leaves for making roofs of their houses.
6. Some of them collect a kind of leaf which is used as plates. They sell it in the local market.

The forest provides ground for pasturing their cattle. Rearing of cattle among them is treated as a source of income. For plough cultivation however cattle are required as per their traditional custom. They consider cattle as an unavoidable part of life. Thus, in the past, forest provided food and shelter for them, but now it still supplies them with one required material for their shelter and helps them economically by supplying forest products. The forest may therefore be treated as a source of a secondary income.

The Forest and the Forest Spirit World of the Bhoksas

The Bhoksas consider forest as an indispensable part of their life. They know ins and outs of the forest. They wish to acquaint their children with the forest even at their childhood for better understanding of the accessible parts of the forest and to use those parts conveniently. They divide the accessible portion of the forest into three parts, viz.,

(i) *Ucha Jungal* – The upper part of forest.

(ii) *Maddaya Jungal* – The middle part of the forest and

(iii) *Nicha Jungal* – The lower part of the forest.

The upper parts of the forest are close to the villages and are utilized as grazing ground for their domestic animals.

Bhoksas have their regular contact with this portion of the forest, particularly in the second half of the day. In the first half, adult males are engaged in the agricultural fields, whereas adult females are busy with the household activities; so only in the second half, they get time to go into the forest with their domestic animals for grazing. But in agricultural seasons, when all the adult males or females are fully engaged, then children generally go into this part of the forest with cattles for grazing purposes. Generally the young school going children have to perform this job of herding their domestic animals for helping their families. This part of forest is not rich with edible roots or fruits or firewood. Because of regular grazing of cattle in this part of the forest, these do not get a chance to grow there. Besides, the herdsmen, if they find any fruit or root, they collect it.

The middle part of the forest lies next to the upper part of the forest where men or women usually go for collecting dry wood for fuel or for collecting wooden poles for reconstruction of old houses or to construct new houses. Generally Bhoksa women do the job of collecting fuel wood, and at the same time they also collect roots, fruits, barks etc. in this part of the forest. Sometimes one or two males go into this part accompanying their women as guides or as protectors. For the collection of wooden poles, one or more groups of men go together into the forest and select the required wooden poles, then cut them down and return home with the wooden poles.

The lower part of the forest is treated as the interior part as well as the dangerous portion of all the accessible parts of the forest. In the month of August to September they go into this part in a group for collecting the *Bind grass, Munch* and *Chalta*. Generally each year they visit this part of the forest, one or two times or sometimes more, depending on their requirement. Neither women nor the young children or a person alone could be allowed to visit this part of the forest. This is because; this part of the forest is full of wild animals that may attack any time.

Due to their living in the proximity of the forest, the tradition of the Bhoksa community is tuned with the environment of the forest. Their day to day contact with the forest has forced them to develop a strong belief that some spirits are in the forest that can do harm and can also do good to them. Among the forest spirits, some of them are malevolent in nature and do harm to the people. However, they favour the people in case they are pleased over by them.

According to the Bhoksa, the accessible parts of the forest are ruled by the three malevolent spirits, e.g., *Bhagaya, Okhaya* and *Majhi,* and one benevolent spirit i.e. *Sarawala.* Spirit *Bhagya* is well known for its malevolent nature. Though it won't directly affect man but its effect comes on the society of the Bhoksa people in a harmful way. It may do harm to the cattle. It is believed that a person who is killed by a tiger, his soul transforms as a *Bhagaya* spirit. At the time of roaming of the soul of this spirit, if any cattle or cattles fall on its way then the cattle or cattles could get affected by its malevolent nature. The cattle affected by malevolent nature of the spirit, fall on the ground and dies. But it is also believed by the Bhoksa people that only *Bharara* a local sorcerer, can save the cattle from effect of *Bhagaya,* if he is informed at the moment of attack.

The spirit *Majhi* is a malevolent spirit. This spirit is malevolent to the mankind. It is believed that Majhi is the soul of wicked men or women who died in an accident in the forest or outside the forest. If anybody falls under the influence of this malevolent spirit then it is assumed that the person will die within a few days. Even if he stays in his house with the hope that Majhi could not affect him. Majhi pretends in a voice of his dearest friend at the dead of night and calls him out. Hearing the voice of a friend, if he does not go outside the room then he may save himself because Majhi has no power to do harm anybody inside a room. The Bhoksas are scared of the bad influence of Majhi.

Spirit *Okhaya* is malevolent to the mankind but not as harmful as Majhi. It is believed by the Bhoksa that if a man dies in the forest without getting food and water, then the soul of this dead person transforms as an Okhaya spirit. This spirit rules over the jungle only; outside the Jungle it has no power at all. If anybody falls under the influence of Okhaya spirit, then he loses his way leading out from the forest even if, he may be a man of reputation for his skill to be at ease in the Jungle. The man has to spend a day or days together in the forest till his friends rescue him from the forest. Spirit Okhaya does not kill anybody directly; he only makes fun a person by making him suffer for food, drinks and by keeping him in anxiety and in the uncertainty of life.

The spirit *Piawala* is reputed for its good deeds. This spirit helps her worshippers in finding out cattle from the jungle which might have been lost while grazing in the forest. It is believed that this spirit is the soul of a virtuous women or *padhania* (wife of the village head) of the village. She helps her villagers by dint of her heavenly affections towards them. When cattle go astray then the Bhoksa make a promise to this spirit of her worship for finding the lost cattle. She is quite popular for her good deeds as she delivers the goods and is frequently propitiated by them.

The Bhoksas and their Environment in the light of Cognized Model

Although the Bhoksas believe that all these four spirits rule the accessible parts of the forest, yet the Nature and activities of these spirits reveal that each of these spirits has certain link with a particular part of the forest. The attack of Bhagaya spirit is reportedly prevalent in the upper part i.e., the part near to a locality of the forest. Thus the attacks of the spirits the *Okhaya* and the *Majhi* are reported to be more frequent in the middle and the lower part of the forest respectively. So it is not improper to say that the belief concerning the forest spirits in relation to the natural environment has some direct or indirect link with the different parts of the forests which is to be taken under consideration from the empirical knowledge.

The spirit Bhagaya harms cattle. The cattle are reared in the upper part of the forest. So, the scope of attack on cattle by the Bhagaya spirit is possible only in the upper part of the forest.

Owning to the proximity of the village, and due to their frequent contacts with the upper part of the forest, the Bhoksa feel most secured in this part of the forest, though according to them, influence of the spirits such as the Okhaya and the Majhi are there. Due to this, during grazing, they keep an eye on their cattle so that they are not lost. However, the spirit Biawala is there to protect cattle from the expected loss. Actually the upper part of the forest is not so thick and finding lost cattle in this part is not impossible. However, their beliefs of spirits have made an adjustment with the natural condition of the forest. As discussed earlier, the spirit Okhaya could affect a group of man. The villagers go into the middle part of the forest for collection of dry wood or wooden beams. The collections may be done in a group but this could lead to a dispute among members of the group on the choice for better dry wood or for the good quality beams. At the same time, it is not expected that sufficient dry woods for the groups could be available in a place. They have to move here and there in search of the required forest products. So the spirit Okhaya may get scope of attack on a person in this part of the forest when a person moves alone into deep part of the forest for collection of required forest products, and it is not improbable for a person to get lost in the forest or being attacked by wild animals, such as bear etc. So the belief of Okhaya spirit forces them to work in a group and to prepare them mentally to cope with the unexpected danger in the forest.

The Bhoksas are tremendously scared of evil tendencies of Majhi spirit. Majhi can attack a person even if he is in a group. The Bhoksa go into the lower part of the forest only in the months of August and September. This is the period when sufficient required materials are available in limited area. As described earlier, the lower part of the forest is infested by wild animals, such as Tiger, elephant etc. and other wild animals, and also by the Majhi spirit. So, lower part of the forest may be considered as dangerous in the light of the belief of spirit as well as, because of the preponderance of wild animals.

From the above discussion, it may be said that the belief of particular spirit is linked with particular part of the forest. As they go into the depth of the forest, the belief concerning spirit which ruled this part is that they are more dangerous than those who rule the adjacent part of the forest where wild animals are not in abundance. Now it is not unlikely to conjecture that belief of spirit and Natural Environment of the forest are independent to each other. Their belief of the spirit that in anticipation gives their community members a scope to adjust themselves with probable risk or danger of the accessible parts of the forest environment and helps them to utilize the forest produce safely.

Conclusion

In this paper, an attempt has been made to represent the forest spirit cosmology in relation to natural environment of the forest in the light of cognized model. As discussed earlier, the Bhoksa believe in four spirits each of which rules particular part of the accessible forest and thus reveals some inter links with the Natural Environment. As the Bhoksa are traditionally a forest dwelling community, so the belief concerning the spirits has, perhaps roots in the mischievous nature of the forest environment and these beliefs are self imposed by them to save their community members from the unexpected danger of the forest. But from the study, it may be said that each of these spirits has some interlink with a particular part of the natural environment of the forest. This is done in response to the signals from the ecosystem and beliefs in the super nature are undertaken with respect to supernatural, but these actions have corrective effects upon the ecosystem. So, it is not improper to regard this cosmology as functional, perhaps even adaptive codification of reality. The Notion of the study in the light of cognized model is not to confirm the physical structure of the forest environment, but whether or not, it elicits behaviour contributing to well-being of the actors and to the maintenance of ecosystem of which they are a part. Further more, it seems that there is no simple direct relation between the amount of testable empirical knowledge in cognized model and the appropriateness of the behaviour that it elicits. It is by no means certain that the representatives of nature provide them by science are more adaptive or more functional than those images of the world inhabited by the spirit who the Bhoksa respect. Indeed, the supernatural veil is perhaps to provide them with some protection against human parochialism and destructiveness.

References

Atkinson, E. T. (1973), *The Himalayan Gazetteer*, Vol. II, Pt. 2, New Delhi, Cosmo Publications.

Herskovits, Melville, J. (1955), *Cultural Anthropology*. New Delhi, Oxford and IBH Publishing Co.

Rappaport, Roy A. (1971), Nature, Culture and Ecological Anthropology. In *Man, Culture and Society*. Harry, L. Shapiro (ed.).

Turner, A. C. (1933), *Census of India* 1931 United Provinces of Agra and Oudh. Vol. XVIII, Part-1 Report. Allahabad, 1933.

Part-2

Survival Strategies in the Himalayas

5 Human Adaptation in Kashmir Himalayas– A Case Study of the Economy and Land Use at Low and Middle Altitude

P. N. Lal

Introduction

Broadly speaking there is a correlation between altitude, topography, rainfall, soil and slope of land and the cultural and economic life of the people of a region. In the Himalayas, at low altitudes people are dependent on agriculture. But with the increase in altitude the economy based on agriculture may be replaced by other activities like pasturing of animals or trade. Even within the agricultural zone we may distinguish a remarkable change in the cropping pattern; paddy, maize and millets at low altitudes may be replaced by buckwheat and barley at higher altitudes.

Similarly, instead of moving from low to high altitudes, if we move from west to east in the Himalayas there is a change in the cultural and economic life of the people. Pasturing of animals is a major activity among many communities in the west but it is limited in the eastern Himalayas. Similarly seasonal migration is an important activity in the west but, in most cases, it is not necessary in the east. Seasonal migrations are necessary for the adjustment with the change of weather but in some cases migration is in the reverse order for the utilization of high altitude pastures. For example, in Sikkim the Lepchas stay in winter at their permanent high altitude settlement (10,000 feet) and migrate to still higher altitudes

(12,000 feet) in summer for cultivation of cash crops. The Monpas of Kameng district of Arunachal Pradesh staying at high altitudes do not come below 10,000 feet as their yaks can't survive below this altitude.

We have studied four villages situated at different contour intervals in the Kashmir Himalayas. The village Dansal and Shadali are situated in Dansal block of Jammu district and their altitude varies from 2000 to 2500 and thus represent situations at low altitudes. The other two villages namely Wussan (4500') and Akora (6000') are situated in Kangan block of Srinagar district and Khoerpore block in Anantnag district respectively and represent conditions at mid-altitude of Kashmir Himalayas. The villages have been selected on the following considerations. During the field work it was observed that at low altitudes, the villages are of small size and highly dispersed. But at middle altitudes fairly large size agglomerated villages are found. Another consideration was that the Hindus constitute the major population at low altitude but at middle altitude the Muslims predominate. Besides, we have observed that there are two sharp divisions among Hindu and Muslim cultivators living within the same village so far as skill and technology of agriculture is concerned. The Hindus are gradually moving away from cultivation of crops towards horticulture and business activities. But the Muslims are drawing more and more towards agriculture and animal husbandry. They are taking to modern agriculture such as terracing, irrigation, use of inputs like hybrids seeds, fertilizers, pesticides and weedicides. They also depend more on manual labour and reciprocal help during different stages of agricultural activity. The Hindu farmers, on the other hand, are progressive and taking to modern agriculture gradually.

Methodology

Cadastral maps of the surveyed villages were obtained from the village Patwari and use of different plot of land was noted from the land records. Besides household census and a questionnaire was also canvassed in the village for getting the data. In some cases, group interviews were conducted on problems of land use. Opinions of Hindu and Muslim elites were taken on agricultural developments.

Physiography

Dansal block of Jammu district, where Dansal and Shadali villages are located, is situated in a hilly tract towards south-eastern side of Pir Panjal mountain range which separates this region from Kashmir valley. The physiography of the region is of Siwalik type. A number of rivers and streams arising from Pir Panjal flow through this region and fall in Chenab which is an important river of this region. The terrain has been badly dissected by the action of the rivers. The boulders and pebbles brought by the rivers are strewn in the valleys. Here and there isolated hillocks and deeply cut ravines predominate the landscape of this region. The villages are situated on the higher terraces of the ravines made by the Jhajjar river. It is an important tributary of Tawi river that finally meets the Chenab.

The village Dansal is situated on the right bank and Shadali on the left bank of Jhajjar Nala. The size of the villages is governed by the physiography of the site. Dansal (107 Acres) is smaller in size than Shadali (873 Acres) (see Table 1). The former has compact settlement while Shadali is dispersed due to terrain conditions.

Table 1
Land Available Per Person (in Acres)

	Total Geographical Land (in Acres)			*Ratio of Land Available per Person (in Acres)*	
Villages	*Total Village Area (in Acres)*	*Irrigated land (in Acres)*	*Total Population*	*Village Area*	*Irrigated Area*
Dansal	107	-	206	0.5	-
Shadali	873	-	255	3.4	-
Wussan	896	470	1954	0.4	0.2
Akora	1021	470	1376	0.7	0.3

The average slope of Dansal is below 10^0 hence it is gentle. But Shadali is relatively steep and the slope ranges from 10^0 to 20^0.The range between minimum and maximum altitude of

Shadali village (2500′-3500′) is higher than Dansal (2000′-2500′) because of the Shadali hill range that lies near the village. Although the village Dansal is small in area but it accommodates 206 persons. It can be compared with Shadali having a population of 255 persons (See Table 2). The site of Dansal is found to be more favourable for cultivation and other activities. Moreover this village is situated near the metallic road running between Jammu and Jindra.

Dansal is dominated by Dogra Hindus who are divided into caste groups such as Pandit and Rajput. The scheduled castes such as Megh, Mahashe, Harijan, Lohar, Kumhar, Teli and barbar stay in separate hamlets away from this village. The village Shadali, on the other hand is dominated by Gujjars who are Muslims. It was observed that Pandits and Rajputs were the main land owners of this area but gradually they sold out their land to Gujjars and scheduled castes. Some of the Gujjars also work as sharecropper in the fields of the Rajputs.

The physiography of villages at middle altitude is dominated by the action of glaciers and action of the rivers on the Karewars in the past. The village Wussan (4500′) is sited on the Karewa table land. It is flat topped terrace like feature developed on the morainic deposits of Pleistocene glaciations. River Sindh passes by this village and meets River Jhelum. The village Akora (6000′) is located by the side of Lidder river which also meets River Jhelum. Both the villages are situated in the Kashmir valley. The Greater Himalayan range running west to east separates this region from Ladakh.

The range of minimum to maximum altitude of Wussan village (3000′-5000′) is more than Akora (5500′-6000′) as the former is located on a Karewa table land. The average slope of Wussan is steep (Above 30°) but it is gentle at Akora (Below 10°). As such the village Akora is larger (1021 Acres) than Wussan (896 Acres).

Wussan village is dominated by Muslims, but in Akora, Hindus and Muslims constitute the village population. Due to availability of dry terraces and a sizeable Gujjar population in Wussan the cultivation of maize and paddy is important. But

Table 2
Population Composition of Study Villages

Villages	*Total households*	*Total Population*	*Distribution of Population by Broad Age Groups and Sex*							
			Children (0-14)		*Adults (15-59)*		*Old Persons (60+)*		*Total*	
			M	*F*	*M*	*F*	*M*	*F*	*M*	*F*
Low Altitude Village										
DANSAL	43	206	36	45	53	54			98	108
SHADALI	48	205	77	81	21	63	95	98	103	152
Middle Altitude Villages										
WUSSAN	224	1954	461	411	491	420	93	78	1045	909
AKORA	275	1376	328	302	335	366	7	38	670	706

in Akora only paddy is the predominant crop due to the availability of gently sloping land.

Soil, Natural Vegetation and Climate

The soil of villages at low altitude is brown and developed under deciduous forests. They are dark brown and vary from silt loam to dry loam with small percentage of gravels. The soil at middle altitudes are classed as sub-montaine and developed under evergreen conifers. Immature soils are found as altitude increases. Alpine pastures appear at higher slopes of the mountains. Thick soil cover is found in the valley bottom and on the terraces.

Wussan village at middle altitude is located by the side of Srinagar-Leh road. There are 10 hamlets locally known as Mohallas or Pora for example, (1) Shah Mohala, (2) Zerikhan, (3) Wandarpora, (4) Sheikhpora, (5) Bela Wussan (Gujjars), (6) Chakproa, (7) Pett Pora (Pandit), (8) Gondi Wussan, (9) Chanir, (10) Khodhar. The hamlets are inhabited by particular clan groups such as Shah, Sheikh, etc. Pandit stays in separate hamlet inside the village. The Gujjars who are migrants to this village have made their houses on the higher slopes of the hills. Akora village, located by the side of Anantnag – Pahalgaon road, has hamleted settlement. Hindus and Muslims live in hamlets separated by stream and rivulets. There is no Gujjar population in this village.

House Type

Houses at low and middle altitudes differ in shape, size and the material used. It is made to suite the climate the material available and the cultural background of the people. At low altitude a Hindu house differs from that of the Muslim in style. A Hindu house has a courtyard in front of the living room. The house is made of mud plastered with clay. Foundation is made of stones. The roof is made from log, branches of tree and leaves which are plastered with mud. The roof is flat.

Gujjar houses of shadali village are rectangular and divided into rooms. Each room accommodates a nuclear family. Parents with their unmarried sons and daughters stay in one room.

Married sons stay in the adjacent room. Each family cooks in the living room. The room adjacent to the living room is used as cattle shed. Most of the houses at low altitude are single storey. Each house stands within the cultivated field of the owner.

At middle altitude the houses are made from brick stone and wood. They are invariably made of three storeys due to climatic conditions. During winters, the family stays at the ground floor. In summer, they move to the second floor. The third floor is used for keeping fodder and household articles. The Gujjars living at middle altitudes make small house for themselves. These are known as 'Kothis'. It is a single room with low roof made of stones. It is poorly ventilated. Inside the house is dark and full of smoke.

Economy

From the Table 3 it is found that agriculture is the main occupation of the people in the villages. But its dependency varies at different altitudes. In Dansal and Shadali villages at low altitudes, the families depending only on agriculture constitute 27% to 30% of the total number of families in the village. But in Akora village at mid-altitude dependency on agriculture is 63%. Agriculture labour and share cropper is

Table 3
Family wise Occupational Structure

	No. of Families		
Types of Primary Occupations	*Dansal*	*Shadali*	*Akora*
Total No. of families	43	48	275
Only Cultivation	13	13	175
Agriculture Labour and Share Cropper	0	32	0
Business	8	0	10
Service	5	3	61
Gold Smithy	3	-	-
Barber	1	-	-
Oil Pressing	2	-	-
Tailoring	4	-	-
Carpentry	-	-	8
Others	7	-	21

Table 4
Production Rate of Cereal Crops

DANSAL	*SHADALI*		*WUSSAN*	*AKORA*
Productionper Acre Quintal	*Production per Acre Quintal*		*Production per Acre in Quintal*	*Production per Acre in Quintal*
-	-	Paddy	15-20	20-25
6	4	Wheat	-	-
7	5	Maize	8-10	Due to Karewa Soil
3	2	Pulses	-	-

conspicuous by absence at Dansal and Akora villages but it is found in Shadali village. The reason is that after the agrarian reforms in Kashmir, the majority of the share croppers have become owner cultivators. Business and service are the other sectors of economy that is conspicuous in all the villages. Occupations such as goldsmithy, barber, oil pressing, tailoring are found in Dansal but it is absent at Akora.

Agriculture

From the agricultural land utilization Table 5 it is found that irrigated land constitute about 52% of the total geographical area of Wussan village. The unirrigated land covers about 5% of the total geographical area of the village. In Akora village, on the other hand, irrigated land constitutes about 47% of the total geographical area of the village. The un-irrigated land is conspicuous by absence in this village. The above record definitely shows advancement of wet paddy terraces in Akora village than at Wussan village. The reason is that in Wussan village the land is undulating due to Karewa topography which is not found in Akora village. Besides, the Gujjars living in Wussan village cultivate the dry terraces for maize crops.

Terraces are definitely advancement in agriculture. In Akora village due to proper water management and diversion of streams and rivulets, terraces have been made at different slopes for the cultivation of Sali paddy .The upper terraces which receive the first flow of the stream water are classed as Abi-Awal (First class paddy land). After filling this terrace, the

Table 5
Land Classification and Ecological Factors

Name of the Village	Total Geographical area in acres	Type of land	Actual area in acres	Area as % to total geographical area	Average slope in degrees	Average altitude in feet	Soil	Predominant Crop	Distance From Block HQ.
(1)	(2)	(3)	(4)	(5)	(6)	(7)	(8)	(9)	(10)
AKORA	1021	ABI – Awl	470						
		ABI – Doyum	1						
		ABI –WARI	22						
		ABI – Soyum	30	46.03%	Below 10^0	4000-5000	Sub-Montane Sandy Loam	Sali Paddy	2 Km
		BAG – ABI	4						
		Banger –Quadim	62						
		Zere – Saya	1						
		Sansar – Jadid	3						
		Banuar – Quadim (Willow)	68						
		Gair – Mumkin	360	35.26%	15^0 - 20^0	5500-6000	Clayey Loam		

Contd...

Name of the Village	Total Geographical area in acres	Type of land	Actual area in acres	Area as % to total geographical area	Average slope in degrees	Average altitude in feet	Soil	Predominant Crop	Distance From Block HQ.
(1)	(2)	(3)	(4)	(5)	(6)	(7)	(8)	(9)	(10)
SUSSAN	896	Irrigated	470						
		Un-Irrigated	41						
		ABI – AWAL	189						
		ABI- DOYUM	53	52.46%					
		ABRI – WARI	9						
		ABI – SOYUM	7	4.58%	Below 10^0	3000-3500	Sandy Loam	Sali Paddy Maize	5 Km
		ABI – SOYUM (MAIZE)	173						
		BAG – ABI	5						
		BANJAR QUADIM	118						
		MAIDAN	30		200-25^0				
		LOBRU	11						
		ZERE – SAYA	6		200-25^0	3500-4500	Clayey Loam	Kitchen Grazing Maize Pasture	
		BANJAR-JADID	2		20^0-25^0	3500-4500	Clayey	Pasture	
		BANJAR QUADIM (WILLOW)	4				Loam	Basture Willow	
		GAIR-MUMKIN	256	28.57%	Above 25^0	Above 4500	Stony Soil		

Contd...

Name of the Village	*Total Geogra-phical area in acres*	*Type of land*	*Actual area in acres*	*Area as % to total geogra-phical area*	*Average slope in degrees*	*Average altitude in feet*	*Soil*	*Predo-minant Crop*	*Distance From Block HQ.*
(1)	*(2)*	*(3)*	*(4)*	*(5)*	*(6)*	*(7)*	*(8)*	*(9)*	*(10)*
DANSAL	107.37	CULTIVATED	51.5	47.66%				1 Km	
		(a) SAGARH			Above 10^0	2500-3000	Sandy Loam	Wheat-Barley	
		(b) BRIYAL			5^0-10^0	2000-2500	Sandy Loam	Wheat	
		(c) TANALA			below 5^0	2000	Clayey fodder grass	Maize	
		CULTURABLE WASTE (a) Current fallow (b) Old fallow (c) Forest	41.37	14.03%					
		UNCULTURABLE WASTE (a) Abadi (b) Stone Outcrop (c) Water bodies (d) Path							
SHADALI	873	CULTIVATED (a) Briyal (b) Tanala	117	13%	20^0-25^0	3000-3500			
		CULTURABLE WASTE (a) Current fallow (b) Old fallow (c) Forest	156	19%					
		UN-CULTURABLEWASTE	600	68%					

water is diverted to lower terraces and then to still low terraces. Such terraces are classed as Abi Doyam and Abi-Soyum. Sometimes the lower terraces are filled with mud brought from the upper terraces. The excess mud is taken out from the field and stored at one place. It is dried and sold to others. A truck load of mud is sold for rupees 100 to 300. This is done mainly by Muslim cultivators.

Terraces which are situated away from the streams and beyond the reach of the water have been converted into kitchen gardens. These are called as Abi-Wari. It covers 22 acres in Akora and only 9 acres in Wussan village.

Shady trees such as Chinar and other fruit trees found in Akora and Wussan villages stop sun-rays from falling on the ground. The land under such trees becomes unsuitable for cultivation. Such land is called 'Zere Saya' and is used for pasturing the cattle. It covers 6 acres in Wussan and only one acre in Akora.

About 36% of land in Akora and 28% land in Wussan villages have been classed as 'Sair Mumkin'. This type of land is not suitable for cultivation as it is stony and steep. Small grasses grow over such land which is used for pasturing the sheep and goats and cattle of the village. Gujjars living in Wussan village have captured portions of Gair Mumkin land and converted it into maize fields. This trend is responsible for low percentage of Gair Mumkin land in Wussan village.

In Dansal and Shadali villages at low altitudes irrigation is not possible due to revines. Agriculture generally depends on rainfall. Here the slope of the land generally determines the quality of the field. Village Dansal is gently slopy. Here about 48% of the total geographical area of the village is under cultivation. But Shadali village which is steep slopy and on ravines has only 13% of its land under cultivation.

In both the villages people cultivate three types of land (Table 5). These are known as Sagarh, Briyal and Tanala. Land with gentle slopes and thick soil cover is called as Sagarh. The homestead is made in this land and the field around it is developed for the cultivation of wheat and maize and pulses. The land which is moderately slopping and away from the homestead is called Briyal land. It receives less attention as it gives only one crop in a year. It is kept fallow for about six months. The lands situated by the side of stream are water logged. Such land is called as Tanala land. It is used for growing fodder grass. This land is kept reserve for the Gujjars who visit this village during winters. They purchase this land at the rate of Rs. 400.00 per acre for pasturing their sheep and goats.

Land Ownership

Terraced fields are private properties. Sons inherit the land from father. As such a plot of land is fragmented into smaller pieces as generation passes. From the Table 1 it is observed that terrace field per person in Akora is higher (0.3 acres) than Wussan (0.2 acres).

Grazing land within the village is owned by the village community. But the willow tree, and fruit trees such as cherry, apprecot and walnuts are owned individually. The only exception is the chinar trees which are given special attention. It is a tall and shady tree and enhances the beauty of the place. It is owned by the Government and nobody is allowed to cut it.

Government reserves some land in the village for the purpose of development and welfare of the local inhabitants. Portions of the river and streams and stretch of forests are managed by the Government. In Akora village the forest department has planted kicker trees in an area of 4 acres. Residents of this village can collect dried leaves and fallen branch of trees. Grazing of cattle is also permitted. Trees are annually auctioned by the forest department.

Stretch of the river Lidder and Streamlets falling in it are also owned by the Government. In Akora village a portion of 'Trout' Nala is developed by the fisheries department. Permits are issued to interested parties for catching trout fish. Some portion of Lidder river passing by Akora village is auctioned by the Irrigation department for collecting sand and boulders. This contract is given to a few Muslims of Akora village.

Rate of Production

Rate of production (Table 4) of crops vary at low and middle altitude villages. It depends on the quality of the soil, cropping pattern and climate. Wheat, maize are the cereal crops at low altitude. Rate of production per acre of wheat at Dansal is 4-6 quintals per acre. Maize on the other hand gives 5-7 quintals per acre. In the village, maize is sown in relatively smaller acreage than wheat but it gives larger production. Mustard is a cash crop and grown in the Sagarh and Briyal land. Recently it is getting more attention and sown in larger area of the field. Rate of production of paddy at middle altitudes is higher than wheat or maize at low altitudes. The acreage rate of production of Sali paddy in Akora village is 10-12 quintals per acre. Families having 5 acres irrigated land produce surplus rice.

Transhumance: A Case Study of the Bakarwals

Bakarwals are a nomadic people who utilize the middle and low altitude zones by transhumance. It is practiced by the Bakarwals for adjustment to the seasonal changes. As their economy is based on the domestication of sheep and goats hence they have to move at different altitudes for getting pastures. With the onset of winter, the Bakarwals slowly move to lower altitudes with their sheep and goats. They cross the Pir Panjal range and stay at the margin of foothill villages. By the middle of April, that is, after the Baisakhi festival, they leave the foot hills and slowly move to the upper regions. Their high altitude camps are located near Amarnath and Dras at altitudes of about 10,000 ft. to 12,000 ft.

At lower altitude, such as, at Dansal and Shadali villages, Bakarwals sell wool to local traders. With the money received, they purchase maize or wheat flour, rice, salt, sugar, tobacco and clothes. Wool is also given to Harijans living near Dansal village for making woolen blankets on wages. These blankets are carried by the Bakawals and sold at Udhampur or Srinagar markets. They also give their maize land to Gujjars for cultivation and get a share of the produce from them.

In their high altitude encampments, the sheep and goats are fattened. They collect milk and prepare ghee, butter and cheese. It is sold at Angu village at an altitude of 8000ft. towards Amarnath. On way, they visit Akora village and make temporary camp at the outskirt of this village.

Bakarwals are Muslims by religion. Their society is patriarchal but the place of woman in their society is important. They attend to most of the domestic duties such as milking of goats, shearing of wool, tending horses, leading the party. Traces of Polygamy have been noticed. Marriage is settled with the consent of the girl. The prospective bridegroom has to work at the house of the bride for few months and his behaviour is watched. Separation and divorce is common among them.

Conclusion

Now we have some idea about the direction of economy in the two altitudinal regions under study. Horticulture is becoming profitable to the residents of Akora and Wussan villages of middle altitudes. It requires less labour and moderate investment. For maintaining an apple orchard of about half acre will require 60 apple saplings. This can be purchased at a cost of Rs. 200. Fencing of the garden will cost rupees one thousand. The owner will have to wait for five years when the trees will bear fruits. During this period inter cropping of pulses, peas, and cats, is possible within the orchard. After 5 years, 60 apple trees yield fruits of about eight thousand rupees annually. Attracted by its profitability the Hindus of Akora village have converted the land fit for maize cultivation into apple gardens. The example of Kaniyalone village may be cited here. This village is situated at a distance of 2 km from Akora. This village sells apples worth Rs.16 lakh annually.

Villages at low altitudes are handicapped in maintaining fruit gardens due to unfavourable climate. Therefore the only alternative open to them as animal husbandry and selling milk and milk products. Gujjars of Shadali village domesticate buffaloes and sell milk and cheese to the nearby towns. From this village alone about one quintal butter chena is sent to Nandani for transport to Srinagar. Hindus of the village are drifting away from agriculture towards services and business.

References

De Terra H. and T. T. Palerson (1939), Studies in Ice Age in India. Carneigee Institute of Washington.

NCAER (1969), Techno Economic Survey of Jammu and Kashmir. New Delhi.

Singh, R. L. (1971), India – A Regional Geography Varanasi : National Geographical Society of India.

Wadia, D. N. (1939), Geology of India, London : MacMillar & Co.

Walter R. Lawrence (1967), The Valley of Kashmir. Srinagar.

6 Forest and People in Upper Sutlej Valley

R. GUPTA AND T. LAL

The Western Himalaya like other hilly areas has a vast treasure of natural resources. This mountain tract is very sensitive from the point of view of its strategic location and complex ecological situation. Forest resource of the region is very important considering the socio-cultural activities of the people living here. Forest in the Western Himalaya extends between the river Indus in Jammu & Kashmir and river Kali in U.P. Himalaya about 900 Kms. The forest lore is so intimately woven in social fabric of the people that the existence of hill society without its forest can not be imagined. For all their basic needs viz. timber for their houses, fuel for their hearths, fodder for their cattle and pasturage for their herds, people are totally dependent upon the forest.

In the present paper an attempt has been made to consider the relation of the people with the forest in the upper Sutlej Valley of Western Himalaya. The Sutlej river within the Himalayan Mountains runs about 450 kms. which generally takes south westernly direction passing through the districts of Kinnaur, Kulu, Simla, and Bilaspur. The river forms the administrative boundary of the Simla and Kulu districts. The length of upper Sutlej Valley is about 130 kms. which falls in Kinnaur district of Himachal Pradesh.

Kinnar district was formed as a separate administrative unit by upgrading Chini and Rampur tehsil of the old Rampur

Bushahr State (Mahasu district of H.P.) on 1st May 1960. The district derives its name obviously after the tribal name, Kinner, the dominant segment of the local people. Kinnaur is situated in the eastern Himachal Pradesh and lies between 30°05'45" and 32°05'20" N latitude and 77°45'0" to 79°0'50" East longitude, having a total geographic area of 6553 sq. kms. It is surrounded on the north by Lahul and Spiti district, on the east by China and on the South and West by Simla and Uttarkashi district of Uttar Pradesh. The total population of the district is 58,154 as per 1981 census. The population density of the valley is 9 person per square km as per the census of 1981.

The Sutlej Valley under study is secluded, rugged and mountaneous to extra ordinary degree, consisting of a series of mountains, precipitous ravines descending rapidly to the bed of the river. This entirely mountaineous region is more or less equally divided by the Sutlej river, the river entering the Kinnaur district from north east and leaving at its western end. Sutlej river in its passage through Kinnaur district crosses more or less three parallel mountain ranges – the Zanskar mountains, the Great Himalaya and the Dhauladhar ranges. The crest of these mountain ranges lie generally up the perpetual snow line with many peaks rising between 5180 m and 6777 m, except where passes break the high ranges.

The climate varies with the altitudes. Climate is moderate in summer, while in winter, the more inaccessible portion of the tracts is not exceptionally cold. Location has great bearing on the winter climate as most of the high altitude villages are situated on sunny sides. So, the climatic conditions vary not only with the altitude but also with the factors like the direction of the valley faces, their width etc. With the complex physiographic conditions, the district has a temperate zone climate with long winter from October to May when snowfall occurs, and a short summer from June to September.

Practically monsoon rains are spent before they reach Kalpa and most of the precipitation is in the winter in the form of snow. Avalanches in the area are frequent at high altitudes and at times have ploughed long lines through forest, being especially destructive at the slopes of Kailash. To the east of

Wangtu, rainfall decreases as border is approached. The climate of Pooh sub-division of the upper Kinnaur is semi-arid. In January 1979, snowfall recorded at Kalpa was 243 mm while the rainfall recorded was 58.08 mm (May), 7.20 mm (June), 11.06 mm (July), 7.87 mm (August), 11.6 mm (September), 7.1 mm (October), 18.9 mm (November). At the same place, there was 91.00 mm snowfall in the month of December 1979.

The Sutlej Valley once used to be rich in Fauna. But with gradual increase of cattle stock, population density, and decrease in forest area, the wild life has depleted. Now the principal fauna are brown bear, musk deer, antelope, goral, ibex, wild sheep, etc.

The forest is the principal natural resource of the district. Forest covers 281.14 sq. km. area of the district. Deodar, spruce and Kail are the important flora species of this area. Very little is known before 1850 about the forest of the district. Frequent fires for cultivation till then had left to the present day the mark of their revenges. In 1850 however, a native trader purchased deodar tree at the rate of two anna each, from the Raja of Rampur Bushahr State. He was followed by European traders who were felling deodar, even in the accessible forest area. Raja granted "parwana" to these traders. A bag of rupees was sufficient to purchase an indefinite number of trees. All timber was extracted in logs generally of 10′ to 12′ in length for making railway-slippers in the plains. Little care was taken to avoid the enormous wood waste. Dr. Cleghan, in 1862, estimated that only one quarter to one third of the logs of forest reached to the sales depot. The Raja found great difficulty in dealing with the traders who constantly avoided their obligation. A lease was prepared by the government, in the year 1864 to 1877 which affixed royalty being paid to each tree fall. Dr. Brandis (Afterward Sir Districh) in company with various other forest officers made rough Survey of Bushahr forest and has left on record some very interesting remarks. He calculated that between 1859 -1863, 30,000 deodar trees were felled from accessible part and a large proportion of the forest from lower hills had been completely destructed. In the lease period, from 1877 to 1920, the same was revised by the government which agreed to pay a fixed annual sum to Raja on a fifty years lease base, renewable at the will of the government. Forest settlement and demarcation was done in 1884 by Mr. Minniken who prepared the records of rights and the revision of the demarcation with a view to the exclusion of buffaloes belonging to Gujjars for which villagers represented. Tikka Raghu Nath Singh carried out a revenue settlement in 1885 in which, for the first time, fields were actually measured and mapped. From 1920 onwards regular forest settlement plans are available.

The climate and the altitude are the important factors affecting the distribution, density, and quality of forest. Climatically the area under study may be divided into two parts. First one the area which is getting rainfall due to monsoon can be classified as wet zone, and the second one is dry zone which does not get any monsoon rain. This climatic factor is well represented in forest area of the region.

The wet zone forest occurs on the well drained sites and on ridges and spurs generally forming an admixture with Kail, Spruce and fir. In the depressions broad leaved species like horse chestnut, hazelnut, maple, bird cherry and walnut are found. On the left side of the Valley, forest comes much lower down towards the river than they do on the right bank due to isolation of direct sun light restricting the spread of vegetation. From river side at 1220 metres to alpine pastures at snow line, on the right bank consists of grass land and forests, are on the higher altitude. Upto 1600 m (approx) Chir pine is found, whereas on sheltered ravine banks between 1600 metre to snowline, cedrus deodar and pinus flourish.

The dry zone forest includes the forest of Kalpa and Kilba Kailash range. This extends from Sutlej valley of Nachar to the cliffs of Kalpa sub-division. In this zone low level forest comprising Neoza pine form an open forest along both banks of Sutlej valley.Neoza forest occur both in demarcated and undemarcated forests. The unedible seed of the Neoza pine play an important role in the socio-economic activity of the people of this district. Neoza grows in the altitudinal limit of 1500 and 3300 m beyond monsoon zone. This pine demands little fertility of the soil and is capable of growing on excessively dry barren hill sides with shallow soil and even on the bare rocks. Above the Neoza pine, there are deodars forming pure forest belt throughout the greater part of the area. Further above, there are blue pine and spruce, followed by silver fir between 3000 to 4000 metres.

Apart from wet zone and dry zone forests in the parts of east Kalpa, Pooh upto the junction of Spiti and Sutlej river and Hangran sub-tehsil, semi-arid zone forest exists. In this zone at considerable temperate and elevated place, deodar grows, but its expansion is limited and is concentrated in few patches.

After discussing the major forest zones, we may now consider the classification of forest from the points of view of supervision and administration. Forests are thus classified as reserved, protected and undemarcated as given in the following Table 1.

Table 1
Area Under Forests (*In Sq. Kms.*)

Year	*Reserved Forest*	*Protected Forest*	*Undemarcated Unclassed Forest*	*Total Forest*
1972-73	-	208.41	5805.48	6013.89
1973-74	-	208.41	5805.48	6013.89
1974-75	-	208.41	5804.54	6012.95
1975-76	-	208.41	5804.54	6012.95
1976-77	-	208.41	5804.54	6012.95

Source: Division Forest Officer, Kinnaur.

There is no reserved forest in the district. Protected forests are under the control of forest authority, while undemarcated/ unclassed forests, which are also called as panchayat forest, are under the control of village panchayat and forest authority. Local administration is also responsible for the maintenance of the later. Felling or any other activity in the unclassed forest may be done after having a joint decision of all the parties. This classification legally permits the right of the users to timber and other domestic requirements including grazing rights. The residents of the valley are permitted to exercise their rights and avail the concession laid down in the forest Settlement report in protected forests. The report also explains that the right exercised in the demarcated forest can be exercised in the same way as in the undemarcated forest.

People and Forest

In the Himalayan zone the people and forest are so much closely associated with each other that it seems difficult to separately study them in isolation. Since ancient times from generation to generation, the forest dwellers had utilized the forests for cultivation, grazing and fuel purposes without difficulty. At that time, forests were in abundance and population was sparse. But due to rapid increase in human and livestock population and high influx of outsiders for wood cutting and cattle grazing it was felt necessary to define the rights of the users in the forest. The right of the users is mentioned in the report on Forest Settlement of Sutlej valley in Bushahr State.

The record of the rights for demarcated forest provides grazing facilities to domestic animals including the pack animals. Timber for building purposes are given as per the provision laid down by the Government. Also there are provisions for the collection of firewood, dry and felled wood. Villagers may even collect the torch wood, fruits, honey, edible and other seeds from the forest. Other concessions authorize the villagers to collect neoza for sale and personal use. Besides, wood for repairing the water channel, cremation, devotion may also be collected free of cost. Collection of earth for plastering, stone for building purpose, maintenance of existing water mills are also permissible.

The concession rate for the timber is quite cheaper to the local people in comperison to the market rate. Following table indicates the wider rate difference in the amounts paid by the right holders and in market.

Name of Tree	*Rate for the right holder*	*Rate in market i.e. for non-right holders*
Deodar	Rs. 0.50 to Rs. 5/- per tree	Rs. 4.90 to Rs. 612.50 per tree
Kail Neoza	Rs. 0.30 to 2.00 per tree	Rs. 2.94 to Rs. 367.50 per tree
Chir	Rs. 0.25 per tree	Rs. 1.96 to Rs. 245.00 per tree
Rai Tosh	Rs. 0.13 per tree	Rs. 0.98 to161.70 per tree
Walnut	Rs. 1.50 per tree	Rs. 3.00 to Rs. 165.00 per tree

Source: Chief conservator of forest, 1965.

The rate of any particular variety of tree varies as per the diameter, which is given in the following table.

Grading of the tree	*Diameter in cms.*
V	10 to 20 cms
IV	20 to 30 cms
III	30 to 40 cms
IIA	40 to 50 cms
IIB	50 to 60 cms
IA	60 to 70 cms
IB	70 to 80 cms
IC	80 to 90 cms
ID	90 to 100 cms

This is considered in the valuation of any variety of trees. At the pastures of Runang, Tasang, Kasang and Hipa of Kalpa range, Gharghat and Rani Kanda pasture of Sangla and Bhabha, Tarranga, Aaari, Nachar and Panwai pastures of Nachar besides the local cattle, also the livestock of Gujjars and Gaddis graze in the summer. Rate charged for nonright holder graziers are as Rs. two for each Horse, donkey, and mule, Rs. 0.37 for each goat and Rs.0.19 for each sheep in the forest area. In Himchal Pradesh, forest department itself is exploiting the forest as per their working plan. In the year 1976-77 the timber, 9.57000 cu mts was marketed with the market value of Rs. 3,029,000. In the same year, besides the timber the values of other minor products of the forests were Rs. 5485.12 (fodder and grazing). Rs. 4107.25 (gums and resins) and Rs. 5,529.18 (other forest products).

As the fruits grown at high altitudes have taste, colour and aroma of their own, the fruits of the Sutlej valley now find ample market. In 1976-77, Kinnaur produced 3,802 tonnes of fruits in 1800 hectares of land. Since these are quickly perishable products, packing cases are essentially required, and the fir, spruce and Chir wood for making packing cases is supplied to the villages at subsidized rates.

A Conservational Approach

The forest of the district is valuable and has to be preserved for maintaining the steady flow of water in Sutlej and also to keep its water free from silt. The harm caused due to grazing of sheep and goat is incalculable particularly in the dry zone where grass and herbs growth is scanty. As the herds pass through the forest they break up the soil with feet causing it to slide down, exposing the roots of deodar seedlings to sun heat and causing them to dry up and die. Wild animals and birds also damage the forest by their movement and eating away the neoza seeds.

The local people are primarily agriculturist and pastoralists. Their land utilization practices are primitive resulting in serious erosion, some time threatening the very existence of the habitation. Apart from the extensive use of the right holders in the forest the entrance of outsiders with the construction of roads is posing another threat to this valuable resource. Road building besides providing employment to the local people has also accelerated the ravage of the forest, because forest produce can be easily marketed by the outsiders. With the construction of roads the vegetation over entire strech buried under a layer of earth and once the earth is loosened landslide starts. Afterwards with the loosening of rock structure and starting of the landslide, the hill regions are subject to frequent flood, earthquake, and other natural calamities.

Due to excessive utilization and exploitation of the forest and geological sequences the district alongwith nearby district of Lahul and spiti was rocked by earthquake tremors on 19th January 1975. This has resulted in considerable damage of the life and property of the area. Pooh sub-division was worstly hit by this. Seriously affected villages were Leo, Neko, Sialkhar, Sumra, Hango, Chuling and Malling.The earthquake registered 25 deaths. The people of the valley had faced the situation boldly and returned to their field for cultivation shortly.

In view of the ecological imbalance caused by the mass level deforestation and excessive use of the forest products, it is necessary to formulate some measures to protect the interests of people and forest. For the proper forest forming and environmental conservation, some suggestions are as follows:

1. Preparation of long term systematic and scientific plan for the forests.

2. Forest plan should be associated with regeneration of the forest, for which a balanced approach is necessary.
3. Some undemarcated forests may be classified into demarcated forests.
4. Availability of the alternate sources of fuel and torch wood to the local people to save the forest.
5. Protection of steep slope, loose mountains maintaining a permanent forest cover on them.
6. Regularisation of the unrestricted use of the forest for grazing the land.
7. Forest products must not be only considered as the source of revenue to the Government, but it should be regulated with the intensity of reforastration measures.
8. Views of the local people must be taken for the major decision on forest policy and their rights must be protected.
9. Alternate source of the packing case for fruits etc. may be made and packing case may be reutilized.
10. Practice of laying emphasis on perishable fruits need to be changed in favour of almond, neoza, walnut and other dry fruits.

In the past, people of the valley had the feeling that the forests were their ancestral property. But large scale felling and collections for outside use have created a feeling of insecurity in them. Since natural resources are being supplied to the outsiders without protecting their own interests, the local people also started damaging the forest in their own way without any conservational measure. As a result the friendly relation of the forest and people discontinued. This created ecological crisis in the region with landslides, earthquakes, bare rocks and soil erosion, etc. Hence it is necessary for us to prepare our forest policy, securing and protecting the feeling of hill dwellers. Their long experience with the forests will obviously be helpful for forming a conservational policy of this valuable resource. In the Himalaya the forest movement like 'Chipko' is widely spreading which is a movement of the local people to restrict the use of forest. It is the time when we should consider the demand of the people and their movement sympathetically which will protect our local regional and national interest. Indeed forest conservation in the Himalaya is part of a global problem. Forest precedes civilization and desert follows. Thus, our forest policy should call a halt to the succession of desert to our civilization. This is the high time to follow the slogan of 'agriculture for plains and silviculture for hills'.

References

Anons (1971), *State Gazetteer*, Kinnaur, Himachal Pradesh, Ambala.

Anons (1977), *Statistical Abstract* District Kinnaur. Directorate of Economic Statistics, Simla-1.

Anons (n.d.), *Existing Basic Facilities in Kinnaur District*. A monograph Published by Directorate Eco., and Statistics, H.P., Simla.

Clower, H. M. (1921), Report on the *Forest Settlement: Sutlej Valley Bashahr State Part – I* Lahore, Punjab: Suprd. Govt. Press.

Gupta, R. (1977), Terrace Cultivation in Uttarkashi District of Garhwal Himalaya (unpublished). Paper presented in *Tribal Economy* Seminar of Anth. Suv. I, Calcutta.

Tandon, J.C. (n.d.), Revised Working Plan for the Kinnaur Forests 1961-62 to 1975-76, Vol. I, Part-I.

7 Environmenal Diversity and Polyvalent Economy in the Western Himalayas

M. K. Raha

Introduction

"Along with many other factors which directly or indirectly contribute in shaping the pattern of livelihood of the people, the role of ecology is unquestionably a vital one" (Das and Raha: 1976: 36). The environment, in which the human being lives, has definitely much to contribute in shaping the human culture. Wherever he lives, be it desert, coastal area, arctic region or the high mountain, he cannot ignore his surroundings. For his own safety and survival he has to adapt himself and adjust with the conditions of the local environment. The influence of the environment thus becomes apparent in his material, as well as, socio-cultural life.

Many scholars have noticed the way a group adapts to the conditions of the ecology it lives in. Of the recent studies, Savishinsky, while working among a band of the Hare Indian in sub-Arctic Canada, noticed the influences of arctic environment on their life style, particularly their three main survival pursuits : hunting, fishing and fur trapping (1978: 1-25). Knight has also shown how intimate is the relationship between ecology and economy and ecology and social organisation among various trapping groups in the sub-Arctic settlements of Canada. He has also analysed the role of ecological factors in the changing economy and social organisation among these people. He has also suggested a set of economic and environmental factors to account for regional differences in the size, mobility and composition of those trapping groups (1968: 107-109). "The environment nearly always determines the most important elements of social organisation" (Barnard, 1979: 131). While analyzing the ecological influence on the settlement patterns of the Kalahari Bushman, Barnard has shown the influence of micro-environmental differences on their settlement pattern (*op. cit:* 132). A further case in point is that of the immigrant Oraons and Mundas living in esturine Sundarban (southern extremity of West Bengal facing Bay of Bengal). About a century ago these people came from lateritic upland of Chotangapur plateau (Bihar) to the alluvial esturine Sundarban as labourers and settled there. In course of time, they gradually adjusted themselves to the physical and cultural environment of their new domain and renovated their culture according to the need of the environment (Raha et al, 1978: 70).

In the foothills or Tarai region same picture is noticed. There the ecology-culture inter-relationship is as prominent as it is elsewhere, and this has even been depicted in the folk songs, verses, poems etc. (Raha et al: 1975). Identically in the Himalaya or any mountainous region the mountain ecology has a direct bearing with the various aspects of culture of the local inhabitants. It is felt that the transhumant mode of life and the pastoral economy of the Bhotia and the Anwals of high Himalayan valleys of the district of Pithoragarh have direct bearing with the local ecology (Das and Raha, 1976: 36-45). Similarly the Ladakhi society and its culture also reveal clearly the imprints of the local environment (Mann, 1978: 60-76).

All these and many other studies have impressed upon the fact that ecology of a region acts as one of the decisive controlling factors in the direction of moulding various aspects of the society, sometime indirectly or directly or compulsively as the case may be (Das and Raha, 1976 : 36). The same is the situation with the high altitude society of the Kinnaura of western Himalaya. In this article, I have tried to show the relationship between the Himalayan ecology and subsistence economy of this high altitude people and how they are exploiting the local environment for their survival persuits.

Space Environment and People: Strategic Issues

Kinnaur is the northeastern frontier district of Himachal Pradesh and having border with Tibet. Prior to May 1, 1980 it was a Tehsil of erstwhile Mahasu district. In the pre-independence era it was a part of the erstwhile Bhushahar state, one of the princely states of the Himalayas. The district has three sub-divisions namely Nachar, Kalpa and Pooh, and a total of 77 villages, situated between 7,000 ft. to 14,000 ft. (approx) above the mean sea level.

The area is thoroughly mountainous and very inhospitable. "Face of the country presents high hills and low dales and is marked by preciptous sky high mountains with their peaks usually covered with perpetual snow (Singh: 1965: 3). A series of mountains and precipitous ravines descending rapidly to the bed of the Sutlej and its tributaries, are seen in Kimaur. Three mountain ranges, the Zanskar, the Great Himalaya and the Dhaula Dhar, have encompassd the district. Within this mountains district there are several valleys, the largest one being the Sutlej valley. Several important villages are situated in this valley. The Sutlej is the principal river of the district. While passing through Kinnaur, it divides the district into two halves. This river is fed by a number of tributaries like the Spiti, the Ropa, the Taiti, the Baspa and the Yula etc. Besides, there are a number of rivulets and streams in this district.

The district has 6013.89 sq. km. of forests having ecological zones, viz. (1) the moist zone covering the lower Kinnaur, (2) the dry zone spreading over the central region and (3) the arid zone comprising the major part of upper Kinnaur. A number of wild animals are found in some of these forests. Owing to the peculiar geographical conditions, of the district, "one experiences change from the heat of the tropical zone almost to the freezing tempeature of a Lapland winter" (Singh: 1965: 3)". From the month of March the temperature begins to rise till June or July (which is considered as the warmest month) whereafter the temperature of the district drops gradually, the drop being very rapid after October" (Raha and Mahato: 1975: 21). The snowfall starts even in November and the whole district remain snowbound till April. The rainfall, which is no theavy, is not uniform throughout the district; it decreases rapidly from the southwest to the northeast of the district. As a result the most part of Pooh sub-divison is almost arid, while the monsoon reaches in its southwest part. The average rainfall of the southwest part (Nachar district) is 710.0 mm while it is only 400.0 mm in the northeast part; it is even less in the extreme northeast. Similarly, the snowfall (average of the district being 322.1 mm) also decreases from southwest (434.2 mm) to northwest about 200.0 mm) region.

Like its three eco-zones, the district has three corresponding culture zones. The northeast part or the Upper Kinnaur i.e. Pooh sub-division which corresponds to the arid zone, is dominated by the Mahayan Buddhism; the southeast part or lower Kinnaur i.e. Nachar sub-division which corresponds to the moist climate, is influenced by the local Hinduism and the central part or Kalpa sub-division which, corresponds to the dry zone bear both Buddhism and local Hinduism (Raha and Mahato: 1975: 16, Raha: 1978: 84).

According to 1971 Census, the district of Kinnaur has a population of 49,835 (26,407 males, and 23,428 females) which is 1.44% of the total population of the state. Of this population, 32.93% live in Pooh sub-division, 38.56% inhabit Kalpa sub-division and the remaining 28.50% reside in nachar sub-division. The majority of the population (68.41%) belongs to the scheduled tribe (the Rajput or Kanet section). The scheduled castes population consists of the Koli, the Lohar, the Badhi and the Nangalu, who together form only 19.40% of the total population of the district. The density of the population is low. It is only 8 people per sq. km. according to the 1971 Census. Social stratificaion on the basis of hierarchy is a characteristic feature among the Kinnaurese (Raha and Mahato: 1975: 260), who may be divided into two broad sections the Khosia and the Beru. The numerically dominant Khosia includes the Rajput or Kanet who are practically the most important element being the land owners and enjoy a superior position. The Beru group consists of the Lohar or the black smith, the Koli or the weaver, spinner and agriculturists, the Badhi or the carpenter and the mason, and the Nangalu or the basket maker (Raha: 1978: 88-90). The members of the Beru group serve the Rajputs and have a inferior social status.

Resources: Development and Utilization

Economy in the Past

From time immemorical till early sixty, the economy of the Kinnaura was based on three important sources, viz. agriculture, animal husbandary and trade. For generations, these three major activities governed the life and activities of the people of this high altitude society. Like many other societies of the high Himalaya, in this society also there exists a direct link and involvement of the natural environment with the life of the people residing there.

As the area is rugged and mountainous, the cultivable land was only available in the valleys and mountain slopes where terrace cultivation was the only possible means. Moreover terracing was also required in order to utilize the irrigation water (rain, show and spring) in its highest capacity. Further because of the peculiar geographical position no vast tract was available for cultivation. The soil was rocky and coarse and was definitely having a very low fertility. The rainfall was scanty and irrigational facilities were undoubtedly insufficient. Further due to heavy snowfall during winter, the whole area remains snowbound almost during winter; the whole area remains snowbound almost from December to April, when no agricultural work was possible. As a result the Kinnaures had no option but to seek for two major alternatives. Firstly, they started utilizing land wherever they get, and as such the Kinnaura have three different types of cultivable land. (1) The high altitude land or Kanda land which are usually situated in high altitude area (12,000 to 15,000 ft. above mean sea level) and far off from the village. This type of land is usually single cropped land. (2) Cultivable land around the village or Kimsaring which usually produces two crops a year and

(3) Neoglang land or lower altitude land situated below the village level and usually a double cropped land. Inspite of their maximum utilization, what they produced from all these three types of land, was not sufficient. As such, they stepped in for the other alternatives, i.e., trade and animal husbandry, particularly the rearing of sheep and goat. The low production from the land was not the only reason for their option for the trade and rearing of sheep and goat. The other reason was definitely their demand for some basic needs of daily use, such as, salt, butter, wool etc. which were essential for their survival in extreme climate. Fraser, in the first quarter of this century, noticed that the Kinner used to get very little of grains from their agricultural field (1820 : 263), and in exchange of what other things they could produce, they used to take cereals of different kinds from the neighbouring more fertile areas. Through trade they used to bring salt, wool, pasmina, tea, borax, butter etc. from the other side of the border in exchange of match lock, sugar, tobacco, cloth, indgo, copper, power paper, iron, grains, spices etc. from the neighbouring plains areas.

The Kinnaures were good traders. They were "almost exclusively the commercial couriers between Hindustan and Tartary, and also between Tartary and Cashmere, frequenting the routes from Leh in Ladhak, Lhassa and Dogurcha and Nepal on trading speculation. The Kenawar merchants carry on trade not only with plains and neighbouring Chinese provinces but they are also the chief carriers between Garha, Ladhak and Cashmere, and even push their commercial enterprises as far as Lhassa on the south-east, exchanging commodities between that place and Nepal, and between Cashmere, Yarkhand, Kashgar, Garha, and the various cities and people of these quarter" (Fraser 1820: 264: 274).

To carry the merchandises in the neighbouring areas or trade centers across the border or also to different fairs, they definitely required carriers. In these difficult high altitude terrains where there was no road, but only very narrow tracts, sheep and goats could be used as effective pack animals. Besides, the demand for wood for protection against the biting cold also made the rearing of sheep and goats an essential alternative. Thus, the animal husbandary developed as one of the important sources of their livelihood, and added to their flock of sheep and goats, some other animals like cattle, mule, yak etc.

Besides the Rajput or Kanet whose past occupations have been described above, there are four other ethnic groups, who also have their own taditional occupations. As referred earlier, the Koli were agriculturists, weavers and leather workers, the Lohar were iron and silver workers, the Badhi were carpenters and also mason and the Nangalu usually make basket from Chihor crippers. All these artisan castes were mean to serve the Rajputs through a traditionally connected bond.

The three major survival persuits of the Rajput as mentioned above continued to exist till the closure of the border with Tibet in early sixties. The closure of the border definitely had tremendous impact on the life and culture of the people is this district and brought about a number of changes in the socio-economic life of the Kinnaura. This event not only stopped the trade with the Tibet, but also brought about changes in other economic persuits and also in their life cycle. Earlier, through trade, they imported items of daily necessities, and such other items both for their own consumption, and for ale, in different fairs and markets. With money thus earned they purchased goods for merchandise and carried those to the trade centers across the border. But after the closure of the border, they became wholly dependent for all these goods in the neighbourhood. Besides, they became totally dependent on pastures of Indian side while the alpine pastures in Tibet became out of their reach. However, the Govenrment took a number measures to recover this economic depression. A number of developmental programmes were started, new communication and transport systems established and the inhabitants gradually adopted new economic pursuits like service, labour, business, horticulture and so on.

Present Economic Situation

The present economy of the Kinnaura is based mainly on agriculture and animal husbandry. The other traditional occupation, trade with Tibet, got disrupted with the closure of the border in early sixties" with the construction of roads (after 1960) and opening of the modern communication and transport systems when the area shook off its age old isolation, and with the promulgation of new administrative system, intensification of modern education and introduction of new developmental programmes, many people of the district inclined towards diversified occupation" (Raha: 1977: 6).

The census of 1971 shows that 60.52% of the total population of Kinnaur are workers. The majority of the workers (62.72%) are engaged in agriculture. The sex wise involvement in this occupation indicates that more women than men have adopted this occupation. While only 46.71% of the males are wholly engaged in cultivation as high as 84.27% of the females are involved in this profession. It clearly shows the keen interest the Kinnaura have towards agriculture. In the present day they have accepted this as their main source of livelihood. Their dependence on agriculture is unquestionable. Even a decade ago that they had the same interest towards agriculture, has been reflected in the returns of the census of 1961 which shows that 66.46% of the total Kinnaura workers (67.17% of the total population) were cultivators. Sex wise distribution of the working class during the same census period shows that 51.90% of the males and 81.62% of the fair sex remained engaged to this persuit. Our survey in three villages from three subdivisions (Nachar, Kalpa and Pooh) also reveals that the overwhelming majority of the male workers and almost all female workers remain engaged in agriculture. While 88.79% of the male workers in chango and 89.93% in Kongos are somehow involved in cultivation, in case of Rogi it is 79.68% (Raha and Mahato 1975: 165-169).

But "with the opening of the roads and starting of various constructional and developmental works, a good number of male workers got non-agricultural jobs like labour, service etc. within and outside the district. As a result these male workers have to abandon the age-old agro-based occupation and to engage in some other jobs. This is clearly indicated by the sufficient increase in the frequency of the male workers from 1961 to 1971 in other services. While only 8.74% were involved in other services in 1961, it increased to 22.31% in 1971. Our survey also shows that in Chango while 19.15% workers are some-how engaged in non-agricultural jobs including service, in Kongo it is 18.70; but in Rogi because of its proximity with the district Head Quarters, Kalpa, the frequency of workers involved in non-agricultural jobs is as high as 25.78%. This shows that the present day Kinnaura are getting interested in the non-agricultural jobs more and more. The educated persons are hankering for the while collered jobs like service; and more and more of them are actually accepting service as their livelihood.

As to the people of Kinnaura cultivtion being the most important type of occupation, we would now turn our attention towards land holding system in Kinnaura. "It is something unique that very few inhabitants are landless. Most of them own land. Of course, the size of landholding varies. 98.6% of the total households of Kongos have land, 96.9% of Rogi and 76.2% of chango households possess the same" (Raha: 1977: 10). If the land holding of the individual ethnic groups is examined, it is seen that while all the Rajput households of Kongos and Rogi own land, 97.4% of them residing at Chango are the owners of land. Identically among the next dominant group, the Koli, 96.7%, 95.5% and 80.0% of the households at Kongos, Rogi and Chango respectively own land. The same is the condition with the other ethnic groups like the Lohar or the Badhi. Only at Rogi half of their households possess land.

It is clear from the data that in Kinnaur the Rajputs have more land under their disposal, and their average per household holding is also much higher than other ethnic groups. The table, below, gives a clear picture about the average per household land holding of different ethnic groups from three different villages of Kinnaur.

Table 1
Averae per Household Landholdings

	Average landin acre owned by		
Village	*Rajput*	*Koli*	*OEG**
Kongos	3.09	1.61	0.48
Rogi	7.02	1.33	0.60
Chango	2.14	0.62	1.35

*OEG means 'Other ethnic groups.

The table shows that the Rajputs have more land in their possession than other ethnic groups. Of the three villages, the Rajputs of Rogi village has much higher acreage of land than their compatriots living in the other two villages.

Ecological Involvement

As already stated the district of Kinnaur has three distinct eco zones. The Nachar sub-division because of its monsoon rain, comes under moderately moist zone; Kalpa sub-division is the dry area as it gets some, though very much insufficient monsoon rain whereas Pooh sub-division is arid as almost no monsoon rain can reach this place.

On examining the involvement of the environment in economic spheres of the Kinnaura society, it is revealed that the two, ecology and economy, are intimately interwoven, particularly in the Himalayan situation. From Table 2 it is clear that while in Nachar area where the environmental condition is quite congenial to the agro-economy as it is in the monsoon zone and in a comparatively lower altitude area, the people remained more involved with agriculture and were least bothered about trade. Animal husbandry was also developed moderately. The reason possibly is that the people had to devote more, both man power and time, in agriculture, so to spare time and manpower for a pursuit like trade, was not considered profitable whereas in Pooh area which is arid and high altitude zone and as such the environmental and soil conditions were not at all congenial to agriculture, people preferred trade and animal husbandry over agriculture. This is because of the difficult terrain, unfertile soil condition and lack of irrigation facilities. These have led to a very low agricultural production. The low agricultural production, people demand for various daily necessities, some of which are essential for the extreme climatic condition and their nearness to the trade centers of the country across the border, probably allured and compelled the inhabitants of Pooh to involve more in trade and animal husbandry. The environment here has played a role in the selection of the economic persuits and the survival strategies of the Kinnarua.

Table 2
Ecology and Economy Reltionship in Kinnaur

					Environmental Condition			
Subdivisions	*Area (in Sq. Km.)*	*Altitude (average)*	*Rainfall (Avg. mm.)*	*Snowfall (in mm.)*	*Vegetation*	*Weather*	*Population 1971*	*Involvement insurvival persuit*
Nachar	42.1	7000	710.0	434.2	Thick	Monsoon area wet.	12,120	Trade – Minimum Animal husbandary Moderate. Agriculture Maxium
Kalpa	51.7	9500	322.2	629.1	Moderate	Dry	15,612	Trade Moderate. Animal husbandary Moderate Agri: Maximum
Pooh	46.6	11000	270.1	235.2	Thin to Nil.	Arid	13,248	Trade Maximum. Animal husbandary Maximum Agri: Minimum

Ecology, Animal Husbandry and Trade Sndrome

Another distinct case of the environmental involvement is the development of woolen industry. As the whole area is situated on the high altitude, where extreme cold prevails throughout when the whole area remain heavily snowclad, people felt the perpetual need of wool and woolen garments. To fulfil this demand they opted firstly for the rearing of sheep and goats to make wool available at home and secondly imported wool from Tibet through a trade link. As a result almost simultaneously, these two persuits, rearing of sheep and goats and trade of wool developed. Further as these two persuits gradually developed, an industry of wool also developed in this district and people started producing wool and woolen garments not only for their own consumption but also for selling the excess in the neighbourhood or in the fair.

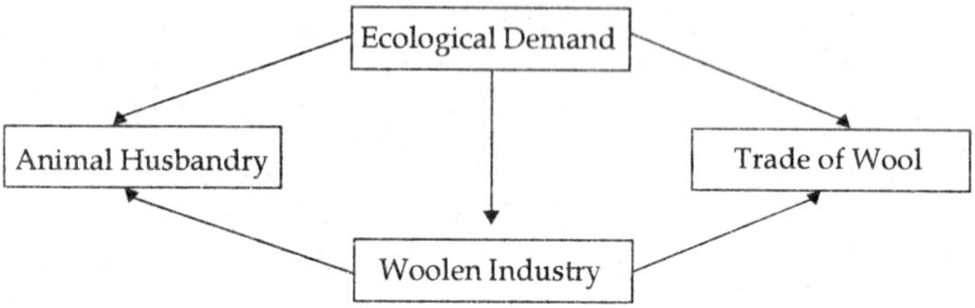

Survival Strategies

It is seen that the peculiar Himalayan ecology in Kinnaur subscribes to the growth and development of some survival persuits there. Because of the difficult environmental and soil conditions, the people there could not remain satisfied with their main productive economy i.e. agriculture the output of which was definitely meager incomparison to the demand. The production was low because of the unfertile soil, restricted agricultural facility, production of inferior coreal etc. As agricultue alone was failed to satisfy their demand for survival, they were left with no option but to find out other alternative survival resources. Ultimately they could find that trade and animal husbandry would suit them in varied ways in this

Himalayan ecology. So in order to balance this deficiency they finally turned to trade and animal husbandry. This drift was absolutely necessary for their survival.

Another reason for their option for trade and animal husbandry, in which the local environment had played a role of a compelling factor, was the non-availability or insufficient supply of some basic necessifies which were very much essential for their survival in the high Himalayas. These items were wool, salt, butter, cereals, meat etc. In order to get these they had to depend on trade and animal husbandry. To win over the extreme winter one of the most essential items was wool; and for this essential life saving item they definitely felt the necessity of the developmnt of trade of wool and woolen industry.

It is thus seen that human being in a given ecosystem always fights for survival and moulds his survival strategies and mode of subsistence according to the demand of the local environment. Further and deeper studies are essential to see how people react to the existing eco-system and adapted themselves to suit the demand of the situation. I think Savishinsky (1978: 32) and Vayda and McCay's (1975: 293-306) view is quite relevant in this regard. "While recent studies in human ecology have provided sophisticated pictures of the relations between particular socities and their natural environments, we can refine these pictures ever further by examining the variable ways in which individuals, families, sub-groups within a society react to and interact with other components of their ecosystems".

References

Barnard, Alan (1979), Kalahari Bushman Settlement Pattern in *The Social and Ecological System*, (Ed) Philip Burnham and Roy. F. Ellen, Academic Press, London.

Das, J. C. and M.K. Raha (1976), "Ecology, Economy and Transhumance: A Study of an Immigrant Society in the Himalayas", *Bulletin of the Anthropological Survey of India*, Vol. XXV, No. 3&4.

Fraser, J. (1820), Journal of a Tour Through Part of the Snowy Range of the Himalayan Mountain and to the Sources of the Rivers Jamuna and Ganges, London.

Knight, R. (1968), "Ecological Factors in Changing Economy and Social Organisation Among the Rupert House Cree", Anthropological Papers No. 15, National Museum of Canada, Ottawa.

Leynsecle, P. Von (1979), Ecological Stability and Intensive Fish Production: The Case of the Libinza People of the Middle Ngiri (Zaire) in *The Social and Ecological Systems* (Ed.) Philip Burnham and Roy F. Ellen, Academic Press, London.

Mann, R. S. (1978), "Ecosystem and Society of Ladakh", *Jr. of Social Research,* Vol. XXI, No. 1, 1978.

Raha, M. K. (1977), "Changing Economy of the Kinnaurese" (Unpublished), Paper Presented to the minar on *Tribal Economy,* Anthropological Survey of India, Calcutta.

Raha, M. K. (1978), "Stratification and Religion in a Himalayan Society" in *Himalayan Anthropology* (Ed) James F. Fisher, Mouten Publishers, The Hague.

Raha, M. K. and S. N. Mahato (1975), The Kinnaurese of the Western Himalaya (Unpublished Report).

Raha, M. K., J. C. Das and S. Paul (1975), Verses from Western Duars: An Eco-Cultural Analysis, *Folklore,* Vol. X, No. 2.

Raha, M. K., J. C. Das and J. Singh (1978), "Ecological Perception of Esturine Sunderban and the Process of Cultural Readjustment: The Oraon Case" in *Xth International Congress of Anthropological and Ethnological Sciences* (Abstract) Vol. 3.

Riches, David (1979), "Ecological Variation on the Northwest Coast: Models for the generation of Cognatic and Matrilineal Descent", in *The Social and Ecological System* (Ed) Philip Burnham and Roy, F. Ellen, Academic Press, London.

Savishinsky, Joel, S. (1978), "Trapping, Survival Strategies and Environmental Involvement: A Case Study from the Canadian Sub-Archtic", *Human Ecology,* Vol. 6, No. 1.

Singh, R. C. P. (1965), District Handbook, Kinnaur, District Himachal Pradesh, Census 1961, Simla.

Vayda, A. P. and McCay, B. J. (1975), "New Directions in Ecology and Ecological Anthropology" in *Annual Review of Anthropology* (ed) B. J. Siegel, Vol. 4. Annual Reviews Palo Alto.

8 Cultural Adaptation to Mountain Environment: A Study from Garhwal Himalaya

Jitendra Singh

Mountains, one of the major features of the globe's geography, posses a great variety of environmental niche, suitably adjusted and inhabited by the people with diversified adaptive strategies, have very little and sporadic representative in anthropological studies as compared to those inhabiting tropical and subtropical forests, savanas, river valleys, Islands and coastal regions. Adaptation to various challenging environmental conditions of the mountains have long been a difficult task to its people, who in order to adjust themselves with the existing situations, had to adjust themselves with the existing situations, had to evolve certain unique devices that in due course have become traditional cultural diversities of the people, occupying different environmental niche. Varieties of factors responsible for varying mountain environments are well defined in the writings of Brush (1976).

"The outstanding feature of mountain ecosystem is altitude and a steep environmental gradient alongwith diurnal temperature climate in tropical areas, steep slopes and environmental stress factors cold and hypoxia - related to altitude. With the increase of altitude climatic conditions change: heat radiation increases resulting in lower temperature and a high diurnal temperature range, evaporation and isolation increase; exposures to wind increases greatly but varies on windward and leeward slopes and orographic rainfall patterns change, with leeward slopes and intermountanous valleys receiving generally less moisture than windward slopes and high valley areas. The effect of these changing climatic conditions on the vegetation of mountain areas is clear: a succession of vegetation belts or life zones".

The vegetation zones largely correspond to climatic zones which considerably effect and mould accordingly the life style of the people. Delineation of complex relation between climato-vegetation zones and human beings, generated as adaptive responses, contextual to material cultural and food procurement strategies among the Garhwali people of different Himalayan zones of Uttarkashi district, as evident from the studies of Badeti (lower altitude), Deora (middle altitude) and Dharali (high altitude), is the objective of present article.

Geo-Morphological Environment

The district of Uttarakashi is perched on the extreme northern edge of the state of Uttar Pradesh and on the Western corner of Garhwal Division, between 30°3′ and 31°18′ N and 77°49′ and 79°24′ E. On the north it touches Himachal Pradesh for most of the distance and Tibet in the rest. To west, south and east, it is bounded respectively by Dehradun, Tehri Garhwal and Chamoli districts of the Garhwal Division of Uttar Pradesh (Singh, 1987).

The entire district comes under Central Himalaya with a tangled series of mountain ridges with innumerable spurs separated by narrow valleys. The general direction of the main mountain ridges is from north-east to south-west, radiating from a loafty series of peaks boarding Tibet, which vary in height from 20,000 to 23,000 feet, above see level.

The district is traversed by a number of streams and rivulets, which together give rise to three main river systems - the Bhagirathi, the Yamuna and the Tons and three synonumous valleys respectively. The valleys are deep and narrow and mountain sides have steep gradients.

The climate ranges from tropical heat to severe cold. Places exposed to sun become warm during summer days, while nights are cold throughout the year. There is a great variation in temperature. Snowfall occurs as low as 4000 ft. in winters. Middle and lower altitude enjoy heavy rainfall during rainy season while only occasional drizzling occurs in high altitudes.

Interplay of local configuration and climate is largely responsible for the variation in seasons in the three altitudes. In middle and lower altitudes there are three seasons in a year– the *Sitkal*, the *Rudi* and the *Vaskai*. In the lower altitude *Sitkal* (winter) remains from mid-October to mid-February; the *Rudi* or *Khadsau* (summer) ranges from mid-February to mid-June, and the *Vaskal* (Rain) from mid-June to mid-October. However, in middle altitudes *Sitkal* persists a little longer (mid-October to mid-March); *Rudi* lessens (mid-March to mid-June) and *Vaskal* almost same (mid-June to mid-October). But high altitudes enjoy only two seasons - the long spell of *Sitkal* or *Heund* (mid-October to mid-April) and the rest months are considered to be the summer.

On the basis of rainfall, elevation, wind and temperature, etc. variants, the habitable mountain environment of the district is to be categorized into three broad vertically graded climatic zones. The first being the lower altitude (below the elevation of 4,000 ft.) or the Mansoon zone with tropical climate; the seen second is the middle altitude (i.e., between 4000 to 7000 ft.) or the Mansoon zone with temperat climate, while the third, the high altitude (i.e., above the elevation of 7000 ft.) or the Arid zone with colder climate. Corresponding broader vegetation zones are also to be demarcated. The lower altitudinal tropical mansoon zone is characterized by the natural growth of forests predominated by Pine trees, which in the middle altitudinal temperat mansoon zone are mixed with Banj (Oak) and Buran trees and those in high altitudes of arid and colder climate are totally replaced by the forests of Deodar trees. Categorically the mountains of the district are rocky but the rocks are not bare, they are sufficiently covered with thick crusts of soil rich in humus and hence are quite suitable for the growth of different kinds of vegetation.

Social Environment

The Garhwal Himalaya, in which the district of Uttarakashi lies, was formerly under the jurisdiction of Garhwal Kingdom. Garhwal has frequent references in Sanskrit texts like Skand Puran and Mahabharat in which it is respectively named as the territory of 'Kedar' and 'Kulind'. In these texts people of the area (Sabha-Parva) have also been enumerated, who took their names derived according to adoption of means of livelihood and topography etc. such as Poshup Kirat (pastoral Kirat), Ekasan Khas (settled Khas), Tangan, Partangan (traders of borax and horses), Tushar (people of snow land), Darad, Jyoja, Pradara and Parad. However, these names now a days have disappeared into the depth of time, though most of them still survive as Gotra name, of the people of different castes and sub-castes of hierarchical and dichotomous society. The idea of social dichotomy of Beet (Upper) and Dom (Lower) groups and bases of its differentiation such as division of labour and ritual purity, commerciality and marital choice etc. which have further stratified the former group into Brahmin and Rajput castes, each with several sub-castes, while the later into Mistri, Bajgi and Dom castes, was certainly a derivative of 'Varn' system brought and infused by the different people of the plains settled down in mountain areas.

Culture Environmental Orientation

Impact of varying environmental situations over the culture of the inhabitants of different zones can not be ignored. Generally all of the different aspects of life style automatically opt for suitable adoptations against the adversities of environment. But human habitations, their dress and food procurement strategies etc. aspect of material culture emit conspecious reflection of a particular type of environment as compared to values, beliefs, rituals and ceremonies etc. other parts of culture. There are recurrent processes which cross cut zonal boundaries as parallel adaptations to similar or dissimilar conditions of mountain environment. Due to relative geographical proximity of the communities of different zones and their mutual interaction and similar background, many of the analogus patterns are absorbed through the processes of common cultural genesis on diffusion. Unless otherwise specified, the description will generally be in terms of ethnographic present and comparative account is to be given if it does occur regarding adaptive responses in the three zones of the district.

Environment and Habitat

Owing to the occurance of gradient – a characteristic feature of the mountains, sufficient plain ground is not available for the village settlement and hence settlement pattern is irregular, scattered and graded. Choosing of settlement site is a matter of versatile experience for identifying firm hillocks devoid of avalanche and landslides. Besides, it should be made facing river valleys and along the sides of many slopes and perrenial streams for having maximum sun rays and constant supply of potable water. Mountain slopes are cut to make levelled plinth for the habitation and if space permits a levelled courtyard is also made in front of the house otherwise at the sides.

A typical *Kudu* or *Kuda* (dwelling) is self contained, compact and constructed under one gabled roof to escape cold and rain. Usually dwelling are two storied, but to accommodate increasing family members, the dwelling is raised upwards to add further stories totalling upto three. It is a beautiful adjustment to economise plinth area, roofing material and of course to avert maximum exposure of the house to the conditions of mountain environment. The dwellings are constructed by the building material available in the terrain i.e., wood and stone. The mountain houses, so to say are portable and admirably suited to sustain sesmic thrusts, avalanche and landslides. During the times of need (such as natural erosion or supernatural wish) the houses are dismentaled and with the same building material a new house is re-constructed over a new suitable site. The *Ovara* (ground floor) of the house, which to some extent is underground as a rule is spared for cattle. In this room a wooden *tanda* (shelf) is made to accommodate sheep and goat. There is a *Nissand* (stair case) in ovara to connect *Tanda* and *Manjula* (first floor). From inside, though the ovarasa has also a *Dar* (door) opening in the courtyard. In the two storied house, the *Manjula* is used as kitchen-cum-sleeping room while in three storied, it is used as sleeping-room and the *Baund* (second floor) is used as kitchen-cum-sleeping room. At the floor levels of *Manjula* and *Baund*, there are alround projections, which are fitted with surrounding railings to make it *Chauk* (Varandah) where the doors of *Manjula* and *Baund* open and are connected to each other and to the ground with a stair-case furnished with *Photda* (closing lid). The varndah surrounding the house are used for sitting, gossiping, basking, drying of household things and storing of fuel and foddar etc. The triangular space under the gelded roof is also covered to make an apartment for storing fuel and other household things. The inner walls of all the store are fitted with detachable *Khoti* (pace for bee-hive) having a small opening outside for allowing the bees to enter inside. The *Chhain* (Roof) is made of thick wooden poles and planks which in lower and middle altitudes are covered by nailing rectangular silt pieces. The upper most silt layer on roof is extra waterproof and protects the wooden plank layer from destruction due to moisture in monsoon zones which is of no use in arid zone. The walls of the house are plumbered on well dovetailed wooden frames filled in by stones and mud mortar and plastered with the paste-made by mixing of mud, cow-dung and straw. The doors are so small that for entering one has to crawl down. The houses are completely devoid of windows and vantilation but they have a small opening in the roof to excuse out smoke, which is shut down during rains and snow. People sleep together, bedding on wooden floors around the hearth having constant burning weeds or in the houses having hearth in the above floor and cattle in the lowest with the integrated central idea of keeping the house warm. The rooms are lighted by *Chhulha* (pine nodes) which also give warmth. All these factors contribute to retain warmth and curtain exposure to environment.

Environment and Grain Protection

The *Kothar* (granary) construction again focuses an unique adaptation to protect grains from the adverse conditions of the mountain environment. The Kothar an independent structure, looks like a small hut with front varandah, irrected in courtyard. The entire grainery is made by hard woods in such a careful way that it becomes completely air-tight and water-proof. Cereals and pulses used as staple food obiously amount much and stored in underneath *Ganja* (vertically elongated cells) numbering six in one door types while twelve in two-door types. Each *Ganja* has storing capacity from 20 to 23 maunds of cereals. The seeds are stored in *Bhindvali* (upper horizontal cells attached to store walls) numbering three in one-door-types while six in two door types. Each of the Bhindrali has carrying capacity of approximately two and half mounds of grains. In the rest of the open space inside the Kothar, other household belongings are also safely stored. The deer flap of the store has a provision of internal locking system and simultaneously it is connected by a big and thick *Sankal* (iron chain with bells) to the sleeping room to alarm the family members about the opening of the grainery.

Environment and Dress

The traditional dress pattern of the people of all the three zones reflects an adequate and advantageous adaptation to evade mountain cold and to compromise with the fluctuations of environmental conditions. The *Bhandi* (woolen) clothings prepared by the Koli experts with the wool of their own sheep are capable of preserving their body-heat as well as they are suited for rough use without the risk of wear and tear and being dirty. And similarly woolen beddings inclusive of carpets, wrappers etc. are well suited for the mountaneous environment. The woolen garments need not to be washed frequent, as compared to cotton or others and that washing itself in cold environment is not as easily possible and hence these are amply suited in the terrain. The *Paitravan* (woolen shoes) with woolen sole not only keep the feet warm but also saves the wearer from skidding over snow and slopy smooth rocks. Wrapping of one's waists by elongated woolen cord regularizes steps during walk and keep the body alert, is another effective adjustment to mountain environment.

Environment and Food Procurement Strategy

Mountain environment has multifarous manifestations on the food procurement strategy i.e., largely agriculture, basic to this area. The nature and season of sowing and harvesting of agricultural crops, alongwith related different operations, implements and technology etc., everything reveal full adjustment with the surrounding environment. For mountain agriculture, the sunny slopes, river basins, and hill taps are suitably exploited. In mansoon zones, due to heavy rains, the agricultural fields, being situated at the slopes, are always erosion-rpone. So to cope with the situation of erosion and keeping the fertile layer of soil rich in humus intact, the slopes are vertically cut and thus gained soil is spread horizontally over pebble fencing to get a labelled terrace. These terraces are exploited for growing safe crops in which irrigation is also possible provided there is water source. The concurrance of terraced fields and terrace cultivation is certainly high in the steep mountains because terraces increase with the increase of gradients, and decrease with the decrease in gradients. Despite the occurrence of steep mountain gradients in arid zones, system terrace cultivation is not found. The reason is obiously only scanty and sporadic drizzling and practically no rain to cause soil-erosion. Hence the agriculture is done by cultivating the slopy mountain sides and to protect the crops from grazing only, pebble fencing is done. But in the river-basins of the arid zone sometimes, for channelizing irrigation, terraces are made for levelling the fields.

The arid zone or the high altitude region is adopted for taking one crop a year as the fields remain frozen with snow for about half of the year. But the mansoon zone inclusive of lower and middle altitudes gives two crops, *Unali* and *Sard* annually. In high altitude, agriculture calander starts with the beginning of cultivation in early *Baisakh* (mid May), but sowing of seeds takes place in mid *Baisakh* (early June) and the crop ripend, harvested and thrashed upto mid of *Asoj* (early October), closing the calander as early as possible, so that they must get enough time to collect and stock fuel and fodder from the forest sufficient for six months consumption, before the commencement of winter. The crop grown mainly are Potato, *Chhimmi, Marsa, Seechana, Cheena, Phafra, Makki* and *Rai* alongwith cabbage, raddish, turnip, etc. vegetables.

In the middle and lower altitudes almost similar agricultural calander is followed, but the crops ripen earlier at lower elevations and later with the increase in the gradients. The *Unali* (Rabi) crop is sown from *kartik* to *Mangsir* (October-November). Through these crops variety of cereals, pulses, oil-seeds and vegetables are grown such as wheat, paddy, *Jhangara, Batthu, Marsa, Kaundi, Chhna, Mandua, Tor, Urd, Bhatt, Gahat, Gram,* barley, beans, potato, Lahi, Til, mustard, and many others suitably. The areas which remain frozen during winters but are fit for the cultivation of wheat, barley etc. are sown to ensure germination before snowfall. These seedlings remain frozen under snow for the whole winter and with the clearance of snow by melting at the commencement of spring they enjoy abrupt growth due to prevalence of favourable conditions and within a short span of time they come to flowering which ultimately leads to fruit bearing. This is a unique adaptability against the unfavourable conditions of the mountain environment.

Adaptation to mountain environment emanates from the small sized fields and a few agricultural implements. The wooden plough with a small blunt iron share is so adjusted for the rough cultivation in that mountaneous environment as to furrow and uproot even boulders, yoked by sturdy bullocks or Jebu in a narrow yoke is again suited for the narrower turns of terraced fields. The *Jal* (plainer) is not known in high altitudes but in middle and lower, it is smaller and very rarely used to level the fields as it is not fit to move in a narrow and uneven mountain fields. Therefore for breaking clods a mallet like instrument with long handle called *Dilara* is used. For weeding and hoeing fields, small handled and pointed *Kutli* or *Kutla* ((piercing hoe) are adopted in preference to flat and sharp eged cutting hoe. Containers of different shapes and sizes are made by wood, *Ringal* and skin of goat and sheep not frequently in the environment.

Rotation of crops is also established according to the need of mountain environment. In middle and lower altitude two year cycle of rotation of crops of paddy, wheat, and mandua, takes place. Rice is sown in April and reaped in September, followed by the sowing of wheat in October which is reaped in April. Then Mandua is sown and reaped in October after which the land remains fallow till next April. Usually for this purpose village lands are divided into two parts. The half land in which paddy is sown is called *Satiyora* and that of Mandua as *Kodora* but in the turn of wheat sowing it is called *Gunwara*.

In arid zone, which is single cropping Chhimmi is followed by potato, Cheena, marcha and kaundi in the following years and this rotation of crop is obviously a five year cycle for a field.

To prepare the field for seed, it is ploughed once in the case of coarser crops and twice or maximum thrice for finer crops. The fields for taking finer crops are only smoothed over by the plainer otherwise only clods are broken with *Dilara*. The *Unali* (Rabi) crop is neither harrowed nor wooded like *Sardi* (Kharif) which requires these treatments one or two times since the seedlings reach the height of a few inches until coming to earth. Manuring is not considered necessary in Talaon or *Sera* (land with perennial water supply) is considered sufficient to maintain fertile standard. But the other lands are manured immediately before sowing seed mainly by Gaunt (cowdung) and *Mol*, and old cowshed litter or leaf mould. Cattle and sheep goats are allowed to stay at fields for manuring. Practice of irrigation, however, in mountain environment, is limited to supply water to *Chwar Dhan* (irrigated paddy) in *Sera* lands and possibly to wheat crops, otherwise unirrigated fields lying over even hill-tops are well suited for the bumper yields of *Ukhad-Dhan* (unirigated paddy) and wheat.

Harvesting is also adjusted according to requirements of mountain environment. The paddy is cut off by *daranti* (sickle) close to root while wheat and barley plants are cut about the middle. In the case of Mandua or Jhangora only ears are cut first and afterwords stalks are cut for fodder when they dry. The stalks are bundled and stocked over trees poles as there is no place for storing straw places inside the house. Thrashing in mountain terrain is also amply adjusted and due to lack of spaces only ears, legumes, and coss separated from the stalks in the fields itself are brought to smaller, stone paved thrashing yards-cum-courtyard for processing. The grains are trodden out of oxen who are allowed to wave around a pole on the heaps of ears in usual way and winnowd by pouring it out of basket held high upon to a mat below. Paddy is husked daily for use by pounding it in a stone mortar hallowed in courtyard with a stick about 3" in diameter and 5′ long holding in middle while operating in standing. Grains of pulses are not broken before cooking. Flour is prepared by Gharat (water-mill) especially *opted* for the environment and oil is extracted by a special adaptive mechanism based on the principle of Osmosis. Oil pressures of any kind are not traditional to the mountains. The oilseeds are broken into finer pieces in mortar and thong gathered in a wooden flat container especially made for extracting oil, where it is kneaded with regular sprinkling of water and pressing. In due course oil cakes soak water and expel oil which is collected separately.

Environment and Pastoralism

Pastoralism is well suited for mountain environments in Garhwal as there are abundance of forage facilities but is never an isolated subsistence strategy. It is largely compensatory adaptation subsistantiate agricultural economy if commercialized, as in high and middle altitude than in lower altitude. Environment is not suitable for yak, chanwar and Gaya in lower and middle altitudes and for buffalo in middle and high altitudes. Wheras horse, cow, bullock, Jebu and herds of sheep and goats are effectively adapted to all places. Usually people keep these animals to cater agricultural and domestic needs, viz; mule and horse for riding, and transportation, cow and buffalow for milching, bullock for ploughing, and sheep and goat for the transportation and supply of wool, meat and milk. Some well to do families traditionally Rajputs, own herds of sheep and goat for commercial purposes. One family member along with two-three labour graziers and fellow graziers of village or neighbour together move these herds year the round from alpine meadows to foothill forests in a regular geographical and calendrical cycle for free and nutritious forage as well as to escape extreme environmental fluctuations. During summers they gradually drive their herds towards alpine pastures and with the onset of cold and snow they return to their villages. This is the time that exactly coincides with the harvest of *Sardi* (Kharif) crop and sowing of *Unali* (Rabi). So the graziers get enough fodder in the vicinity of village and fields where they keep their herds for manuring. This time they stay in their village for about a month. In the mean time the sheep are sheared and the owner-member shift their duties with a new member who drives the herds for winter pastures at foothills. During movement, the garziers follow and graze the fellow or harvested land on their way. The graziers are highly welcomed by the enroute villagers and are invited by them to halt during nights in their fields for manuring and as a return they get food and hospitality etc. Thus by receiving once developed symbiotic relations the graziers gradually reach the forests of foot hills in *Mangsir* for grazing the herds throughout winters. With the start of summer, in the beginning of *Chait*, the graziers purchase certain essential commodities from the markets of foothills and march in usual manner towards their respective villages to reach during harvesting of *Unali* (Rabi crop) and sowing of *Sardi* (Kharif) crop. At this time also the sheep are sheared and allowed to stay during nights in the fields, ready for sowing for manuring. The owner-grazier shifts their duties and in the beginning of *Baisakh* start for alpine pastures.

Before the advent of mechanized transport, in this region he goats and ram were adopted as pack animals for the transport of grains and goods from one mountain zone to another through the narrow undulating mountain tracks frozen with snow far beyond the reach of heavy packs. Although in interior areas of the district sheep and goat still constitute the only means of transport, but the amount of rental fetched by this little hired transport is almost insignificant.

With the closure of Tibet trade the goat and ram herds lost their significance as pack animals. The trade with Tibet was another coincidence of pastoral adaptation, started by the exchange of graizers' goods, in the same alpine meadow and this developed and flourished for centuries as *Balthia* (exchange) till its stoppage. Now the pastoralists are giving more importance to own and rear goats for multiplying herds for the commercial supply of wool and meat.

Environment and Horticulture

Environment is largely responsible for the growth of different types of vegetations in different zones. The apple orchards along with frequent *Chuli* and *Akhrat* trees are adapted for the climate of high and middle altitudinal zones. Pears, lemon, banana, and orange etc., are adjusted to the environment of middle and lower altitudes, while mango and guava are suited to lower altitudes. In pretty past people did horticulture for the catering to their own requirements, but now a days some of these, especially apple orchards, are being planted for commercial purposes as environment is favourable for these as well as the idea of cash crops has also cropped up in the minds of the people under modern forces of social environment.

Environment and Hunting, Gathering

Mountain environment is home land of varieties of vegetations, birds and animals. Among these, many are hunted and gathered by the inhabitants for consumption in addition to cultivated grains, poultry and domestic animals. People supplement their diet by eating meat of much esteemed game animals like Kakar, gural and deer, Chakor, Monals are run down and captured and every body will eat pheasants and Guchchhi (mushroom that grows over the root of Deodar Tree). Different types of wild fruits, berries, roots and leaves are collected and eaten. Herbs are known to local people which are collected and used for medicinal purposes. *Shilajit* (resin of rocks) is also collected and used as medicine. Musk deer were also hunted in forests of snow covered mountains for taking out musk and used for fragerance and is famous for its medicinal properties. But now, due to enforcement of certain forest policies, people can not game the animals.

Concluding Remarks

It is clear from the preceeding account, how the inhabitants of Uttarakashi district of Garhwal Himalaya have adjusted themselves according to prevailing environment of their respective three climate-vegetational zones, so far as traditional material culture and food procurement strategies are concerned. Many of the strategies of adoption cross cut zonal limits due to similar requirements, availability of similar building material and in this respect diffusion of idea and technology is also important. Modern education system, extension of modern amenities, implementation of policy programmes and frequent contact with mass media and outsiders etc., have exerted greater influence over the surrounding environment, as well as social environment and consequently it has changed. The people once adjusted to traditional environment as discussed above are also trying to successfully mould themselves according to new environmental factors.

References

Brush, S. B. (1976), Introduction to Symposium on "Cultural Adaptations to Mountain Eco-System" *Human Ecology*, Vol. 4, No. 2.

Singh, J. (1987), *Nritatwik Darpan Me Uttar Kashi Ke Garhwal Samaj aur Samskriti Ka Pratibimb* (in Hindi) Calcutta: Anthropological Survey of India.

Part-3

Biological Aspects of Adaptation

9 Human Skin Tanning – A Study on Populations of Punjab Plains and Simla Hills

I.J.S. Jaswal

Skin colour is an important characteristic in human biological studies and had found place almost in every anthropological description of populations. Recent advances in the methodology of physical anthropology have renewed the interest in human pigmentation. Skin reflectance spectrophotometry has made it possible to apply biometric tests to this polygenic trait, which has helped in quantifying the skin colour and removed the handicaps of "colour chart comparisons" method.

The disturbances produced by diseases in skin pigmentation, endocrinal effect on colour and theories relating to the selective pressures in the evolution of pigmentary variations have attracted the attention of biochemists, physiologists, geneticists, ecologists and anthropologists towards skin pigmentation.

An attempt has been made to study the skin tanning variations in the human populations in the present paper.

Subjects

The populations surveyed are the Brahmans, Khatris, Rajputs, Haryana Jats, Jat Sikhs and Baniyas of North India. The five endogamous groups except Rajputs have been studied from Punjab plains, where temperature registers extreme fluctuations and the average rainfall is about 115 cms. Rajput sample has been taken from Shimla Hills of Himachal Pradesh, which is a mountainous region varying in elevation from 1000 metres to 3000 metres above sea level. The climate is cold and it snows during winters. An adult sample of 102 Brahmans, 176 Khatris, 97 Haryana Jats, 101 Jat Sikhs, 104 Baniyas and 70 Rajputs was taken ranging from 20 to 25 years of age.

Methodology

The present investigation was conducted with the EEL Reflectance Spectrophotometer. Only three filters i.e. 601 (425 nm) 605 (545 nm) and 609 (685 nm) were used. The skin reflectance was recorded at two sites - (i) the middle of the forehead above glabella and (ii) the medial aspect of upper arm. Percentage reflectance was noted against a magnesium carbonate block as standard. The site of investigation was thoroughly cleaned and care was taken not to include the related individuals in the sample.

Results

Table 1 shows melanin equivalent and tanning in six endogamous groups examined. Melanin equivalent (i.e. reciprocal of the reflectance at 685 nm) gives the concentration of melanin at the site of reflectance (Harrison, 1957). As expected, the melanin concentration at upper arm site was much less than at forehead. Variations in melanin equivalent at upper arm and forehead revealed that the Baniyas had maximum concentration of melanin pigment of all the populations investigated, at both sites. They were followed by Jat Sikhs, Haryana Jats, Rajputs, Khatris and Brahmans in the decreasing order of melanin concentration, in the region of upper arm. Rajputs shift to second position after Baniyas with respect to forehead pigmentation. The sequence of other populations remains unaltered.

Tanning coefficient (ratio of melanin equivalents at forehead to upper arm) is a measure of tanning due to differential exposure of body parts to sunlight (Kalla and Tiwari, 1969). To rule out the differences becauses of occupational variability, all the subjects were selected from the same walk of life, who are exposed to more or less identical situations during their daily chores. The highest value of tanning coefficient was recorded in Rajputs followed by Baniyas, Haryana Jats, Khatris, Jat Sikhs and Brahmans in the same order.

Table 1
Melanin Equivalent and Tanning

Population	*Sample Size*	*Melanin Equivalent* *Upper Arm*	*Forehead*	*Tanning Coefficient*	*Mean Exposure Index*	*R/G Ratio*
Brahmans	102	0.01906 (0.001570)*	0.02143 (0.001971)	1.126 (0.0797)	6.01 (2.818)	0.79
Khatris	176	0.01908 (0.001516)	0.02166 (0.002532)	1.136 (0.1033)	5.67 (2.816)	0.91
Rajputs	70	0.01936 (0.001624)	0.02353 (0.003464)	1.217 (0.1565)	6.92 (3.032)	1.21
Haryana Jats	97	0.01958 (0.001729)	0.02227 (0.002352)	1.140 (0.0973)	5.38 (2.729)	1.01
Jat Sikhs	101	0.01992 (0.001896)	0.02240 (0.002225)	1.127 (0.0801)	5.20 (2.347)	0.90
Baniyas	104	0.02073 (0.001777)	0.02435 (0.002369)	1.179 (0.1147)	5.65 (2.603)	1.16

*S.D. in Paran thesis.

Tobias (1961) used reflectances at all the nine wavelengths of EEL to calculate the Mean Exposure Index. For the purpose of present study the index is slightly modified and the M.E.I. calculated, is the mean of the differences of reflectances at the forehead and upper arm at three dominant wavelengths (425 nm, 545 nm and 685 nm). The order of populations with respect to Mean Exposure Index (Modified) was Rajputs, followed by Brahmans, Khatris, Baniyas, Haryana Jats and Jat Sikhs in the descending order.

R/G ratio has been calculated by taking the ratio of differences at red filter (685 nm) and green filter (545 nm) between readings at upper arm and forehead (Huizinga, 1968). Rajputs had the highest R/G ratio, followed by Baniyas, Haryana Jats, Khatris, Jat Sikhs and Brahmans.

Discussion

From photobiological point of view, melanin pigmentation of human skin can be considered having two components - constitutive and facultative. The constitutive skin colour designates the amount of cutaneous melanin pigmentation generated in accordance with cellular genetic programme. The facultative skin colour characterizes the increase in melanin pigmentation above the constitutive level e.g., elicitation by direct exposure of the skin to ultraviolet light or induced by endocrine changes etc. (Quevedo et al., 1974). The relative relationship between the two gives us the idea of tanning. Though it is difficult to analyse these components biochemically and photobiologically, but an attempt may be made to study as far as one can go. Skin colour has been found to be correlated with some of environmental variables like latitude, temperature, humidity and altitude (Roberts and Kahlon, 1976). The adaptive role of pigmentation has also been pointed out in relation with ultraviolet radiations, vitamin D synthesis, heat exchange and resistance to certain diseases (Post et al. 1975). The skin colour of human populations is the resultant of interaction of these complex factors.

Melanin is the most important skin pigment and its concentration is inversely proportional to the percentage reflectance at red filter. The melanin equivalent at covered body site is taken to be the constitutive skin colour and that at the most exposed repetition site to be depicting facultative tan over and above the constitutive upper arm covered and forehead uncovered. Further the sample was taken out of the resident students of educational institutions, who are exposed to similar outside activity and live under more or less similar conditions. The ratio of melanin equivalent at forehead and upper arm has been taken to be a measure of tanning, called tanning coefficient. The maximum tanning has been shown by the high altitude population - Rajputs. Baniyas come next to Rajputs, but the constitutive skin pigmentation of Baniyas is much more than that of Rajputs. The other four groups Brahmans, Jat Sikhs, Haryana Jats and Khatris show low value of tanning coefficient as compared to the other two groups. Similar results are obtained when tanning is studied by R/G ratio. Rajputs have the highest value of R/G, followed by Baniyas. The remaining four groups cluster around a lower level. The third measure i.e., means exposure index (modified) does not show much discrimination, though Rajputs again top with the highest value of M.E.I.

It may be noted that tanning coefficient takes into consideration only one wave length i.e., 685 nm and is primarily based on the changes taking place in the differential distribution of melanin pigment at covered and uncovered sites. R/G ratio takes note of green filter (545 nm) also, which gives good measure of absorption by the haemoglobin component. M.E.I. gives the average difference between two levels of skin colour at all the wavelengths. The utility of any measure is determined by specific situations and the constitutive skin colour of the populations studied.

The highest tanning among Rajputs of Shimla Hills may be because of the environmental factors. At high altitudes and near the Equator, the ultraviolet intensity is greater than at sea level or at northern latitudes. The continued differential exposure at covered and uncovered body parts gives rise to higher tan among Rajputs. This calls for further investigations on human groups living under varying environs.

Among the remaining five populations of Punjab plains, Baniyas show highest tanning coefficient and R/G ratio. They have the maximum constitutive melanin pigmentation also. This is suggested to be because of higher level of initial pigmentation and also due to genetic propensities towards higher tanning. This was also pointed out by Kalla (1969 and 1972). He found that the skin tanning, on an average, tends to increase with the increase in the initial pigmentation and suggested that, in skin tanning potential, the parent child correlation is found to be much higher than in the normal skin pigmentation, indicating a stricter genetic control of tanning. The similarities between the remaining four groups can be explained because of their more relatedness. The Khatris and Sarswat Brahmans are closely connected and racially the Jat Sikhs and Hindu Jats of Haryana are identified as belonging to the same stock (Ibbetson, 1883).

It is concluded that the variation in skin tanning is the result of adaptations of human populations to different environments and is also determined by the genetic make up of the population.

References

Harrison, G. A. (1957), The Measurement and Inheritance of Skin Colour in Man. *Eugen. Rev.*, 49, 73-76.

Huizinga, J. (1968), Human Biological Observations on Some African Populations of the Thorn Savanna Belt. *Kon. Ned. Akad.* Wetenach., C., 71, 356-390.

Ibbetson, D. (1883), *Punjab Castes.* Census of India, Lahore, Government Press.

Kalla, A. K. (1969), Changes in Skin Tanning with the Changes in Initial Pigmentation of Skin, *J. Anthrop. Soc. Japan,* 77, 1-10.

Kalla, A. K. (1972), Parent-child Relationship and Sex Differences in Skin Tanning Potential in Man. *Humangenetik,* 15, 39-43.

Kalla, A. K. and S. C. Tiwari (1969), Skin Tanning Variations with Age. *Anthropologist,* 15, 33-40.

Post, P. W., F. Daniels, Jr. and R.T. Binford, Jr. (1975), Cold Injury and the Evolution of "White" Skin. *Hum. Biol.,* 47, 65-80.

Quevedo, Jr., W.C., T. B. Fitspatrick, M.A. Pathak and K. Jimbow (1974), Light and Skin Colour in Sunlight and Man-Normal and Abnormal Photobiologic Responses, T.B. Fitzpatrickr (ed.) University of Tokyo Press.

Roberts, D.F. and D.P.S. Kahlon (1976), Environmental Correlations of Skin Colour. *Ann. Hum. Bio.,* 3, 11-22.

Tobias, P. V. (1961), Studies on Skin Reflectance in Bushman–European Hybrids. Proc. *Second. Int. Cong. Hum. Genet.,* 461-471.

10 Effect of Sickling on Reproductive Performance

MADHU BALA SHARMA & DIPESH CHAUDHURY

Adaptation is simply a measure of reproductive success. The study of reproductive history gives us an idea about fertility, mortality and morbid condition of the population. Besides a number of factors such as age at marriage, age at menarche, health status of women and capacity to reproduce viable offspring and the occurrence of hereditary disease could also affect the reproduction. Genetic differences of fertility between the normal and carrier of hereditary disease are well documented by a number of investigators. The heterozygous carrier for genes of Diabetes, Huntington Chorea, Phenyl Ketonuria, Tay Sachs Disease, Cystic fibrosis and Sickle cell trait have more fertility than the normal (Reed & Neel, 1959; Woolf et al. 1975; Myrianthopoulos and Aronson, 1966; Danks *et al.*, 1965; Conneally et al. 1973; Allison, 1966; Edington, 1955; Livingstone, 1957; Firschein, 1961).

In the present study the following attempts have been made to study the reproductive performance of the sickler (AS) and Non-sickler in the Gond population.

1. To investigate whether the trait lesion could effect early or late menarche.
2. To find out the average conception of sickler and non sickler.

3. To find out the average reproductive wastage of the sickler and non sickler.
4. To find out the sex ratio among the offspring of sickler and non sickler.
5. To test the malarial hypothesis with respect to reproductive performance of sickler and non sickler.

Material and Methods

The hapernized blood was collected from 58 unrelated Gonds of New and Old Fotarah, Surender Nagar and Gitti Khadan within the corporation limits of Nagpur. The blood was analysed for haemoglobin variants by horizontal paper electrophoreśis using Barbitone buffer Ph 6.8. The samples reported to be of AS type were further tested for sickling by using freshly prepared two per cent solution of sodium meta-bisulphite ($Na_2S_2O_5$) in the manner described by Donald and Castle (1948).

The data on reproductive performance and sex of the offspring from ever married sickler and non sickler individuals were secured by interview. The Demographic information including age at menarche, age at marriage, age at first birth were also collected. All the individuals interviewed belong to same socio-economic group and most of them were illiterate, very few of them have got their basic education.The practice of family planning methods is not very frequent in the tribal population.

Results

Menarcheal Age

The menarcheal age is an important event in the physiological life of a women as it marks the beginning of reproductive period. Table 1 describes the percentage distribution of sickler and non-sickler women in different menarcheal age groups. The highest percentage of women was observed to have their first menstruation at the age of 13, in both sickler and non-sickler. The mean menarcheal age in both sickler and non-sickler was 13.5±0.06 and 13.5±0.87 respectively, the difference is not statistically significant.

Table 1
Menarcheal Age in Sickler and Non-Sickler Women

Menarcheal	*Sickler*		*Non-Sickler*	
age in Years	*N**	*%*	*N**	*%*
11	–	0.0	1	2.6
12	3	15.0	5	13.1
13	8	40.0	16	42.1
14	5	25.0	8	21.0
15	4	20.0	5	13.1
16	–	0.0	2	5.3
17	–	0.0	1	2.6
18	–	0.0	–	0.0
	20		38	

*N = Number

Adolescent Sterility

The adolescent sterility refers to an interval between the menarcheal (age in those cases where the marriage took place before menarche) or from the age at marriage (in cases where the menstruation occurred before marriage) and the age at first delivery. In the presnt study completely sterile women and those who got married recently i.e., approximately 6 months before the survey, were not included for the calculation of adolescent sterility period. The adolescent sterility period in non-sickler was slightly more than the sickler.

Table 2
Adolescent Stertility in Sickler and Non-Sickler

Period of sterility	*Sickler*		*Non-Sickler*	
(in years)	*F*	*%*	*F*	*%*
1	9	45.0	17	45.95
2	5	25.0	7	18.92
3	1	5.0	7	18.92
4	1	5.0		
5	3	15.0		2.70
6				
7			1	2.70
8				
9			3	8.11
10				
11 and above	1*	5.2	1*	2.70

Total Number of Conception

Table 3 shows the total number of conception. It is a most relevant indicator for getting the idea of reproductive performance. However, it was found that in men average there was no difference in the number of conceptions between the sickler and non-sickler, though the sickler mothers showed higher trend (4.7%) than the non-sickler (4.4%).

Table 3
Total Number of Conception (Reproductive History)

Age in Years	*Sickler* N	*Sickler* %	*Non-Sickler* N	*Non-Sickler* %
20-22	4	4.2	12	7.2
23-25	10	10.6	12	7.2
26-28	3	3.2	18	10.8
29-31	11	11.7	14	8.4
32-34	5	5.3	6	3.6
35-37	6	6.4	3	1.8
38-40	29	30.8	29	17.4
41-43	-	0.0	4	2.4
44-46	7	7.4	26	25.6
47-49	12	12.7	-	0.0
50-52	7	7.4	12	7.2
53-55	-	0.0	20	11.9
56-58	-	0.0	-	0.0
59-61	-	0.0	11	6.6
Average conceptions		4.70		4.40

Reproductive Wastage and Infantile Death

Reproductive wastage and infantile deaths were more common in non-sickler mothers (29.9%) than sickler mothers (23.4% (Table 4).

Sex Ratio

Table 5 shows that sickler mother had more male children than the non-sickler mothers. The sex ratio between the sickler and non-sickler was 121.2 and 28.5 and 110.5±20.2 respectively.

Table 4
Still Birth, Abortion, Miscarriage and Infantile Death

Age group	*Sickler*		*Non-Sickler*	
in years	*Miscarriage, abortion, still birth and infantile death*		*Miscarriage, abortion, still birth and infantile death*	
	N	%	*N*	%
20-24	3	13.6	3	6.0
25-29	2	9.1	2	4.0
30-34	3	13.6	3	6.0
35-39	–	0.0	8	16.0
40-44	7	31.8	8	16.0
45-49	4	18.2	11	22.0
50 - above	3	13.6	15	30.0
	1.1 death/mother		1.3 death/mother	

Table 5
Sex Ratio

Sickler			*Non-Sickler*		
Male	*Female*	*Sex ratio*	*Male*	*Female*	*Sex Ratio*
40	33	121.21±28.5	63	57	110.52±20.2

Discussion

Selective advantage in modern genetics is expressed as a function of relative reproductive fitness. The concept of relative reproductive fitness of individuals with specific traits or carrier of specific genes, although simple enough, has proven surprisingly difficult in practical applications because the genetic situation on which the concept of fitness has a deciding bearing are often variable and subtle. Relative fitness in its simplest term can be expressed as the ratio of the mean number of children of two groups-affected group and the normal.

In the present study the difference in fertility of sickler and non-sickler are not statistically significant. But the observed differences are in the direction of higher fertility among the sickler than the non-sickler, strengthening the hypothesis that hyeterozygots has a selective advantage over the homozygous normal. Similar results are also reported by Edington (1955) from Ghana and Firschein (1961) from British Honduras. It has been indicated above that differences in the number of live births is possibly due to excess of spontaneous abortions and still birth among the normal. This in turn could account for the maintenance of HbS geneat equilibrium in the Gond population.

The mechanism of this advantage which the heterozygous Hb^A Hb^S person enjoys in the malarious environment is not known with certainity. In the following section the possible effect of HbS gene which could account for this is discussed. The red cells of Hb^A Hb^S individual sickle only, when the partial pressure of oxygen falls below 15 mm (Allison, 1956). This occurs only in unusual condition. The red cells carrying the P. falciparum adhere to the walls of blood vessels or are present only in the internal organs. This situation may lower the partial pressure of oxygen within the cell so as to induce sickling in Hb^A Hb^S. Because of this misshape the red cells are removed from the circulation and disposed off more rapidly than would otherwise occur, thus limiting the extent of malarial infection Miller, Neel and Livingstone, 1956 and Clark and Tomlinson, 1949 state that because of its large vascular spaces and slow circulation, the placenta after the third month of pregnancy would be an important site for the maturation of parasites. Therefore Hb^A Hb^S mother may be less likely to get the malarial lesions of placenta that cause abortion again, because the parasitized erythrocytes are removed from the circulation. Edington (1955) also showed that the still birth rate for hospital population of mothers Hb^A Hb^S was slightly lower, but the figures were not at acceptable levels of statistical significance. The data of Platt (1971) does not indicate an increased incidence of abortions and still births among the non-sickler. The Hb^A Hb^B has the selective advantage only in the malarious environment. Otherwise it is disadvantageous to the carrier. One finding that could have biological significance reported by Polednak and Jenerich (1978) that is higher frequency of abruptio placentae in sickler Vs non-sickler (Odds ratio = 3.0). However, the pathological studies indicate that large placental infarcts and decidual necrosis (Possible of hypoxomia or ischemic origin) may cause abruptio placentae (Naeye, 1971). It is noteworthy that placentae of mothers with sickle cell trait reportedly show the agonal sickling of red cells which could result in anoxic conditions and vascular occlusion in the placenta. Foetal mortality may be high in severel cases of abruptio placentae (Naeye, 1971). Platt (1971) has observed significant increase in the perinatal mortality under the anoxic stress in sickler Vs non-sickler. On the contrary whalley et al. (1963) found no increase in placental abruptions in Black woman with sickle cell trait then in the normal.

The sex-ratio among the Heterozygous Hb^A Hb^S is significantly higher than in the normal. The present findings are in agreement with those reported by Firschein (1961). The fact that there is no significant difference in mortality of children between the two classes of mothers, suggests that one should not expect a great difference between the two groups in the sex of children dying during first five year.The higher sex ratio among the sickler may be due to differential selction operating in the zygote carrying XY and XX chromosomes.

Conclusion

In nutshell, it may be said that there is a tendency for increased fertility and less incidence of reproductive wastage (still birth and abortions) among the sicklers when compared to the non-sicklers in the malarial environment. The sex ratio is significantly higher among the progeny of the sicklers than that of the non sicklers.

References

Allinson, A.C. (1954), Protection by the Sickle Cell Trait against Subtertian Malarial Infection, *Br. Med. J.* I, 290.

Clark, H. C. and W. J., Tomlinson (1949), The Pathologic Anatomy of Malaria. In Malariology Ed. N.F. Boyd. Phila : W.B. Saunders Co., pp. 874-903.

Conneally, P. M., A.D. Merritt & P. L. Yu (1973), Cystic Fibrosis: Population Genetics. Texas Reports on *Biology and Medicine,* 31: 639-650.

Danks, D.M., J. Allian and C.M. Anderson (1963), A Genetic Study of Fibrocystic Disease of the Pancereas. *Ann. Hum.Genet.* (Lond.) 28: 323-356.

Edington, G.M. (1955), The Pathology of Sickle Cell Disease in West Africa. *Trns. Roy. Soc. Trop. Med. Hyg.*, 49: 253-267.

Fireschein, L. (1961), Population Dynamics of the Sickle Cell Trait in the Black Caribs of British Honduras, Central America. *Am. Jr. Hum. Genet.*, 13 : 233-254.

Livingstone, F.B. (1957), Malaria and Sickling, *Brit. Med. J.*, 5021 : 762-763.

Miller, M. J., J.V. Neel and F.B. Linvingstone (1956), Distribution of Parasites in the Red Cells of Sickle Cell Trait of Carrier are Infected with *Plasmodiumfalciparum. Trans. Roy. Soc. Trop. Med. Hyg.*, 50: 294-296.

Myrianthopoulos, N.C. and S.M. Aronson (1966), Population Dynamics of Tay Sachs Disease. I. Reproductive Fitness Andselection. *Am. J. Hum. Genst.*, 19 : 313-327.

Neeye, R.L., W.L. Harkness and J. Utts. (1977), Abruptio Placentae and Perinatal Death: A Prospective Study, *Am. J. Obstot. Gynecol.*, 128 : 740-746.

Platt, H. S. (1971), Effect of Maternal Sickle Cell Trait on Perinatal Mortality. *Brit. Med. J.*, 4: 334-336.

Polednak, A. N. and D.T. Jenerich (1980), Birth Characteristics of Blacks with Sickle Cell Trait: A Case Control Study. *Hum. Biol.*, 52: 15-22.

Reed, T.E. and J.V. Neel (1959), Huntingtons Chorea in Michigan. 2. Selection and Mutation. *Am. J. Hum. Genet.*, 11: 107-136.

Whalley, P.J., J.A. Pritchard and J.R. Richards (1963), Sickle Cell Trait and Pregnancy, *J.A.M.A.*, 186: 1132-1135.

Woolf, L. I., M. S. Mc. Bean, F.M. Woolf and Canalane, S.F. (1975), Phenylketonuria as a Balanced Polymorphism: The Nature of the Heterozygote Advantage. *Ann. Hum. Genet.*, (Lond.) 38: 461-469.

11 A Preliminary Statement on an Iodine Deficient Environment and Disabilities

SANJIB K. CHAKRAVARTY & S. H. AHMAD

A preliminary survey was conducted on a section of the Gallong in Tirbin circle of Siang district, Arunchal Pradesh, where a number of individuals were affected with various congenital and acquired malformations viz., nodular and toxic goiter; congenital defects of central nervous system ranging from mental subnormality to severe mental retardation; neuromotor disorders often associated with deafness or deaf-mutism and cretinism; stunted growth and dwarfism in varying degrees of severity. These malformations were associated in combination among both the goitrous and non-goitrous individuals. Deficiency of iodine was presumed to be the major factor in causing abnormalities, and the total situation was ascertained to be a state of hypothyroidism.

The Gallong form an endogamous unit of the generic group- Adi. The clan exogamy and village exogamy is practised among the Gallong. Preferential matings are rigidly avoided and polyandrous form of unions is prescribed. Thus spouses in this patriarchal society are drawn from considerable distances in different directions; the median marriage distance is estimated to be 15.7 km (Ahmad and Chakravarty, 1977).

It is suspected that the soil and water resources in this area lack the required quantity of iodine. Besides, manuring is never associated with the crude method of cultivation (shifting) which they practise. So, the inhabitants of the area are essentially deprived of the required quantity of iodine for their anabolic processes. The chief varieties of vegetables included in their diet, viz., green rape leaf, turnip, cabbage and other kinds belonging to Brassica species are goitrogenous. The people still prefer to consume common salt, even though the local Government has imposed a ban on the sale and consumption of common salt and have taken steps for popularizing and providing iodised salt.

From the analysis of the intensities of selection potential (Crow, 1958), it is observed that selection is operating at a considerable magnitude chiefly in the direction of mortality ($I = 1.07$, $I_m = 0.75$, $I_f = 0.18$) (Chakravarty and Ahmad, 1978). Thus the adaptive fitness of this section of the Gallong, in the environment they are exposed to is debatable.

Considering the total situation, the geo-physical environment of the area can be adjudged as the possible causative agency behind the broad spectrum of malformations. Very little responsibilities could be attributed to heredity, intra-uterine environment, social environment and other such agencies. Of the total population surveyed 12.9% of males and 17.8% of females were found to have goiter (Ahmed and Chakravarty 1977).

The inability of the thyroid gland to procure iodine disturbs the processes of thyroid hormone synthesis in varying degrees. It is also well known that thyroid deficiency through the lack of production of thyroine affects the production of growth hormone by the pituitary gland. Therefore, through a chain of processes, deficient functioning of thyroid gland results in retarded ossification of the cartilages etc. giving rise to stunted growth and dwarfism. In this study area seven individuals (6 Males, 1 Female) were found to have stunted growth and three (2 Males, 1 Female) were identified as dwarfs.

Apparently the morpho-metric differences between the normals and the individuals showing retarded growth are striking. A total of fourteen anthropometric measurements were considered which will help in highlighting the distinctive features between the two categories of individuals (Table 1). It

Table 1
Anthropometric Measurements of Normal, Stunted and Dwarf Males
(In mm)

Measurements	*Normal (N=22)* X	*Stunted (N=6)* X	*Difference to normal*	*Dwarf (N=2)* X	*Difference to normal*
Stature	1583.3	1418.2	-165.1	1159.0	-424.3
Sitting height	849.2	793.2	-56.0	561.0	-288.2
Head length	192.4	197.7	+5.3	185.0	-7.4
Head breadth	144.1	146.3	+2.2	136.0	-8.1
Head-Circumference	560.4	565.7	+5.3	34.5	-25.9
Nasal height	53.4	49.7	-3.7	51.5	-1.9
Nasal Breadth	38.5	38.0	-0.5	36.0	-2.5
Total facial height	121.1	119.2	-1.9	116.5	-4.6
Total Arm Length	681.6	600.0	-81.6	564.0	-117.6
Arm Span	1586.8	1440.7	-146.1	1293.5	-293.3
Chest breadth	278.0	260.7	-17.8	220.0	-58.0
Chest Circumference	844.8	769.2	-75.6	685.5	-159.3
Weight (Kg)	52.6	41.2	-11.4	26.5	-26.1

was observed that there was marked reduction in all the linear, facial and trunk measurements among the individuals with retarded growth. The individuals with stunted growth showed a deviation from the above trend in respect of head measurements, where they register higher values and comparatively bigger head. However, the dwarfs exhibited extreme reduced values for all the characters, except in nasal length and chest depth as compared to the stunted individuals. The relative proportions of chest depth to chest breadth and chest circumference were found to be maximum among the dwarfs and thereby showing a feature of pegion shaped chest, compared to normal and stunted individuals. Weight relatively reduced from normal individuals through stunted to dwarf and the variations were as per stature and other body proportions.

Thus from the above study it becomes clear that the environment (geo-physical) of a particular area has a direct correlation/effect on the healthy state and well being of the population. It is suggested that a thorough study should be undertaken in the areas of iodine and other deficiencies and their subsequent effect on the unwanted genetic/acquired load on populations, for suggesting measures in increasing the healthy component.

References

Ahmad, S.H. and S.K. Chakravarty (1977), Physical Anthroplogy of Village Ragi Doke in Siang District of Arunchal Pradesh. Report Submitted to Anthropological Survey of India.

Chakravarty, S.K. and S.H. Ahmad (1978), Body Dimensions, Fertility and Selection in a Section of the Gallong with Endemic Hypothyroidism and Congenital Defects of the Central Nervous System. Paper Presented in the Seminar on 'Genetical Demography of Indian Population January 1978. Anthropological Survey of India, Calcutta.

Crow, J.F. (1958), Some Possibilities for Measuring Selection Intensities in Man. *Human Biology,* 30: 1-13.

12 Skeletal Maturation of Rhesus Monkey – An Assessment in Natural and Captive Environments

A. K. Bhatia

The behavioural studies on monkeys show that the behaviour of monkeys from natural wild environment differs from those which are bred in captivity. In natural environment an animal is subjected to varied stresses and strains in comparison to the one which is bred in captivity under set conditions of nutrition and handling. This might also be effecting other biological processes like growth, as the same is the outcome of the interaction of individual's internal and external environment. With this consideration in mind the present report intends to assess the differences in terms of skeletal maturation between rhesus monkeys from natural and captive environment.

Material and Method

The data is based on 341 rhesus monkeys (males 182; females 159) procured from the postgraduate Institute of Medical Education and Research, Chandigarh. The monkeys are supplied to the Institute by the animal suppliers who in turn trap the monkeys from their natural wild environment. The monkeys range in age from newborns to about 7 years of age. The ages of the monkeys were estimated on the basis of body weight, sitting height and dental status (Gavan and Hutchinson, 1973).

Using the standard positioning techniques, the following nine radiographs of left side only for each monkey were taken on INDU medical films at an anode film distance of 36 inches in the Radiological laboratory, Department of Anthroplogy, Punjab University, Chandigarh.

1. Antero-posterior view of the elbow
2. Antero-posterior view of the shoulder
3. Lateral view of the elbow
4. Postero-anterier view of the wrist and hand
5. Antero-posterior view of the knee
6. Antero-posterior view of the hip
7. Lateral view of the knee
8. Dorso-planter view of the foot
9. Lateral view of the foot.

On the basis of this radiographic data, the median ages for complete fusion were calculated for each epiphysis by graphical method of probit analysis.

The results obtained were compared with the ages of epiphyseal fusion reported by Ven Wagenen and Asling (1958) on a mixed longitudinal data of 68 females and 48 males, all born in the monkey colony at Yale University (Department of Obstetrics and Gynaecology) and maintained under standardized laboratory conditions of optimal nutrition and health.

Results and Discussion

Table 1 compares the ages of various epiphyseal unions between the monkeys from natural environment (present study) and captive environment (Van Wagenen and Asling, 1958). As is clear from the table the fusion of various epiphyses is generally delayed in wild monkeys in comparison to the laboratory bred monkeys.

The delay ranges from 0.1 month (distal ulna) to 17.4 months (metatarsals) in males and from 2.2 months (proximal tibia) to 16.8 months (metacarpals) in females. However, in case of centers from proximal humerus distal femur, proximal tibia and tibial tuberosity in males and proximal humerus, distal ulna, femur - head and lesser trochanter in females, the fusion occurs earlier from1.4 to 4.4 months in females when compared with the findings of Van Wagenen and Asling (1958).

Table 1
Comparison of the Ages (in months) of Epiphyseal Union between Captive and Wild Rhesus Monkeys

	Males			*Females*		
Epiphyseal Centre	*Captive Monkeys (Van Wagenen and Asling)*	*Wild Monkeys (Present Study)*	*Difference*	*Captive Monkeys (Van Wagenen and Asling)*	*Wild Monkeys (Present Study)*	*Difference*
Upper Extremity						
Proximal humerus	72.0	67.6	-4.4	63.0	58.8	-4.2
Distal humerus	24.0	38.0	+14.0	24.0	31.6	+7.6
Proximal radius	48.0	54.9	+6.9	36.0	48.9	+12.9
Proximal ulna	51.0	58.8	+7.8	39.0	53.7	+14.7
Distal radius	60.0	69.1	+9.1	60.0	63.0	+3.0
Distal ulna	69.0	69.1	+0.1	60.0	57.5	-2.5
Metacarpals	51.0	65.3	+14.3	42.0	58.8	+16.8
Phalanges	51.0	61	+10.0	45.0	51.4	+6.4
Lower Extremity						
Femur head	45.0	50.1	+5.1	39.0	37.1	-1.9
Lessertrochanter	45.0	50.1	+5.1	36.0	30.9	+5.1
Distal femur	69.0	67.6	-1.4	51.0	57.5	+6.5
Proximal tibia	69.0	67.6	-1.4	54.0	56.2	+2.2
Proximal fibula	54.0	59.1	+15.1	51.0	61.6	+10.6
Tibia tuberosity	78.0	75.8	-2.2	63.0	67.6	+4.6
Distal tibia	51.0	60.2	+9.2	45.0	54.9	+9.9
Distal fibula	51.0	64.5	+13.5	45.0	53.7	+8.7
Calcaneal epiphysis	45.0	60.2	+15.2	33.0	48.9	+15.9
Metatarsals	48.8	65.4	+17.4	45.0	58.0	+13.0
Phalanges	48.0	62.8	+14.8	45.0	51.7	+6.7

In the sequence of epiphyseal union, though the broad sequence of epiphyseal union is by and large same viz., elbow, hand wrist and shoulder in the upper extremity and hip, foot ankles and knee in the lower extremity, but the variations within the regions have been found. For instance the shoulder epiphyses i.e., proximal humerus fuses earlier than the distal radius and ulna in males, while in females the epiphyses at proximal humerus fuse later than distal ulna but earlier than distal radius in the natural wild monkeys. In captive monkeys, the proximal humerus fuses after the fusion on distal radius and distal ulna.

The epiphysis of tibial tuberosity fuses after the proximal humerus in both males and females in the wild monkeys, though in captive monkeys the fusion of the tibial tuberosity and proximal humerus takes place in females at the same time at 63 months.

Likewise in the hand and foot regions a clear distalo-proximal sequence of epiphyseal union has been seen in the wild monkeys in comparison to the captive monkeys. In this, phalangeal epiphysis fuses earlier than the metacarpal/metatarsal epiphyses, and within the phalanjes distal phalangeal epiphyses fuse earlier than the middle which are followed by the proximal phalangeal epiphysis (Bhatia 1976).

Similar precocity in osseous development is also seen in the appearance of various ossific centers in captive rhesus monkeys (Bhatia 1976, 1981 and Van Wagnen andAsling 1964).

According to Washburn (1943), the traction epiphyses and those of hand and foot are more variable in old world monkeys. The present comparison shows the fusion of traction epiphysis like proximal ulna, proximal tibia and calcaneal epiphysis to be more delayed as also of metacarpals/metatarsals and phalangeal epiphysis.

Thus the pattern and timings of skeletal maturation varies in comparison to the monkeys in captivity. As stated in the beginning, the monkeys in the natural environment are subjected to various types of stresses and strains in their day to day activities. The life for these animals is more hard in their natural set up where they are exposed to climatic fluctuations, heat, rain, sickness, group isolation and of course the hazardous daily hunt for the food. These monkeys are always under one pressure or the other whether it is natural calamity, food scarcity, prey or inter and intra group struggles.

In monkeys bred under captivity, the shelter, food and mate, the three basic necessities are easily available without much struggle for the same. They are handled and brought up under proper care and health. The struggle for existence is not as hard as for those who are in the lap of Mother Nature.

Perhaps these stresses and strains do delay the growth processes including skeletal maturation of rhesus monkey living in natural environs. The element of better nourishment and diet in the captive monkeys enhancing their osseous development might be operative to some extent but it is the multitude of the natural environmental factors which result in the delayed skeletal maturation in the wild monkeys. Those epiphyseal centers which have inherent tendency to vary more, like traction epiphysis and hand - foot epiphysis, are affected more than other epiphyseal centers. It is probable that those bony regions which show greater differences may be regarded as phylogenetically unstable. They show more plasticity and hence inner and outer environment affects them the maximum.

Refernces

Bhatia, A.K. (1976), Skeletal Maturation in the Rhesus Monkey-Appearance and Fusion of Centers of Ossification in the Upper and Lower Extremity. Ph.D. Thesis, Punjab University, Chandigarh.

Bhatia, A.K. (1981), Skeletal Maturation in Rhesus Monkey-Appearance of Centers of Ossification in Two Extremities. *Ind. Jr. Phys. Anthrop. And Hum. Genet.*, 7(1) : 1-11.

Gavan, J.A. and Hutchinson, T. C. (1973), The Problem of Age Estimation - A Study Using Rhesus Monkey (Macaca mulatta). *Anth. J. Phys. Anthrop.*, 38 : 69-82.

Van Wagenen, G. and Asling, C. W. (1958), Roentgenographic Estimation of Boneage in the Rhesus Monkey. *Ann. J. Anat.*, 103 : 163-185.

Van Wagenen, G. and Asling, C.W. (1964), Ossification in the Fetal Monkey (Macaca mulatta). Estimation of Age and Progress of Gestation by Roentegenography. *Ann. J. Anat.*, 114 : 107-132.

Washburn, S.L. (1943), The Sequence of Epiphaseal Union in Old World Monkeys. *Ann. J. Anat.*, 72: 339-360.

13 Variation in Birth Weight According to Parity and Socio-economic Levels

G.R. LAKSHMI

Birth weight is an important factor in the study of growth and development of infants. The birth weight of neonates depends on a complex relationship between its genetically inherited growth potential and the effectiveness of the support provided by the maternal organism. Enough evidences have been accumulated to describe the birth weight as truly multifactorial. Various studies suggest that it appears the birth weight of the newborn depends on socio-economic condition of the mother, maternal age, sex of the child, parity, gestation period, climate, season, ethnic origin, general health and nutritional status etc.

The present communication envisages the effect of parity and socio-economic environment on the birth weight of the neonates.

Material and Method

301 neonates (live births) from Government Women Hospital, Dehradun, were subjected to metric measurement (Birth weight). The information regarding parity, socio-economic status and family size were recorded. Both the schedule and interview methods were adopted for recording the information.

Results and Discussion

Birth weights of infants according to parity and sex are presented in Table 1. It may be observed that the males

Table 1
Birth Weight of Intants According to Parity

	Birth Weight (Kg.)						
	Male		*Female*		*Total (M+F)*		
Parity	*No.*	*Mean + S.E.*	*No.*	*Mean + S.E.*	*Mean + S.E.*	*Sex Ratio*
1.	59	2.52±0.065	46	2.49±0.060	2.51±0.045	128
2.	55	2.70±0.066	30	2.63±0.076	2.68±0.050	183
3.	30	2.62±0.087	25	2.66±0.071	2.64±0.057	120
4.	15	2.74±0.136	14	2.85±0.145	2.66±0.104	107
5.	8	2.77±0.166	5	2.63±0.206	2.71±0.131	160
6.	4	2.96±0.160	4	3.07±0.231	3.01±0.142	100
7.	3	2.16±0.166	2	2.48±0.235	2.29±0.153	150
8.	-	-	1	1.36	1.36	-
All	174	2.63±0.038	127	2.58±0.039	2.61±0.027	138

generally exhibit higher birth weight than the females with exception to 3rd, 6th and 7th parities. In the 3rd parity, the Mean birth weights of the two sexes are almost similar, whereas, in the 6th and 7th parities the values are more in case of females. However, average birth weight of total parities for males (2.63 Kg) is more than the females (2.58 kg). This is in conformity to the general findings of other workers. Nanda *et al.* (1977), Ramamma and Mukerjee (1977), Rao and Saheb (1981).

In both the sexes a trend of higher Mean birth weight in subsequent parities is noticeable with exception to 3rd, 7th and 8th parities where lower averages are recorded. Regarding 7th and 8th parities, it may be pointed out that the sample size is very low.

Sex-ratio according to parity shows preponderance of males over females in all the parities except for 6th and 8th. Sex-ratio is significantly high in parities 2nd, 5th and 7th parities.

The recent researches have indicated that the uterus is one of the severest, if not the most severe environment to which human life is exposed. Thus the findings of increased birth weight in the subsequent parities could probably be the effect of uterine environment.

In order to see the number of parities and the birth weight in different socio-economic environment, the data have been classified into various income (per capita) groups and compiled in Table 2.

Table 2
Birth Weights of Infants According to Income Groups

	No.of Birth				Birth Weight (Kg.)			
Per Capita Income (Rs.)	*Male*	*Female*	*Total*	*Parity Range*	*Male Mean ± S.E.*	*Female Mean ± S.E.*	*Total (M+F) Mean ± S.E.*	*Mean No. of Family members*
<51	14	10	24	1-7	2.60±0.101	2.44±0.181	2.53±0.094	6.54
5±1-80	21	25	46	1-8	2.60±0.081	2.64±0.115	2.62±0.072	5.71
81-110	26	15	41	1-5	2.45±0.092	2.54±0.088	2.48±0.066	4.24
111-140	27	17	44	1-5	2.49±0.103	2.54±0.090	2.51±0.071	4.84
141-170	17	15	32	1-4	2.89±0.101	2.68±0.094	2.79±0.071	4.06
171-200	16	11	27	1-7	2.72±0.118	2.47±0.077	2.62±0.079	4.40
201-230	6	1	7	1-4	2.79±0.186	2.5	2.75±0.162	4.42
231-260	12	7	19	1-4	2.70±0.162	2.85±0.202	2.76±0.124	3.76
261-290	6	8	14	1-3	2.87±0.327	2.65±0.148	2.74±0.159	6.42
291-320	6	6	12	1-2	2.58±0.138	2.46±0.118	2.52±0.088	3.16
321-350	9	3	12	1-3	2.78±0.124	2.41±0.300	2.69±0.122	3.33
351-380	2	1	3	1-2	2.50	3.00	2.66±0.166	5.33
381-410	3	4	7	1-3	2.83	2.50±0.204	2.64±0.142	2.57
> 410	9	4	13	1-3	2.65±0.231	2.50±0.288	2.60±0.177	4.15

It is apparent that in lower per capita income group i.e., upto Rs. 80/-, a tendancy of higher parity level (upto 8) is noticeable, whereas with the rise of per capita income, a steady decline in the number of pareties is observed, with exception to theRs.171-200 income group, which shows higher parities (upto 7).Thus lower income group has definitely shown more pregnancies than the upper or middle income groups. The number of family members, obviously, is more in low income levels.

A general tendancy of increase in birth weight according to income groups is noted for males. However, where the parities are upto 2, the lower averages for obvious reasons are recorded. In case of the females no consistent trend of increase of birth weight according to income groups is revealed. Combined (M+F) birth weight distribution in the various income groups do not show a trend of increase for the reasons stated above.

To conclude, it may be recalled that the males generally exhibit a higher birth weight than the females in different parities. The birth weight in both the sexes shows an increase according to parity. An ideal sex-ratio (1:1) is achieved in the 6th parity. The socio-economic condition reveals more pregnancies and parities in lower income groups. The males show an increasing trend of birth weight from lower to higher income groups.

References

Nanda, D.K., D. Chowdhury and Sikha Chatterjee (1977), Relationship of Birth Weight and Birth Length with Birth Order and Sex in a Bengali Sample. *Jr. Ind. Anth. Society*, 12: 272-275.

Ramamma, K. and D.P. Mukerjee (1977), Pregnancy and Birth Weight Around Tirupati with Special Reference to Maternal Age and Seasonal Variation. *Jr. Ind. Anth. Society*, 12: 227-246.

Rajendra Rao, K. and S. K. Yaseen Saheb (1981), Birth Weight and Still Birth among the Car-Nicobar Islanders, *Ind. Jr. Phys. Anthrop. And Hum. Genet.*, 7: 53-60.

14 Ecology and Nutritional Stress Among the Gujjar

S. S. Bandyopadhyay

Nutritional stresses in man are clearly a reflection of his ecology, culture and biology. The physical environment has a direct bearing on the nutritional requirements because of the very fact that human activities are subject to ecology of the region. Non-availability of adequate diet affects the quality of life in terms of physical health of individual and certain permanent impairments. The food is the media by which the metabolic activities and energy is supplied for the performance of human activities. The quality of food intake is greatly subjected to cultural factors, viz. socio-economic conditions and to the available sources in an ecozone.

In the present study an attempt has been made to see the effect of socio-economic and physical environment on the nutritional requirement and stresses on the Gujjar population. The Gujjar population have both, settled and migrating ways of life. The pastoral nomadic Gujjars migrate to high altitude hills (about 3000 metre) of U.P. and H.P. during summer months (April to September) for want of pasture lands. Their economy is mainly based on milk and milk products etc.

Material and Method

The material of the present paper consists of daily food intake, socio-economic conditions and work activity on 94 Gujjar households inhabiting the forest areas of Sivalik and Lansdown forest divisions of U.P. Besides, some body measurements viz. statures, weight, were also taken on 236 individuals in the age group of 20-25 years. The measurements were taken on normal individuals only. Standard methods were adopted for collecting the relevant information.

Results and Discussion

Out of 94 Gujjar households, 29 households are permanently sedentarized in low altitude Sivalik forest areas of U.P. Table 1 shows the household size of Gujjars. It may be observed that the migratory Gujjars have a greater proportion of large sized households than the settled ones. The average household size shows a lower value in case of settled Gujjars (7.07) as compared to migrating Gujjars (8.50 and 9.81). The large size of households among pastoral nomadic Gujjars is probably an adaptive feature for the division of labour, settlements in the Himalayan forest areas and migratory pursuits. The sex-ratio shows slight preponderance of males over females in both the migrating and settled Gujjars. However, not much of variation in the sex-ratio is seen in the two Gujjar types.

Table 1
Household Composition of Gujjars

	Household Size							
	1-3	*4-6*	*7-10*	*11 & above*	*Population size*	*No. of Households*	*Average Household Size*	*Sex Ratio*
Migrating to high altitude of U.P. Hills	6	12 (13.6%)	13 (27.4%)	13 (29.5%)	374 (29.5%)	44	8.50	103.26
Migrating to high altitude of H.P. Hills	0	4 (19%)	8 (38.1%)	9 (42.9%)	206	21	9.81	112.37
Settled to Low altitude of U.P. forest area	2 (6.9%)	12 (41.4%)	12 (41.4%)	3 (10.3%)	205	29	7.07	105.0

The sedentarized Gujjar settlements in the U.P. Sivalik hills show that maximum number of families is residing since past ten years or so (Table 2). This shows that sedentarization among Gujjars is a very recent phenomenon.

Table 2
Sedentarization of Gujjars

Migrating families		*Settled families in U.P. forest*	*Years of Settlement*					
			0-5	*6-10*	*11-15*	*16-20*	*21-25*	*26 and above*
U.P. Hills	H.P. Hills							
44	21	29	9	12	2	3	Nil	3

Table 3 shows the socio-economic condition of the Gujjars.It is revealed that on an average the size of herds and Land holding families are lesser in case of settled Gujjars than migrating ones. Subsequently, the average milk produce and selling capacity per family is less (15.81 litres and 12.58 litres respectively) in the settled Gujjars as compared to the other type. The average consumption of milk and milk products seem to be a less in the migrating Gujjars than the settled ones. This clarifies that the migrating Gujjars put greater emphasis on selling of their produce to improve their economic status. Thus migration is motivated by the desire to improve their economy.

Table 4 shows mean stature and weight according to sex and also average caloric need as per the work activity and available calories from food in the Gujjars. It is noted that the mean values of weight and stature are lower in case of settled Gujjars, in both the sexes, as compared to migrating Gujjars. It is as per expectation of the weight being directly correlated with height. Considering work activities, the average caloric requirement in both the sexes seems to be higher for migrating Gujjars.The needed calorie for males in migrating Gujjars comes to 2853-2860 K.Cal. and in the settled Gujjars, it is 2782 K. Cal. The females usually require less calories than the males. Among Gujjar females it ranges from 2177 to 2392 K.Cal. The calories available from the food consumed per day shows a lower value

Table 3
Socio-Economic Condition of Gujjars

		Land Holding		*Herd Milk*										
				Buffalo		*Cow*		*Goat*						
	House-hold No.	*House hold*	*%*	*No.*	*%*	*No.*	*%*	*No.*	*%*	*Total*	*Produced (Lit.)*	*Produced per house-hold*	*Sold per house-hold*	*% consump-tion of produce*
Migrating to high altitudes of U.P. Hills	44	5	11.36	978	92.09	26	2.44	58	5.46	1062 Av. 24.12	1118	25.4	21.34	16.01
Migrating to high altitude of H.P. Hills	21	5	23.8	688	91.61	22	3.19	41	5.19	751 Av. 35.76	457	21.76	17.95	17.50
Settled to low Altitudes of U.P. Forest Area	29	3	10.34	406	90.63	22	4.91	20	4.46	448 Av. 15.45	458.5	15.81	12.58	20.39

Table 4
Stature, Weight and Calorie Need of Gujjar

	Sex	Sample size	Average height (Cm.)	Average Weight (Kg.)	Average Calorie needs (K. Cal.)	Average Calorie available from their food/day/member (K. Cal.)	Difference between required and available (K. Cal.)
Migrating to	Male	70	168.97	60.39	2853	2757	-96
U.P. Hills	Female	55	154.8	50.00	2212		+545
Migrating to	Male	27	169.8	60.02	2860	2594	-266
H.P. Hills	Female	29	157.38	51.48	2392		+202
Settled	Male	30	164.55	54.85	2782	2832	+50
	Female	25	152.99	48.8	2177		+655

in case of migrating Gujjars (2594 to 2757 K.Cal.) than the settled Gujjar (2832 K. Cal.). The difference between calorie needed and available from food shows the nutritional stress in the migrating Gujjar males, whereas surplus calories are available to settled Gujjars. The females generally perform lesser activities than the males, thereby have surplus calories in both the types of subsistence. Here it is presumed that both the sexes consume similar quantity and quality of food. Thus a very significant feature emerges out that the migrating Gujjars have nutritional stress inspite of their better economic condition, whereas the settled Gujjars, who have comparatively poorer economy seems to be well nourished. This nutritional stress among the migrating Gujjars may be causing some gradual harm to the population.

To conclude it may be recalled that the settled Gujjars have greater proportion of medium sized households and poorer economy, but do not have any nutritional stress as compared to the migrating Gujjars. Thus the physical environment is generally putting a heavier load of nutritional requirements among the migrating Gujjars which they are unable to compensate even with their better economic status.

References

Gopalan, C., B.V. Rama Sastri and S.C. Balasubramanian (1977), Nutritive Value of Indian Foods. National Institute of Nutrition New Delhi, *I.C.M.R.*.

John, D. Kirsehmann (1979), *Nutrition Almanag*, New York Mc. Graw Hill Book Company.

Krause, M.V., L.K. Hahan (1979), *Food, Nutrition and Diet Therapy*, London W.B. Saunders Company.

Part-4

Ecological Variation and Changing Lifeways

15 Culture, Environment and Development: An Odyssey in Search of a Balanced Strategy

B. R. Rizvi

There is a general tendency among the participants in this Seminar to define cualture as "human adaptation" (Sahlins 1868: 367) and bring out the various facets of culture and environment relationships. This paper assumes that culture and environment do maintain a dyadic relationship, but how this relationship has been disturbed and ecological imbalances injected by developmental activities having a direct bearing on the societies who have been maintaining a close liaison with the environment from the time immemorial is the main focus of this paper.

Three societies have been selected as case studies where intensive field work was carried out from 1970 to 1981. Data were collected from Kashmir (J&K), Chattisgarh (Madhya Pradesh) and Khammam (Andhra Pradesh).

Kashmir (J&K) Situation

Balahama is the village 3 miles west of Pampore. There are 275 households in the village: 259 Muslim and 16 Kashmiri Pandits. The Muslims are divided into two sect and a number of caste groups whereas the Kashmiri Pandits are divided into two endogamous groups' viz. *Karkun* and *Gor*.

The traditional economy of the village is based on dry farming; wheat and maize are the principal crops. Apples and almonds were grown in orchards surrounding the village as main cash crops. The nearby culvert passing through the village was the only source of water supply. People lived in penury and ignorance. In contrast to this dismal picture, the villages surrounding Pampore enjoyed relatively better off economy as a result of saffron *Kong* cultuivation which was hitherto a monopoly of this area alone.

About 15 years ago a few villagers of Balahama put the saffron tubers (*munji*) underground as an experiment. To their delight they found a rich blossoming in their *Kong* fields. Others too followed the suits and within five years all dry fields under maize and wheat cultivation were converted into saffron fields. According to an estimate each households in Balahama was earning an average of Rs.15,000/- per annum from selling saffron only. Houses were repaired or rebuilt, the village mosque and *Imambara* too were renovated and construction activities were noticed all around the village. The Shias were divided into two parties owing their allegiance to one Agha Sahib of Badgam and Maulana Ansari of Srinagar. The two priests were more of political rivals than divided on any fundamental religious issues. The minority fraction of the Ghias of Balahama, get an opportunity with their new begotton wealth to asset themselves. They too built another *Imambara*. Clashes occurred between the two Shiiate factions during Moharram and the district authorities banned public processions in the village. The people revelled in prosperity but only temporarily till a cement facatory came in an adjacent village at Khrew, which was inaugurated in October 1981.

On December 30, 1981 the residents of Khrew and adjoining villages observed a bandh in protest against dust pollution created by the newly opened cement factory in the area. Leader of the agitation claimed that ever since the factory went into production a thin film of dust had covered the area. It has affected even the drinking water and posed a health hazard. The crops, particularly saffron, had been badly affected and the yield this year was about half of the last year's harvest.

Another grouse was that the factory had not employed many people from the area, though there were a large number of unemployed graduates including engineers at Khrew and adjacent villages. The local people who had been employed were given menial jobs while attractive posts were "reserved" for people hailing from Srinagar and other towns.

Technical experts of the factory claim that the quantum of dust being emitted by the plant is not more that what it is spewed out by similar plants elsewhere in the country. As the factory is not in full production yet, the two major dust collectors are not being operated. They say that the dust level is within permissible limits.

The general impression is that the local people are rather reluctant to work in the factory as it involves heavy and "dirty" work. Most of the local inhabitants are fairly well off because of cultivation of saffron and dry-fruits trees. However, 8 persons of Balahama are working in Khrew cement factory.

The Chattisgarh (M.P.) Situation

The Hill Korwa practiced shifting cultivation of slash-and-burn type (*bowar*) from the time immemorial. Since their abodes were either on the top of planteau or in thick forests on the hill stages, their dependence on forest was complete. Hunting and food-gathering were as important and rewarding professions as bowar. The local forests are of deciduous mixed forests type containing mostly of Shova robuster (sal) and Bassia latifolia (mahua). The Hill Korwa and other neighbouring tribes of the area have depended traditionally on sal and Mahua trees. These trees not only provide them wood but also leaves for making temporary huts (*Koomba*) and plates and bowls for food; sal gum is used for making bird traps (*lassa phands*). *Mahua* tree yields flowers which can be eaten raw or cooked or brewed into *jagra*. The sweet fruits are picked up for local consumption. Oil is also extracted from the Mahua seeds by the Hill Korwa and other tribals of the region.

Swidden cultivation was banned in 1867 by an order of government as the practice was considered harmful to the forests. For improving the quality of life and saving the environmental decay the tribals were encouraged to abondon the practice. A sudden change over from their main livelihood left the people dazed and shocked. A section of the tribe turned into a band of marauder which wanted to subsist by pillage which was often followed with murders. The rulers of Surguja felt perturbed and determined to put down the acts of lawlessness committed by the Hill Korwa. Non-tribal populations were given land and state patronage to deal with the Hill Korwa with an iron hand. The state appointed the loyal Hill Korwa with an iron hand. The state appointed the loyal Hill Korwa as Chiefs (*Lalsohne Mukhya*) and efforts were made to induce the Hill Korwa to come down from the Hill top to the plains and start settled agriculture. A section of the Hill Korwa responded to these efforts and took up plough agriculture. They are called rather scornfully as *dih Korwa* (Korwa living in plains) by the Hill Korwa who did not abandon their traditional forests and hill abode and indulged in swiddening rather in a clandestine manner. This situation prevailed till 1952 when the feudatory states of Surguja and Raigarh were merged with Indian Republic. The situation of bowar was reviewed and the Government of Madhya Pradesh decided that shifting cultivation should be allowed only in cases where people are solely dependent on this, until such times as they will require having to settled agriculture. Simultaneously efforts were made to rehabilitate the Hill Korwa in forest villages. Soon it was found that the Hill Korwa get alienated from their newly be gotton lands: bullocks, which were distributed for ploughing by the government, were eaten up; free food distributed for sowing too were consumed. Houses built by the government and allotted to the Hill Korwa were deserted. The causes responsible for the retrogressive development are very obvious for anthropologists and hence need not be repeated. The Hill Korwa could never become settled agricualturists instead they swelled the size of serf population (herwaha) working for non-tribal landlords (grihats).

Thus a proud people depending for their livelihood on forests were reduced to a group of ignoble serfs by the "outsiders" who regarded swiddening as bad and become an advocate of settled agriculture. There was very little effort to see the whole problem through an "emic" porspective i.e. the perspective of the tribal himself who lives the culture. Solutions sought by the modernizers to the 'problems' - that are non-acceptable to the tribal. He has also not been provided with the alternative ways of earning subsistence (Atal 1981).

Now let us take another lead from the adjoining Bastar District where a fierce controversy is on between developments versus environment. An area around 350 kms radius from Jagdalpur and covering parts of Maharashtra, Orissa and Andhra Pradesh was identified by F.A.U. and Swedish International Aid Agency as suitable for intensive forest plantation. The Ford Foundation recommended intensive forestry over as much as 16,000 sq. kms. out of a total forest area of 22,000 sq. kms. in Bastar. This was the first forestry project in India to receive World Bank assistance. Work started in 1976, but when strong objections were raised against the planting of tropical pines by clear falling and in particular destroying sal and other indigenous species, the M.P. government reduced the area under plantation in the project to 1,000 hectares instead of 3,000. The idea was to plant 20,000 hectares over 20 years to provide 50,000 tons of pulp a year. For these two decades, a paper mill set up at a cost of Rs.250 crores - could use sal and other hard wood till pine was ready for the axe.

The M.P. government agreed to appoint a committee to study the environmental impact of the pine plantation project after its feasibility was confirmed by Sandwell, the Canadian Consultant appointed by the World Bank. The Committee ruled in 1979 that the experimental tropical pine plantation in Kurandi near Jagdalpur showed "excellent promise". The pine monoculture was "geared to conserve water" and would help to keep the climate cooler than the deciduous mixed forests".

The major objection to the scheme is that it will rob the tribals of sal on which they traditionally depended. For the same reasons the tribals in South Bihar are stoutly opposing the State Forest Development Corporation's attempts to cultivate teak in place of sal.

Many administrators and forest officials, however, believe that opposition to the project on this country is either politically motivated or is based on sentiments. An administrator pointed out how vast areas in Baster were already being denuded of sal by the very tribals who were supposed to earn their livelihood from it. "By stopping the scheme they will be putting the clock back", he said further "I am an administrator; I am for development. Any such project is bound to impose a sacrifice on certain sections of the community" (D'Monta 1981). It is true that the tribal is cutting down forest trees with an alarming rate but this is happening not because the adivasi population is growing but because there is an inexerable shift from a traditional forest based economy where his needs were minimal, to an agricultural economy where the pressure on land is bound to increase. Besides, the timbers that adivasi are cutting is for their own fuel and fodder, whereas the real devastation - such as taking place in Bastar today is being perpetuated by the Forest Department, in active collusion with rapecious timber merchants; all the wood is going out of the district - there is not a single paper mill in Baster today.

The other case against pine plantation is that when large scale monoculture plantations are established then the national forest will be destroyed. Although only one 50,000 tonne a day paper pulp plant is now envisaged (its capacity will be increased to 100,000 tonnes). There is no guarantee that if the pine proves successful, there will be no further expansion or even additional plants. Pine has a dense canopy, under which little else grows, furthermore, pine needles pose a serious fire hazard either on the ground or with standing trees, especially as they contain inflammable resin. The protagonists of this scheme present a rosy picture in terms of economic profitability of the project as pine is commercially more available in relation to sal or other indigenous species. It takes only 20 years to attain full stature as against five times as long for sal and three times for teak. Moreover, pine is given better than bamboo in providing long-fibre pulp which is ideal for paper. Such hard economic sense, they argue, should out-weight any other adverse factors. Must such development is necessary be at the cost of environment and by extension the traditional style of the tribals. Planting pines for a paper mill is by very definition not going to employ the tribals displaced as a result. Just 200 people have been given regular jobs in the first phase of the experiment and the proposed paper plant will only hire another 1,000 in all categories. If on the other hand some of this pulp is exported, whom does the scheme really benefit?

The environmental impact of introducing exotics like pine or eucalyptus for economic benefits along should not be dismissed so lightly. Experts have expressed fears and warned that in a well nourished soil this imported species is susceptible to diseses like gamosis. If pine was restricted to denuded areas one would object to it and while it would be more difficult to manage scattered sites instead of consolidated plantation, this would employ very many local people in occupation to which they are eminently suited.

Does monoculture such as tropical pine in Bastar or Chir in the Himalayas (also aided by World Bank) amount to the development of the area or its improverishment? This crucial question ought to be answered before any major forestry or related industrial project is taken up. In the long run, after all, ecology and economy have to go hand in hand.

The Khammam (A.P.) Situation

The Godavari valley is the traditional abode of the Koya. The Polavaran Taluk on the West Bank of the river and Chodevaram, Yallavaram, Chadrachalam and Nugur Taluks on the opposite bank of the river form the part of the Koya land which is further extended into Bastar beyond Nugur and into Malkangiri Taluk of Orissa. The Koya numbering 3,44,437 in Andhra Pradesh are also found in Bastar as stated earlier, where they are known as Dorla and in part of Andhra they are known as Guthi Keya or the Hill Koya.

Here, the author is mainly concerned with the Koya of Bhadrachalam and Nugur Taluks of Khammam district of Andhra Pradesh.

Chatti, a village predominantly inhabited by the Koya is situated 63 kms. north east of Bhadrachalam on the tri-junction of Andhra Pradesh, Madhya Pradesh and Orissa. Sabri river, one of the main tributaries of Godavari flows on the northern border of the village.

The Koya were traditionally swiddeners and the mode of swiddening is known as *podu*. New *podu* is no more in existence excepting sporadic clandestine swiddening in some pockets. The people are now, by and large, settled agriculturists. The main crops sown are maize, paddy, and lentils. Chillies and tobacco are the main cash crops, are of a recent origin. In the year 1953 Godavari innundated a large part of Koya land in one of its most devasting floods. With the flood came the black cotton soil. This event encouraged the neihbouring non-tribals to come and settle down near Koya settlements for cultivation of tobacco and chillies. As the needs for exporting the cash crops arose, first chatti was connected with Bhadrachaeam and Konta (M.P.) with tarred roads and a bridge was constructed in close proximity of the village in 1965 connecting Bhadrachalam with Malkangiri Taluk of Koraput district (Orissa). Being closest to the construction site of the bridge Chatti supplied the bulk of labour force; women constituted the major part of this labourers. With the beginning of construction activities a cycle of changes occurred in social organization of the Koya of Chatti.

The Koya women as a result of their participation in construction activities came into direct contact with outsiders that caused a tremendous change both in their life style and world review. Gradually they started resenting their own male folk for purposes of marriage. They rejected their male folk being lazy, and addict (to liquor and toddy). They also complained of maltreatment of Koya males after marriage with their spouses. Emergence of vast tobacco and chilly farms run by non-tribals offered further job opportunities to Koya women who came into perpetual contact with non-tribal males. The result: A non-Koya trader from East Godavari settled down in a neighbouring village; took vast amount of land from the Koyas on lease and started cultivation of cash crops. In order to offset his investment problems, he subsequently married with four different Koya girls and sought government loans in their names separately. In fact all the four Koya girls were working in his farm as wage labourers and were getting their daily wages.

It was further observed that out of 106 Koya girls within the age group of 15 years to 35 years, 61 (59.53 per cent) were leading the life of spinsters or divorcees and were working as wage labourers.

Divorce has become a common phenomenon in the Koya society.The motives being mutual lack of confidence, ill-treatment meted out by husband and in-laws, incompatibility of age and temprament, ill-maintenance of wife and suspected adultery. 13 cases of divorce were reported from Chatti. An analysis of these cases show that in 7 cases women sought divorce. The average period of conjugal relations between spouses was found 2.46 years. The first divorce took place in 1945, then in 1966. Eleven other cases occurred during last 7 years. The average age group of divorcees was found 27.5 years for men and 28.1 years of women. The average period of stay of Koya girls in their respective families of procreation ranged between 7 years to six months. The percentage of broken families was found 23.27 and the average family size 4.42.

There is clear indication that the institutions of marriage and family among the Koya appears to be in peril. The rate of irregular unions of Koya girls with non-tribal is on increase and also the aversion of Koya girls to marry with their own men and lead a married life. The mechanism of ethnic boundary maintenance is crumbline. The social identity of Koya women is fast changing and the domestic sphere of their activities is shrinking. As a result of considerable enlargement of public sphere activities of Koya women the traditional authority structure of the tribe, from familial level to the collective level of Kulam panchayat is collapsing.

The agencies responsible for integrated tribal development may feel proud of the fact that Koya women are now changing and joining the main stream of Indian society but the fact is that by refusing their own men as life partners they are becoming civilized concubines of non-tribal white collar professionals.

The three pictures of development narrated above have a single factor in common; in pre-development stage the three societies enjoyed a well balanced relationship with environment. The disbalance between men-environment relationship were injected through the planning for development. Neither an anthroplogist nor a common citizen is against the development but the question which has been raised, time and again, is development for whom?

Who should be the real beneficiary of developmental activities? Whether weaker segment of the society should be uprooted or displaced for the benefit of the stronger and more powerful segments? Whether the uprooted societies should act as merely a labour force for carrying out the development activities planned by the outsiders? If development means the movement upward of the whole system as Gunnar Myrdal (1972 : 355) would like to state, there appears to the some lacuna in the planning for and priorities in development activities.

"Man who should have been at the center has been thrown to the outskirts. Our concern with environment has given us a loud slogan: 'Save the environment'. But this particular shout has subdued our relevant wishes. Narrowly defined, environment excludes culture and therefore quite logically students of culture raise a counter slogan for saving the culture. Our overconcern with environment should not become a pretext for strangulating our cultures. What is needed is a generous definition of environment that includes both nature and culture" (Atal 1981: 93).

Forest tribes are evicted from the forest, for maintenance of ecological balance, new afforestation scheme implemented and the pace of industrilization is accelerated for the benefit of market economy, and thus the resultant effect is the imbalance of relationship between the environment and culture. Another implication of emerging disbalance between culture-environment relationship is the politicization of this very issue in the form of Jharkhand, Uttarakhand and the like movements which are injecting a sense of isolation and alienation among the people who are affected by development planning, a direct product of formal economic models derived from logic and laws of mind rather than from facts and laws of nature. If planning for development of primitive and agrarian societies is to be implemented successfully, the planners should lean more heavily towards emperical realities and concrete facts of life rather than depending on priori-assumptions and mental reconstructs.

References

Atal, Yogesh (1981), Rethinking Relevance. *Eastern Anthroplogist,* 34(2): 77-94.

D'Monto, Daryl (1981), Pines for the Forest. *Hindustan Times,* LIX (4). Jan. 4, 1982.

Myrdal, Gunnar (1972), *Asian Drama.* London: Penguin.

Sahlins, Marshall, D. (1968), Culure and Environment. In *Theory in Anthropology* (Ed.) Robert A. Manners and David Kaplan. London Routledge and Kegan Paul. 367-373.

16 Environmental Orientation and the Dimension of Dynamism

D. K. SAMANTA

There are intellectual tendencies currently observed to conceive of human society and of man nature relationship in terms of ecosystemic functioning. Ecosystem is advocated as the key concept for a unified science of human ecology. What permits a system to persist is explained by the concept.

The relationship between man and his environment received the attention of the Greek scholars for the first time a few centuries ago and since then human knowledge in this regard increased several folds. The environment includes physical environment that is geographical set up; biological environment, that is, plants and animals; and, cultural environment consisting of numerous cultural forms. The writings emphasized how these 'environments' influence and condition man, but ignored the process of change, which did not receive its due attention. An attempt is made here to consider the various facts of man-nature relationship and the process of change, which remains a characteristic feature of human society. This dynamic nature of human society in terms of use of natural resources is important as to know the society either in historical and evolutionary context or to explain and analyse the contemporary situation. If one ignores this aspect there is a resultant gap in our understanding of the cultural processes.

In the present paper we examine the social situation as it exists among the Korku at various/different junctures of time. In this study genealogical method of collecting data has widely been employed. The central theme is the dynamic relationship between the population and environment. The Korku are seen in the perspective, of their contacts with other tribal, and non-tribal, groups in the same environment. In the present study the Korku are the nodule and the economy and social relations are the illustrations, while the ways the Korku have adapted them to the changed situation is the locus.

The Korku live in the districts of Betul, Chhindwara, Khandwa, Hoshangabad and parts of Dewas of Madhya Pradesh, and Amravati District of Mahrashtra. Their highest concentration is in Amravati, Betul and Chhindwara Districts. This administrative area comprises the western part of the Satpura ranges and the Tapti valley. The Korku speaks the language which belongs to Munda sub-family. In this part of the country they are the only Mundari speaking group living with Dravidian and Indo-Aryan language speaking neighbourers. Commonly they are well built with a lighter skin colour. They have come into contact with the Caste Hindus long back in some areas of their concentraion. However, the intensity of contact varies.

The land is hilly with undulation and valleys. There is only one system of hills which is the Satpura. The summits attain an average elevation of 3,400 ft., the highest point being that of Bairat plateau at 3,866 ft. The principal river system is that of Tapti which drains the rainwater to Arabian sea. The climatic vicissitude of the area is remarkable being in the tropical climate zone. Rains start in second week of June and last upto the middle of October. Rain is closely followed by a brief spell of warm weather for about two weeks and then the winter commences which continues till February. Summer months are March, April and May and it continues during the first half of June. In general, the climate is cooler than that of the Berar plains. The average rain fall is 1106 mm in one calender year. Ninety percent of the yearly rainfall is due to the impact of south-west monsoons.

The Forest

The hilly tract contains at places certain very dense forest. The quality of soil varies from fertile deep loam of the plains commonly known as black cotton soil to thin red soil of the plateau and the hilly terrain. This has a direct bearing on the crop pattern. Cultivation of *kharif* crops greatly predominate over that of *rabi* crops. The main cereals produced are *jawari*, Maize, linseed and other lighter millets like *kodo, kutki, rajgira*. A few pulses are also grown. The forest areas are rich in teak wood which earns a handsome amount every year. Lac and *rusa* oil are two minor forest products of this area which are used for preparing perfumes. The other important plant of the area is *mahua*. *Mahua* flowers are collected for distillation of liquor. *Mahu* flowers are also consumed as other eatables.

The Korku villages have some characteristic features. The size of the villages on the hills varies from that of the villages of the plains. Villages of the plains are much larger in size, hence are more populous than the villages of the forest and on the hills. For a village site, a plain area is necessary which is not easily available in the forest and on the hills.

For selection of a village site three factors are important. These are high mount to avoid water logging, a waterhole for drinking water facility and land around this site for cultivation. Once these requirements are fulfilled and a village is established, it has some characateristic features. On the eastern fringe is the burial ground having small huts, one for each clan. A little near the habitation area is *Meghnath deo*, which is a big pole of teak wood. The huts are arranged in two linear rows facing each other and with the main street of the village in between. The street is used for village festivals and community dances. There are cattle-shades attached to most of these huts. The place of *Muthu deo*, the village god is in the main thoroughfare at the root of a neem tree. This tree is planted at the time of selection of the village site by the headman or the patel of the village. The rows of huts stretch from east to west.

Each hutment consists of an all purpose room which opens in the veranda on the south and north. The deadbody is taken out through the north door of the hut, while the new born is taken out through the south door and the bride also enter through this door. The huts are constructed on a height of about two feet from the ground. These are rectangular in shape divided into two equal halves. In the eastern half are the hearth and the place for ancestor worship, at the base of the central pole. The walls are made either of processed earth or of bamboo mats plastered with mud and cow-dung. The huts are devoid of any windows, and the two entrances of the hut have bamboo doors. The doors face each other to allow the cross ventilation of the air. As the huts are stretched east to west the impact of hot summer wind is reduced to a great extent to make these huts comfortable. The central pole is always of teak wood. The whole structure rests on a wooden frame. On the wooden frame of the roof there is bamboo matting on which the country tiles are arranged. A poor man's hut has thatched roof on which are tied wooden poles to save it from dispersing away by strong gusty winds. The central pole is very important for the existing hut, and so also the ancestors for the Korku. Hence, the place of ancestral worship is at the base of the central pole.

The cattle-sheds are also made of wood, bamboo and tiles. For purpose of tying the people use barks of some specific plants. There is also a place to store the cereals inside the hut. These containers are made of bamboo splits plastered with mud and cow-dung. The shape of containers is rectangular and drum shaped. The corridors are fenced with bamboo mats. The roof is double sloped to drain the rain water.

The huts to house the memorial posts are also made of wood and bamboo with thatched roof but without any walls.

For making various agricultural, hunting and fishing implements the forest products are widely used. The plough, the handles of axe, spade, garden spade, sowing funnel are made of locally available wood or bamboo. Baskets of various types and for various purposes are made of bamboo splits. Barks are used for every kind of tying. Ropes are made out of creepers and are as strong as to drag huge logs. Forest here is the locus of resource which is exploited as per the need.

The male dress consists of *dhoti, kurta* and turban and ladies wear *sari*. Shoes are commonlyk used in this hilly terrain. These shoes are made of hide of sambar. Sambars are available in this tract.

The Change

The villages where the Korku have come in contact with others particularly with non-tribal groups, and close who live in urban centers there are certain differences from the description I have just given. The continuity of the linear rows of huts are not maintained as is the case of other ethnic groups. Brick walls are frequently observed. Different tiles are used. Dresses are different in material as well as in style of wearing (like *sari* style) to fit in the changing atmosphere. Memorial huts of concrete also have made their appearance. Some of them have large houses with a number of rooms. The privacy for the couples is more emphasized.

Modern and improved agricultural implements have replaced the old fashioned ones. This is as per the need of the cultivation which differs greatly than what is in the hilly tracts, described earlier. In addition to their traditional ornaments, they also have fascination for modern and new designs. Their old designs are considered as tribal by others and hence, they are attracted to the new types of ornaments.

The Korku living in forested hilly areas domesticate goat, poultry bird, cow and dog. Of all these dogs are very important. They are the protector of the Korku, find places in their mythologies. Each Korku village has a number of dogs. During nights dogs cry and announce the presence of a tiger or bear and awake the villagers. The tiger tries to kill the dogs and attempts to lift away cattle. Bear menace is well known in this area; hence, the dogs are their life savers. The dogs are also used during hunting expeditions. The next important domesticated animal is the cow. Bullocks are used as draft animal for ploughing and for various other agricultural operations. Milk is an essential item of the people's daily diet. The goats and poultry are used for ceremonial sacrifices on the occasions of festivals and life cycle rituals.

In the plains the services of dog are not required because of the absence of wild animals. Also alongwith the depletion of wild animal populations the dog has lost its importance among the Korku even in the forest areas. Previously dogs made the people aware of the wild bears that spoiled the crops. Buffaloes are domesticated now than the cow because they give more milk and milk has a better market value due to its more fat content.

The Korku used to practise *dahya* (shifting plough) cultivation in the hilly terrain which usually gives a low yield. This has direct contribution to the population size of the village and also the stability of the habitation sites. They used to move from one habitation site to the other for the purpose of a close supervision of their field activities, along the cycle of cultivation sites. Their crop pattern has direct relation to the prevailing climatic conditions. Mostly they used to cultivate lighter millets, paddy and maize. The imposition of prohibitory rules on shifting cultivation and parmanent allotment of plots has restricted their movements and also their freedom to the land at the place they liked. They have taken up settled agriculture. This has brought about a situation for new adjustments. The ritual calender has many additions and these rituals are observed by other neighbouring ethnic groups practising agriculture. Now they get more yields and the population density is also on the increase in the forest areas. New crop varieties have also been incorporated for more yields. They are also trying to learn the new techniques for further improvement in cultivation.

Hunting was also practised earlier. Games were found in abundance. But this has been prohibited. This has resulted into an increase in the wild animal population and the need for dogs and the new hazards for the cattle. They have to pay a fine in case they kill an animal. This prohibition forced them to think of other resources for their livelihood. Collection of roots and tubers has become necessary during rainy months when the cereals have exhausted. They live on these collections till the harvest of maize. Collection of *mahua* flowers is an important work now.

Fishing is a pastime for the Korku. They use nets to catch fish and also catch fish by poisoning the small stream with barks. Now, the nets are more in use and they have taken to river fishing with improved technology. Various types of nets are used for this purpose. The fishing by poisoning is no longer practised because that is useful only in case of small streams.

With lesser amount of hunting and fishing as additional sources of livelihood, the Korku have become more dependent on settled agriculture. Under the circumstances the ritual pattern relating to economic activities are having addition and new adjustments. For example, the worshipping of rain god has acquired increased importance.

Forestry and road repair and construction works provide main employment resource to the Korku in addition to agriculture. They were reluctant to work as labour initially but now they readily go for forest work and earn cash wages. This is an important source of earning for them. In the process they are coming in contact with other people. Selling of firewood is also practised, but this fetches only a small amount of cash.

The Korku did not have a fascination for leafy vegetables as these were not available in the forest. Now, these are available to them in the market and this made them being interested in cultivation of these vegetables in their fields close to their houses. They have learnt the art and skill of growing these from their non-tribal neighbours, from whom they learned the taste.

Life cycle rituals are important for any group of people. As has been said earlier the new born baby is taken through the southern door of the hut which has a relation with the direction and is considered as auspicious. The preventive medicines as well as curative medicines are prepared from plants and leaves etc. The other way for curing disease is through the propitiation of benevolent and malevolent spirits by the medicineman.

In the Korku marriage ceremony there is a function, called *borebai,* which is performed near a *ber* tree. Again, at the time of *panchachauli* ceremony the bride and the bride-groom throw rice on each other to the tune of the dance. '*Panchachauli*' is to help each other in their economic drive. There are several such associations of natural objects with the marriage ceremony.

The Korku bury the deads. The 'great' funeral feast *sidoli* is observed a few months after the death which includes installation of a memorial post and performance of the great dance. People dance and use filthy words in the songs on this occasion. The memorial post is carved out of a teak wood and is planted at the place marked for clan members. All able-bodied persons participate in the dance and the great feast. Anybody can join the dance even without invitation.

The accessibility to the modern medical aids have led the Korku to ail the facilities at least when the traditional medicine man fails to cure the person of some particular disease. They are no more reluctant to take the advice of the trained doctors. Improved communication results in increased mobility of the Korku and they pay visit to their relatives even at distant places and more frequently. Following the local Hindus they observe Dewali festival and an additional marriage season commences after Dewali festival among them. This marriage season continues for a month. More marriages take place during the season after Holi; still one can marry after Dewali.

The Korku have various types of dance and songs which vary according to season and festival. These songs are sung regularly for practice and training. From the songs one can understand about the forthcoming festival. This regularity is not maintained in the mixed population villages.

The trend of deifying the natural objects is observable. A whole hill range has been named after the name of lord Mohandeo who is conceived of as their creator. River Tapti is considered as their mother, who looks after them. *Khedadeo,* the god of land is worshipped for a better yield.

The clans are named after natural objects. It is believed that being frightened by the almighty they took refuge behind various natural objects like tree, hill. Afterwards their clans were named after these natural objects, where they hide themselves.

The Korkus are divided into four divisions which are territorial and endogamous. However, the rules of endogamy within these divisions are at present not strictly observed.

Discussion

From the foregoing description about the Korku life style and environmental adjustment certain things have become apparently clear. They have a kind of distinct relationship with their surroundings. With the changed and changing circumstances the process of fresh adjustment sets in. There is a conscious effort to adopt the changed situation. Consequently there have been changes in their cultural sources.

The relationship of the Korku and their environment is a process of adjustment and readjustment as per the need and requirement.

The present study proposes an existence of dynamism in the man and environment relationship which undergoes changes under various situations. The adaptive changes under various situations are unavoidable. Further, we find that various sections of group do not have the same relationship with the environment and this varies according to the cultural environment.

References

Banett, John, W. (1975), Ecosystem Analogies in Cultural Ecology in *Population, Ecology and Social Evolution*, ed. Steven Polgar, The Hague, Paris: Mantan Publishers.

Dixon, R. B. (1928), *The Building of Cultures*. New York : Scribners.

Geertz, Clifford (1963), *Agricultural Innovation: The Process of Ecological Changes in Indonesis*. Parkeley. University of California Press.

Harris, Morvin (1960),Adaptation in Biological and Cultural Science. *Transactions of the New York Academy of Sciences*, Series I, 23(1), 59-65.

Stoward, Julian H. (1955), Irrigations Civilizations : A Comparative Study: A Symposium on Method and Result in Cross-cultural Regulations. *Social Science Monograph*, I. Washington D.C. Pan American Union.

Vayda, Andrew, O., R.A. Rappaport (1968), Ecology: Cultural and Agricultural in *Introduction to Cultural Anthropology*, (ed.) By J. Clifton, Boston, Houghton Miffin.

17 The Ecological Succession and the Onge of Little Andaman

R. S. Raypa

The society and economy of the Onge of Little Andaman, though still categorized as hunting and gathering type, has passed through various phases of serious economic change. Theirs can thus well be cited as a case of ecological or temporal succession in Environmental Anthropology. Onge have changed (or were made to change) their food habits, habitat, economy and their cultural milieu in the process of time according to the availability of natural resources and their technical skills. The cultural contacts and cultural fusion with outsiders were also the forces for their temporal succession. The paper deals with the various phases of the ecological succession of the Onge.

The Period of Unwritten History: A State of Ecological Equilibrium

Of the period till the last quarter of 18th century, no written history of the Onge is available. We have seen little descriptions noted by mariners like Marcopolo and some others. These travellers may have passed by these islands but were not able to make any first hand observations on the local tribes. According to their notes and diaries, the Onge as well as all the tribals of Andaman and Nicobar Island were bearers of the "Old Stone Age" culture. Some have described them, though wrongly, as cannibals.

The Onge way of life was entirely dependent on natural resources of the Islands. For them, nature had supernatural power. Thus they could make themselves devotees of the spirits of jungle, the spirit of sea etc. to whom they have faith and fear. Under the mercy of these spirits they could utilize the natural resources but however circumscribed by their needs, tastes and values on one hand and the limits of choice fixed by nature on the other. This adjustment could maintain a well balanced ecosystem.

During the period discussed, fishing, hunting and gathering of wild fruits and digging of roots and yams were the only activities and means of their survival. Due to the lack of advanced technical skills and material culture, they led a very simple life. Bows, arrows, spears and axes all made of wood and fibre in a crude form were the means to get the game, fish, turtle, dugong and roots. They never invented the technique of making fire. They used to keep it alive. Their food consisted of fish, pork, turtle, dugong and crabs were only steamed and not elaborately cooked. The taste of salt was not known. The Onge had mainained hunting zones under the occupation of each local groups consisting of 6-10 nuclear families. Each of the local groups used to stay in a communal hut as their economic activities always needed a group of hunters and gatherers. Divisions of labour were also to be found. Leaving the hunting and fishing jobs to menfolk, the women folk engaged themselves in collection of fruits, roots and firewood, in the catch of crabs and small fishes around the creeks.

The Onge never used any covering on their body except a tassel by women to cover the genital parts and a strip of cloth by man for the same purpose. Both the sexes used clay pasting following their beliefs, for health purposes; for curing diseases and also fur beautification. For beautification, they used some ornaments prepared of bark, leaves, fibre and of sea shells etc.

In all, the phase of their ecological succession was within the limit of a simple culture. Their world was limited to the particular island only. Natural environment had mothered the Onge and Onge economy and society. Even then what environmental adjustments could be made was quite voluntary and intrinsic adaptation.

The Period of Establishment of British Colonization: Ecological Disequilirbium Starts

The British-India people first landed on Andaman and Nicobar Islands and established first settlement of Chatham Island during 1789-98 which later on abolished. Again in 1858, penal settlement was established at Port Blair. In 1867, a ship named "Assam Valley" sailed to Little Andaman but no trace of sailors was found. The Arakan ship was deputed to enquire but it only saw the remains of the sailors. They also faced an attack from the Onge but several Onges were then shot dead. After this, Port Man survived there for two months. In 1905 Bonington made a successful visit. Since then visits of outsiders continued and the Onge lost their isolation. The impact of the conflict and culture contact between the culture of the food gathering Onge and the more advanced culture of the settlers on ecological succession relation to the Onge society is briefly described below.

The Aboriginal's Land was Snatched Out

The Onge and other aborigines were pushed into the interior forests or the isolated islands by the powerful alien groups. The Onge were then compelled to reside in only isolated island of Little Andaman. Thus their forest and sea resources were made limited. The Onge, like other forest dwellers the jarawa, the sentinelese, the Great Andamanese, fought a losing battle. Many of the natives gave their lives in protecting their land; their way of life and their identity. Afterward all their activities dealt with new social and economic adjustments and the problem of survival with limited land and sea resources.

Introduction of Opium and Tobacco

The outsiders, like the Malayasian and Chinese traders in earlier days, introduced the Onge to the use of opium and tobacco. They have become addicted to these narcotics. To check the use of tobacco among them is still a problem though opium addiction has died down due to lack of availability.

Introduction of Andamanese Homes

Once, Andamanese homes were established at Port Blair with an intention to teach new ways of life to the aborigines. But later on their impact proved to be disastrous. At Port Blair countless infectious diseases were introduced to tribals. The Onge till not long back used to travel over to Port Blair via Rutland Island. So they could not saved themselves from these "Secrete weapons of the civilized man" (Pandit 1976).

Introduction of Iron

There was a boon introduced to the Onge and it was iron. It proved to be the foundation pillar of the Onga economy and culture. The sea trade route passed through the Andaman Islands since ancient times. After the arrival of the Europeans including the Britishers, Shipping around these islands became more frequent. The Onge must have collected iron pieces and even tools from ship wrecks and in course of time learnt to make some simple tools themselves. They also obtained iron as gifts and some time in exchange of their produce. Due to the use of iron the Onge technology got improved. They then started to prepare single to 4-5 pronged spears and arrows with iron head in place of wooden ones which might have also carried stone blades sometimes. This new technology made the Onge more efficient hunters. The traditional adze, prepared of wood etc. also got an iron blade. The Onge also could thus use iron tools for making better honey and water containers of wood and in felling and cutting trees more efficiently. The use of iron thus generally improved their capacity to exploit and obtain their food and other resources slightly and it pushed them to a higher stage in their ecological succession.

Introduction of Dogs

Though the Onge were good hunters and also their arrows and spears got improved by the use of iron, but still, to bring the hunt in the range of shooting in dense forests had never been an easy business. The hunting party consisting of 5-6 persons after outings of several days or weeks even sometime used to return without sufficient game for the camp. The difficult job of hunting was, to some extent, made easier by the introduction of the dogs who surrounded the game and make of an easy target for shooting. But at present, the dogs remain also to spread some skin diseases etc. among the Onge. Dao, a long knife of iron, proved to be of great importance to the forest dwellers. Felling of trees and marking of trees for the demarcation of the way had become easy process through the use of dao and axes to collect wooden materials for construction of huts and to give needed and artistic shape to artifacts also become easy and less time consuming. Dao was very useful in preparing bows and arrows, spears, canoes and containers.

Introduction of Nylon and Cotton Threads

Introduction of nylon threads helped Onge in every aspects of their society and economy.Onge had been using fibre threads attached to spears, detachable arrows and as bow string too. But to prepare and collect fibre, that too so durable and strong, was a difficult and time consuming task. The nylon and cotton threads had saved their labour and uncertainty. To prepare fibre very thin and to knit it into fishing net was also laborious and time consuming task. To bind the logs, sticks of wood in preparing sleeping plat forms; in raising and in preparing frame and strucature of temporary huts, nylon and cotton threads come handy. It also helps in attaching or fastening the iron heads and sheft of arrows and spears. In place of barks, nylon cotton ropes are used in bringing loads of fire wood, housing materials, hunted game etc.

Rehabilitation of Bengali Settlers (Repetition of Ecological Disequilibrium)

About 300 families of present Bengladesh refuses and 16 families of Srilanka repatriates were rehabilitated in Little Andaman Island in the year 1967 and onward. Later on Nicobarese numbering 50 families also were rehabilitated in Little Andaman. The Onge, once the only occupants of the island, were pushed to a few corners of the island. The settlers first occupied a large land area then exploited maximum part of the resources of the remaining Onge territory with their bigger man power, higher material culture and more advanced technical skills.

The settlers have spoiled the Onge economy. The contacts have also made a vital change in the Onge cultural life. Besides the Onge population, due to various reasons, is dwindling gradually and facing grim prospects of survival. At the present stage of temporal succession their population has come down to 98 in 1982 from 672 in 1901 while it was 150 in 1951, 129 in 1961 and 112 in 1971.

Welfare Activities by Various Agencies

After 1950 various Govenrment and non-governmental agencies started welfare activities for the benefit of the Onge. In the early fifties a coconut garden was started by Dugon creek. In the mid-seventies a tahsildar was posted at Hut Bay to look after the Onge. Through him, Onge were given rice, wheat flour and some essential articles like iron, clothes in exchange of the local produces viz. honey, resin, etc. The coconut garden could not flourish satisfactorily due to the Onge's apathy. Later on sufficient quantity of rice, wheat, flour, various spices, tobaccos, iron, clothes etc. were given free of cost which is still continuing. In 1969-70, on suggestion of anthropologists at Port Blair the Onge were brought to permanent settlement at Dugong creek and South Bay. Pukka huts were construcated for them. In accordance with the Tribal Act of 1956, like other tribal areas, Onge area was also declared as "Primitive Tribal Reserve Area". Medical facilities also reached them. In 1978, their huts were electrified. In the early eighties a new horticulture garden was established at Dugong Creek.

Each of the families was given aluminium or plastic utensils as gifts. The Onge get clothes such as lungi, pants, half-pants, petticoat, bluses and sarees and they are always encouraged to wear them.

Cultural Contact and New Environmental Adjustment

After 1967 most of the sea and forest resources are being exploited by the settlers in the island. Even cases of illegal entrance and exploitation of the tribal reserve land by outsiders have been reported.

Frequent visits of Government Officials, tourists, V.I.P.'s and labourers also have made an adverse impact upon the Onge psychology and thinking. The visitors compel the Onge to be photographed several times in several postures. Frequent presents of clothes and continuous instigation to wear them have given rise to a feeling of inferiority in the Onge mind. And so they unwillingly wear clothes only in presence of the outsiders. But the ill fitting clothes, make them uneasy in the tropical climate of the island.The over burden of clothes are not a voluntary adaptation and is against their needs, tastes and choice.

Rice, wheat flour, *dal* (pulses), various species, salt, tea leaves are supplied to the Onge free of cost at their doors. These have become now their main items of food, consisting only carbohydrate. They have as a result, now become passive in hunting and fishing which offered them with proteneous food since thousand of years. The Onge wait for gifts of ration and can remain without it for a couple of days, but do not feel much interested to go for hunting and fishing expendition except to catch small fishes occasionally. Simultaniously, honey has disappeared from their diet due to lesser availability. They have acquired the taste of salt and various spices too. Sometime they work in the horticulture garden as daily wage workers. But they have not learnt the techniques of horticulture except the art of bush cleaning by dao. Their apathy, disinterest and lower degree of technical skill do not permit to be horticulturist so quickly. Changes in food items have also to some extent, affected their health and hygiene. The greater impact of free ration supply is on their economy or the food resources as they have become more dependent on outsiders. The Onge have adopted tea and consume it heavily. No milk and sugar are added. They have made themselves habitual smokers of bidis and cigarettes. They some time took more than two meals a day, as the ration they get are ample. Cleanliness and hygiene are not known, Utensils are hardly cleaned and the dogs lick them. Drinking water obtained from wells in their compact settlement is not always clean.

The most critical thing is that they have no means of sources of their food depending on their own efforts and faculties. They have no products also to be exchanged for the food items if free ration supply were to be suddenly stopped.

Though efforts of providing them with huts and bringing them in a permanent settlement were valued and appreciable but now the families settled to look after the Onge have become source of irritation in their settlement. Still a few Onge families leave their puckka huts for jungle for days together. Unsuitability of the new huts or the interaction with outsiders or some folk beliefs may be the reasons for their going out. The trees and bushes have been cleaned out in their settlement in such a way that the settlement has turned out as a desert area.

Medical facilities are being extended at their doors. But the Onge have not yet fully accepted. They never admit sick in hospital. The Onge prefer the traditional medicines. Thus more emphasis to change their world view in accordance with the changed circumstances are needed. Many diseases introduced by outsiders are observed among them, which have been proving one, of the reasons of the dwindling trend in their population.

Cultural contact has another impact on the Onge psychology and way of thinking. Outsiders, often use the words' Jangli, 'Nanga' etc. for them.Such behaviour forces the Onge to think that they are inferior to the outsiders.

Once, the Onge called them as "ENIREGALE" meaning "the real man". But now circumstances have made them to accept their inferiority. Their dependence on outsiders for their basic needs naturally has given them such feelings.

The cultural contact has created apathy towards their traditional way of life. They have even changed their tastes and values. An Onge boy named Raju, who was given part time job at Port Blair, has been badly influenced by alien culture. He seldom visits his native land and kins. He prefers to roam around and to see films at Port Blair. He has become habitual of taking liquor, which has been absent in Onge society. An spoiled individual member in a small community is not a neglible thing as it may have a bad impact.

The Onge now hardly observe their traditional ceremonies. The cultural contact has another impact on the Onge traditional art and crafts. The beautiful wood and bamboo utensils, weapons and tools have been disappearing. Artistic traditional ornaments prepared of bark, fibre, leaves and shells have been replaced by colourful beeds and glass or plastic made bengles.

Conclusion

The Onge, belonging to a Negrito stock of race, living in Little Andaman Island have passed through several stages of ecological succession. Till the end of 18th Century, the Onge, the hunters and gatherers, had a balanced eco system based on forest and sea resources.

The Onge first came into contact with Malayasians and Chinese traders and from them they learnt the use of iron. But at the same time opium was introduced, opening of British colonization in 1859 made another impact on them, which upset the Onge economy and ways of like. The Onge were pushed to limited corners. Onge fought for their land and for resources but at last surrendered to a more powerful culture. Of course, the Onge got iron which made their hunting and fishing weapons powerful and more advanced. They tamed dogs that helped in hunting.

The next stage of ecological succession comes after the arrival of hundreds of families of new settlers in the island after 1967. These settlers have occupied 3/4 part of the island leaving a neglibile scope for the Onge economy. The contact with outsiders during the last three decades has had a powerful impact on them. They are prepared to wear clothes while the tropical climate does not necessitate clothing. Many diseases have been passed on by outsiders to the Onge. Hunting and gathering Onge now take rice, wheat, flour, various spices, dal etc in their meals. Arrival of cost free ration at their doors has made them passive in doing their traditional hunting and fishing activities.

The main sources of the Onge subsistence are based on outsider's help and money. Neither they have vast land and sea area to be exploited nor do they possess the tools and the interest to exploit it. The Onge population has been gradually dwindling. The 98 souls of Onge have no stable economy baded on their own efforts. They lead a life of borrowed culture and live in a beggar economy.

At the present stage of ecological succession, the cultural environment created by the outsiders is more powerful in making the Onge environmental adjustment which is very marginally based on the Onge will, aptitude and choice.

References

Awaradi, S.A. (1978), Anthropological Demography of the Onge of Little Andaman.

ICAES Post-Prelim inary Section, PORT BLAIR.

Bonnington, M.C. (1932), 'Census of India 1931'. The Andaman Nicobar Islands Vol. 2, Cal,Supdtg. Government Printing.

Bose, D.K. (1977), 'The Onge of Little Andaman'. Typed Report 1973-74 (post script '77)

Bose, S. (1964), Economy of the Onge of Little Andeman. *Man in India.* 44 : 298-310.

Cipriani, L. (1953), 'Report on the Survey of Little Andaman during 1951-53. Bull. Dept. Anthrop. Govt. of India, 2(1) : 61-62.

Lal, P. (1956), 'Andaman Islands' A Regional Geography.

Mann, R. S. (1976), Defective Strategy Regarding a Negrito Tribe of the Andaman: Problems and Suggestions. *Man in India.*, Vol. 2, p. 43-56.

Nigam, R.C. (1962), 'The Onge of Little Andaman – Their Settlement and Population. '*Vanvajati*, New Delhi 10 : 85-92.

Pandit, T. N. (1972), 'Tribes of the Andaman and Nicrobar Islands'. PP. 239-59. In *Tribal Situation in India.* (ed. K.S. Singh). Indian Institute of Advanced Study.

Pandit, T.N. & Bose, D.K. (1975), 'The Onge of Little Andaman'. Paper presented in the workshop on *Primitive Tribal Communities.* Ministry of Home. New Delhi, January 16-17, (Monographed-9).

Pandit, T. N. (1976), 'The Original Inhabitants of the Andaman and Nicobar Islands. '*Yojana,* New Delhi 20(13) : 81-96.

Pandit, T.N. (1976), Ecological Adaptions of Various Ethnic Groups in Andaman and Nicobar Islands in (S.C. Sinha, ed.) *Research Programmes in Anthropology*.

Pandit, T. N. (1978), 'The Economy of Onge - A Case Study of a Hunting and Food Gathering Tribes', (unpublished) XICAES, Port Preliminary Session, Port Blair.

Raya, R. S. (1978), 'The Changing Pattern of Ecological Adaptation of the Onge" (Unpublished), Paper read in the XICAES, Port Preliminary Session, Port Blair.

Part-5

Ecology, Economy and Population

18 Demographic Structure and Environment: A Study of the Gujjars

A. C. SRIVASTAVA & R. S. BALGIR

Demographic structure of the population may be regarded as a quantitative measure of man's ability to reproduce and survive. As such it reflects physical and genetic fitness and measures the outcome of cumulative response to varied stresses. It would seem to reflect particularly the interplay of social and cultural forces on biological adaptation to the environment. The concept of 'natural selection' has clarified the role of differential fertility and perpetuation of traits that give individuals an advantage in coping with their environment.

Sympatric populations with different genetic endowments in course of time, in an evolutionary perspective, may represent a trend of genetic convergence because of their similar exposure to extra-genic factors including physical environment. Population fission and migratory habits in the different eco-zones may lead to the further stresses for adaptation. In the present paper the Gujjar isolates living in different topographical conditions, viz. Himalayas and sub-Himalayas, and with varied subsistence, are examined for population structural variations etc.

The Gujjar take their name from Sanskrit word, 'Gujara' the original name of the tract of land in western India, currently known as Gujrat. The Gujjars migrated from Western India, for some unknown reasons, to north-western parts and to some extent in Central India. Cunningham has described their distribution to be found .... in great numbers in every part of north-west India, from the Peninsular Gujrat. They are especially numerous along the banks of upper Jamuna near Jagadari and Buriya, and in the Saharanpur district, which during the last centuary was actually called Gujrat. To the east they occupy the petty state of Sampatpur in Bundelkhand, and one of the northern districts of Gwalior, which is still call "Gujargarh". Initially, the Gujjars were all Hindus, but during the Moghul period, especially during the reign of Aurengzeb, forcible proselytisation of their religion made them to embrace Islam. But a section of them who were not converted did not obey the dictates of Islam, still continues to be Hindus (Ibbe stson, 1916: 183 and Shashi, 1979: 19). At present there are both Hindu and Muslim Gujjar populations in North India, in the state of Jammu and Kashmir, Himachal Pradesh, Punjab, Haryana and Uttar Pradesh. The Hindu Gujjars are in the plains of Punjab, Haryana and Uttar Pradesh, whereas the Himalayan region is inhabited by Muslim Gujjars. There is yet another remarkable difference of subsistence between the Hindu and Muslim Gujjar; while the former are settled agriculturists, the latter are semi-agriculturist and pastoral nomads. The Muslim Gujjar has retained some of Hindu traits, viz., clan organization etc.

Among the pastoral nomadic Gujjars who are known as 'Dudh' Gujjar due to the fact that they raise livestock and subsist on milk and milk products, there is a tendency of partial sedentarisation which has created yet another class of Gujjar known as 'Zamidar' Gujjar. The latter are semi-agriculturist and acquiring more and more of the orthodox Islamic traits, which have created a barrier between them and the Dudh Gujjar in terms of mating.

Material and Method

Demographic data of two Gujjar isolates viz., Muslim Gujjar - pastoral nomads and Hindu Gujjar - Agriculturists, settled in Himalayas and su-Himalayas respectively, constitute the material of the study. The Muslim Gujjars investigated were from villages - Paddar, Proatha, Sera, Kureel and Rajmdu of Chamba district of Himachal Pradesh, with altitude settlements from 1900 to 2100 metres; and the Hindu Gujjars were from the Majrian village of Ropar district of Punjab, with an altitude varying between 600 to 1200 metres. Schedule method was adopted for collecting information in both the groups.

Results and Discussion

Population structure of Gujjar population by age and sex reveals typical young population model. The pre-reproductive segment (0-14 years) comprised of about 33 per cent in case of Hindu Gujjar and 48 per cent in the Muslim Gujjar. Another significant feature of the older segment (50 year and above) of population is that the frequency has considerably decreased in Muslim Gujjar (7.8 per cent) as compared to Hindu Gujjar (18.5 percnt). This lowering of longivity among the Muslim Gujjar can be accounted mainly to environmental causes viz., nomadic way of life in upper Himalayan ranges and residences in forest areas, which causes excessive stress and strain on them.

Considering the sex-ratio in all the major age-groups, it is observed that Hindu Gujjar exhibit an ever increasing trend of males per hundred females in the age groups 0-14, 15-49, and 50 and above. However, the Muslim Gujjars have an almost ideal sex-ratio in the age-groups 0-14 and 15-49. Population sex-ratio confirms to an ideal value in Muslim Gujjar (102.4) in contrast to Hindu Gujjar (145.0) where males out number females in a greater proportion (Table 1).

The size of Gujjar household reveals that both the Hindus and Muslims prefer to have large (7-10 members) to medium (4-6 members) households (Table 2). Small households (1-3 members), however, are about one and half times more in Hindu Gujjar (19.4%) as compared to Muslim Gujjar (7.9%). Thus, comparatively lower frequency of small sized household among the Muslim Gujjar is as per expectation for nomadic way of life, where more number of persons in a group is required to fulfil the need of division of labour and subsistence pursuits.

Table 1
Gujjar Population by Age and Sex

	Hindu Gujjar							*Muslim Gujjar*						
	M		*F*		*Total*			*M*		*F*		*Total*		
Group	*No.*	*%*	*No.*	*%*	*No.*	*%*	*Sex Ratio*	*No.*	*%*	*No.*	*%*	*No.*	*%*	*Sex Ratio*
0-4	42	10.77	25	9.29	67	10.17	168.0	74	17.62	72	17.56	146	17.59	102.8
5-9	39	10.00	37	13.75	76	11.53		66	15.71	75	18.29	141	16.99	
10-14	37	9.49	36	13.38	73	11.08		60	14.29	50	12.20	110	13.25	
0-14	118	30.26	98	36.43	216	32.78	120.4	200	47.62	197	48.05	397	47.83	101.5
15-19	38	9.74	15	5.58	53	8.04		38	9.05	48	11.71	86	10.36	
20-24	31	7.95	18	6.69	49	7.44		48	11.43	34	8.29	82	9.88	
25-29	32	8.21	20	7.43	52	7.89		21	5.00	33	8.05	54	6.51	
30-34	32	8.21	16	5.95	48	7.28		23	5.48	26	6.34	49	5.90	
35-39	21	5.38	22	8.18	43	6.53		24	5.71	17	4.15	41	4.94	
40-44	18	4.62	15	5.58	33	5.01		13	3.10	11	2.68	24	2.89	
45-49	23	5.90	20	7.43	43	6.53		14	3.33	18	4.39	32	3.86	
0-49	195	50.00	126	46.84	321	48.71	154.8	181	43.09	187	45.61	368	44.34	96.8
50-54	24	6.15	11	4.09	35	5.31		14	3.33	4	0.98	13	2.17	
55-59	14	3.59	5	1.86	19	2.88		6	1.43	6	1.46	12	1.45	
60-above	39	10.00	29	10.78	68	10.32	134.5	19	4.52	16	3.90	35	4.22	118.8
50-60 Above	77	19.74	45	16.73	122	18.51	171.1	39	9.29	26	6.34	60	7.84	150.0
	390	100.0	269	100.0	659	100.00	145.0	420	100.00	410	100.00	830	100.00	102.4

Table 2
Household Size of Gujjars

Population		Household				
		Small (1-3)	*Medium (4-6)*	*Large (7-10)*	*Very Large (11 and above)*	*Total*
Hindu-Gujjar	No.	18	26	32	17	93
	%	19.4	28.0	34.4	18.2	100.0
Muslim-Gujjar	No.	8	32	42	19	101
	%	7.9	31.7	41.6	18.8	100.0

Table 3
Mean Age at Marriage among Gujjars

Population		*No.*	*Mean*	*S.D.*
Hindu-Gujjar	Male	156	22.69±0.54	6.72
	Female	159	17.37±0.31	3.85
Muslim-Gujjar	Male	190	19.89±0.28	3.84
	Female	197	16.89±0.24	3.37
Inter Group Homogeneity	Males	t = 4.620		
	Females	t = 1.234		

Mean age at marriage among Gujjars is shown in Table 3. It is observed that females in both the groups exhibit an almost similar mean ages of marriage (about 17 years). But, the males of Hindu Gujjar present a higher mean value (23 years) as compared to Muslim Gujjars (20 years). This higher age of marriage among males of Hindu Gujjar is probably due to sedentary life and available educational facilities.

Reproductive status of Gujjar women indicates a lower frequency of non-attainment of motherhood among the Hindu Gujjars (17%) compared to that of Muslim Gujjar (24%). However, it may be pointed out that these issueless women also include those women who were married recently (Table 4). The average number of pregnancies to mothers (all ages) is slightly higher among Muslim Gujjars (4.1) as compared to Hindu Gujjar (3.8). The frequency of male livebirths and their survival value is higher than the female in both the populations of Gujjars. Surviving children per mother has shown a slightly higher average among the Muslim Gujjar (3.7) than the Hindu

Table 4
Reproductive Status of Gujjar Women

Population	*No.Ever Married*	*Ever-Pregnant*		*Never-Pregnant*	
		No.	*%*	*No.*	*%*
Hindu - Gujjar	159	132	83.0	27	17.0
Muslim- Gujjar	197	150	76.1	47	23.9

Gujjar (3.3). Thus, Muslim Gujjars exhibit a slightly higher fertility performance than Hindu Gujjars (Table 5).

Table 5
Ever Born Children and Wastage According to Mothers (All Ages)

		Ever Born Children Reproductive Wastage							
		Surviving		*Dead*		*Still Birth*			
Population	*No. of Mothers*	*M*	*F*	*M*	*F*	*M*	*F*	*Abortion*	*Live Birth Per Mother*
Hindu Gujjar	132	254	179	29	20	11	5	8	3
		50.2	35.4	5.7	3.9	2.2	1.0	1.6	
Muslim Gujjar	150	289	262	36	21	3	2	4	4
		46.8	42.5	5.8	3.4	0.5	0.3	0.7	

Surviving Children Per Mother — Hindu Gujjar = 3.3; Muslim Gujjar = 3.7

Reproductive wastage is usually high among the Hindu Gujjar (About 5%) as compared to Muslim Gujjar (about 2%). This is quite contrary to the expectation that among the nomadic people in mountainous region the exposure risk to still births and abortions would be greater than the settled population (Table 5). However, similar value (1.6%) of reproductive wastage for pastoral nomadic Muslim Gujjar from Mohand division has been reported by Negi (1978). Thus, the maintenance of lower risk of reproductive wastage in the hazardous conditions and nomadic ways of life could probably be an adaptive feature.

Table 6 shows the distribution of livebirths according to the age of ever-married woman. It becomes apparent that with the advancement of the age of mother the average number of livebirths increases in both the Hindu and Muslim Gujjars. But, in the 40 years and above age of mother, a sharp decline in the average of births is recorded for Hindu Gujjar; whereas, an increase of livebirths per mother is noted in case of Muslim Gujjars. Comparative values of average livebirths per mother, according to age-groups between the Hindu and Muslim Gujjar reveal higher average births in the Muslim Gujjar for all the age-groups. Besides, the higher fertility performance among the Muslim Gujjars – they seem to have, for obvious reasons, concept of larger family.

Table 6
Live Births in Ever-Married Women According to Age

		Age Group of Mothers			
Population		*0-19*	*20-29*	*30-39*	*40 and above*
Hindu–Gujjar	No. of Women	35	110	82	25
	No. of Livebirths	44	241	165	32
	Average Livebirths	1.26	2.19	2.01	1.28
Muslim–Gujjar	No. of Women	56	123	66	24
	No. of Livebirths	88	314	156	50
	Average Livebirths	1.57	2.55	2.36	2.83

Considering mothers of all ages and surviving sibships, it is seen that the Hindu Gujjars possess a maximum sibship size of 8; whereas among Muslim Gujjars a maximum sibship-size of 12 has been recorded.The frequency of mothers in the sibships 6 and above is comparatively higher in the Muslim Gujjar than the Hindu Gujjar.This feature of higher sibship-size among the Muslim Gujjar may have an additive significance to their pastoral-nomadic way of life. The average number of surviving children per-mother is slightly higher in the Muslim Gujjars as compared to the Hindu Gujjars (Table 7).

Fertility patterns of mothers having completed reproductive span and also mothers in performing age are presented in Table 8. It has been observed that the Muslim Gujjars exhibit higher averages of livebirths in both the

Table 7
Mothers and Surviving Children by Sibship Size

Population	*0*	*1*	*2*	*3*	*4*	*5*	*6*	*7*	*8*	*9*	*10*	*11*	*12*	*Total*	*Average Per Mother*
Hindu Gujjar															
No. of Mother	5	18	26	28	22	16	9	7	1	-	-	-	-	132	
%	3.79	13.64	19.70	21.21	16.67	12.12	6.82	5.30	0.75					100.00	
No. of Children	-	18	52	84	88	80	54	49	8	-	-	-	-	433	3.28
%	-	4.16	12.01	19.40	20.32	18.48	12.47	11.32	1.85					100.00	
Muslim Gujjar															
No. of Mother	3	33	23	22	17	16	12	12	9	2	-	-	1	150	
%	2.0	2.00	15.33	14.67	11.33	10.67	8.00	8.00	6.00	1.33	-	-	0.67	100.00	
No. of Children	-	33	46	66	68	80	72	84	72	18	-	-	12	551	3.67
%	-	5.99	8.35	11.98	12.34	14.52	13.07	15.25	13.07	3.27	-	-	3.27	100.00	

Table 8
Fertility Performance of Married Women All Ages

Population	*Women*	*Number*	*Number of Live Births*	*Live Birth per Women*	*Live Birth per Mother*
Hindu Gujjar	45 years & above	65	247	3.80	4.12
	Below 45 years	94	235	2.50	3.26
Muslim Gujjar	45 years & above	44	296	4.68	5.15
	Below 45 years	153	402	2.66	3.65

categories of mothers i.e., 45 years and above, and below 45 years; as compared to the Hindu Gujjars. This probably reflects a greater fertility potential among the Muslim Gujjars, and better opportunities for selection to operate. Another striking feature of the Muslim Gujjars is that, the fertility does not decrease in the high altitude nomadic population; which is in contrast to the general findings of low fertility in the populations at high altitude. Here most probably the lower economic condition of pastoral group has resulted in higher fertility than that of Agriculture based sedentarised population. Broadly speaking, the environment does play a role in shaping the demographic characteristic of a population.

Some population characteristics viz., crude birth rate (CBR), General fertility rate, child-women ratio and net reproductive index for the two Gujjar isolates are presented in Table 9. It may be observed that the values of all these parameters are lower in case of Hindu Gujjars than the Muslim Gujjars. The crude birth rate among the Muslim Gujjar (30.1) is about three times more than that of Hindu Gujjar (10.6). The value of CBR in both these groups are lower as compared to averages for Himachal Pradesh (34.9), Punjab (32.0) and India (34.5) (Agarwala, 1977 : 142). General fertility rate in Muslim Gujjar (168.9) is more than two times than that of Hindu Gujjars (74.5). As compared to GFR-Indian average of 174.0 (Agarwala, 1977: 62) the value is slightly lower in Muslim Gujjars; whereas, it is significantly lower in case of Hindu Gujjar.

The net reproductive index value, which indicates reproductive potentials in a population, is found to be 0.83 in Hindu Gujjar and 1.42 in case of Muslim Gujjar. From this, it is apparent that Muslim Gujjars are at a growing stage and population replacement is possible; whereas, the Hindu Gujjars exhibit a declining trend and perhaps lesser probability of population expansion.

Table 9
CBR, GFR, Child-Women Ratio and NRI Among Gujjars

Population	*Crude Birth Rate (CBR)*	*General Fertility Rate (GFR)*	*Child Women Ratio*	*Net Productive Index (NRI)*
Hindu Gujjar	10.6	74.5	713	0.833
Muslim Gujjar	30.1	168.9	986	1.420

Thus, the two Gujjar isolates, viz., Hindu Gujjar and Muslim Gujjar in the sub-Hiamalayan and the Himalayan habitats respectively, and with different subsistence patterns, are showing marked variations in the demographic parameters. This has resulted mainly due to the interaction of the population with the environment and consequently to the adaptive responses.

References

Agarwala, S. N. (1977), *India's Population Problems.* New Delhi, Tata McGraw-Hill Publishing Co. Ltd.

Crook, W. (1896), *Tribes and Caste of North Western India.* Calcutta.

Cunningham, A. Archaeological Reports, 11 (cited in Crooke).

Ibbetson, D. (1974), *Punjab Castes,* Delhi, B.R. Publishing Corporation, (Reprint of 1916).

Negi, R. S. (1978), Population Structure of a Pastoral Nomadic Community of Himalaya. Proc. National Seminar on *Indian Nomads,* Calcutta, Anthropological Suvey of India.

Shashi, S. S. (1979), *The Nomads of the Himalayas.* Sandeep Prakashan, Delhi.

19 Impact of Environment on Demography and Occupation in the Himalayas and Adjacent Regions

SUBAL CHATTERJEE

It is a general observation that mountains, foothills and plains have different environmental conditions. These conditions are largely determined by the physiographic and geomorphic conditions. The differential ecological situations have bearing on the growth and behavioural pattern of human beings who inhabit there. It is therefore expected that differentiation in ecology will cause differentiation in the cultural milieu of the population. The objective of this study is thus to identify the impact of different environment, if any, on the life pattern of the people inhabiting the Himalayas and the bordering districts. For the purpose, the data of the census of India, 1971, at district levels, have been classified according to the existing physical divisions and the statewise distribution of the mountainous districts. The area of study includes a total of 68 districts which are distributed in six states (Table 1). It was realized that there exists a basic difference in physiography, peopling, religion and culture between the two regions considered, namely, western and eastern.

Physiographically, the eastern Himalayan mountain chains are less steep than those of the Western part. Climatically, the eastern region receives higher rainfall than the Western region. Histroically the western region received influx of populations from the plains of India right from the beginning of Muslim

Table 1

(A)	*Mountain Area (West)*		*Mountain Area (East)*
	Himachal Pradesh		*Sikkim*
1.	Chamba	29.	North District
2.	Kangra	30.	South District
3.	Mandi	31.	West District
4.	Kulu	32.	East District
5.	Lahul and Spiti		*West Bengal*
6.	Bilaspur	33.	Darjeeling
7.	Mahasu		*Arunachal Pradesh*
8.	Simla	34.	Kameng
9.	Sirmaur	35.	Subansiri
10.	Kinnaur	36.	Siang
	Jammu and Kashmir	37.	Lohit
11.	Anantnag	38.	Tirap
12.	Srinagar		
13.	Baramula		
14.	Ladakh		
15.	Doda		
16.	Udhampur		
17.	Jammu		
18.	Kathua		
19.	Rajauri		
20.	Punch		
	Uttar Pradesh		
21.	Dehra Dun		
22.	Tehri Garhwal		
23.	Uttar Kashi		
24.	Pithoraarh		
25.	Nainital		
26.	Garhwal		
27.	Chamoli		
28.	Almora		
(B)	*Foot Hills (West)*		*Foot Hills (East)*
	Punjab		*West Bengal*
39.	Gurudaspur	50.	Jalpaiguri
40.	Hoshiarpur	51.	West Dinajpur
41.	Ropar		
42.	Patiala		*Assam*
	Haryana	52.	Darrang
43.	Ambala	53.	Lakhimpur
	Uttar Pradesh	54.	Sibsagar
44.	Saharanpur		
45.	Bijnor		

Contd...

(B)	*Foot Hills (West)*		*Foot Hills (East)*
46.	Moradabad		
47.	Rampur		
48.	Bareilly		
49.	Pilibhit		

(C)	*Plains (West)*		*Plains (East)*
	Punjab		*West Bengal*
55.	Amritsar	64.	Kochbihar
56.	Kapurthala	65.	Malda
57.	Jullundar		*Assam*
58.	Ludhiana	66.	Nowgong
	Haryana	67.	Kamrup
59.	Karnal	68.	Goalpara
	Uttar Pradesh		
60.	Muzaffarnagar		
61.	Meerut		
62.	Budaun		
63.	Shahjahanpur		

rule. Moreover, due to the existence of several pilgrimage centers, there had been a continuous cultural intercourse between the plains and the mountainous area of the western region. The eastern part, on the other hand, is largely dominated by different tribal groups who had their small isolated regions under their command. Even politically, during the British period, these areas were kept intentionally segregated from the rest of India.

In the western part, the lower and the middle altitude regions are dominated by the Hindu. The higher region is occupied by the Buddhists with pockets of Muslim concentration. In the western part, Buddhism is the dominant religion in the high altitude area and Hinduism in the plains. The large area between plains and high altitude of this part is inhabited by different tribal groups who live largely in isolated pockets. Culturally also, there is a marked difference between the populations of western and eastern regions.

Methodology

The focus of analysis in this paper has been on population pattern, sex ratio, literacy and occupational structure. After posting the data at district level, these have been analysed statistically for each of the six state sub-divisions of the total study area. It is observed that in occupational structure, four most important groups are cultivators, agricultural labourers, people engaged in livestock-forestry etc. and household industry. As such, only these four groups of workers, out of nine groups mentioned in 1971 Census, have been considered for analysis to find out the pattern, if any, of the workers present in the working population.

Analysis

Population Density

In Table 2 the population density per square kilometer is shown. The trend of population density in both western and eastern regions is more or less similar. In the western region, population density in the mountains is 49 per sq. km., being the lowest. It increases to 329 per sq. km. in the foothills and further increases to 363 per sq. km in plains. Similarly, in the eastern region it increases from 16 per sq. km in mountains to 222 per sq. km in foothills and increases further to 298 per sq. km. in the plains. But there is a marked difference in population density between the west and the east. In each area of the east, the population density is much less than that in the west, difference being highest in foothills and lowest in mountains.

Table 2
Density of Total Population per Square Kilometer

	Sub-Division	
Regions	*West*	*East*
Mountains	49	16
Foothills	329	222
Plains	363	298
Total	126	122

Rural Urban Break Up of Population

Table 3 gives the percentage distribution of population by rural and urban area. Rural urban break-up of population in the mountain is almost same in western and eastern regions. The percentage of urban people gradually increases from 14 per cent to 21 per cent and further to 22 per cent in mountains, foothills and plains respectively in the western region. But, in the eastern region, a gradual decrease in urban population is noticed from mountains to foothills and to plains, the figures being 15 per cent, 9 per cent and 8 per cent respectively. So, the pattern of urban population is opposite in respect of two regions. When total populations of western and eastern regions are compared, it is seen that urban population of the west is more than that of the east, percentages being 19 and 9 respectively. Location of forests and the restriction to sell land to non-tribals in non-municipal areas may have some indirect influence on the distribution of rural-urban population.

Table 3

Percentage Distribution of Total Population by Rural and Urban Area

	Sub-Division			
	West		*East*	
Regions	*Rural*	*Urban*	*Rural*	*Urban*
Mountains	86	14	85	15
Foothills	79	21	91	9
Plains	78	22	92	8
Total	81	19	91	9

Sex-Ratio

Census of India expresses sex ratio as the number of females per thousand males. Accordingly, Table 4 gives the sex ratio in six state sub-divisions. Generally, sex ratio is more in the eastern region than in the western region but with only exception in the foothills of the west, where sex ratio in 929, the highest amongst the six state sub-divisions. The highest sex ratio in the eastern region is noticed in the plains (913).

The districts of Punjab, Haryana and Uttar Pradesh have been grouped within the foothills of western region. The males of this region are generally employed in the military and paramilitary forces and thus they stay away from their home.

This might be one of the reasons for a high sex ratio in the foothills of western region. But the general trend that the sex ratio is higher in the eastern region than that of the western region becomes obvious when total male and female population of the west are compared with those of the east. The sex ratio in the eastern region as a whole is 899 which is much higher than 866 of the western region.

Table 4
Sex Ratio (Number of Females per 1000 Males)

	Sub-Division	
Regions	*West*	*East*
Mountains	845	889
Foothills	929	872
Plains	840	913
Total	866	899

Literacy

The rate of literacy in the total population is shown in Table 5. There is not much difference in the occurrence of the literate people among the six state sub-divisions. The highest rate of literacy is in the plains of western region where 28 per cent of the population are literate. When the west and the east are compared, the ratio of literacy becomes equal in both the regions (26 per cent).

Table 5
Percentage of Literates to Total Population

	Sub-Division	
Regions	*West*	*East*
Mountains	26	24
Foothills	25	27
Plains	28	24
Total	26	26

The distributions of male and female literates are given in Table 6. It is observed that about 70 per cent of the total literates are males.

Table 6
Percentage Distribution of Male and Female Literates

	Sub-Division			
	West		*East*	
Regions	*Male*	*Female*	*Male*	*Female*
Mountains	73	27	71	29
Foothills	70	30	69	31
Plains	69	31	71	29

Workers

The number of workers in the total population of the six state sub-divisions is shown in Table 7. The percentage of workers is higher in the mountains of both the west and the east than in foothills and plains. The percentage of workers in foothills of both the west and the east and in the plains of the west is 29, while it is a little less in plains of the east. About 45 per cent people of the total population of eastern mountains are engaged in various types of occupation, whereas the percentage of workers in the western mountains is 36 which is considerably low compared to the east. Since the mountainous area of eastern region gives shelter to more tribal populations, number of workers in this area becomes higher than the number of workers present in the mountains of the west.

Table 7
Percentage of Workers in Total Population

	Sub-Division	
Regions	*West*	*East*
Mountains	36	45
Foothills	29	29
Plains	29	27

The distribution of male and female workers in total working population is given in table 8. Percentage of female workers is considerably low in foothills and plains of both the west and the east. Though 24 per cent female workers out of the total working population of mountains in the western region are engaged in various types of occupations, the proportion of female workers is much lower than that in the mountains of eastern region where percentage of female workers is 35. So, an interesting feature could be observed. Though the percentage of female workers decreases considerably from mountains to foothills and plains in both the west and the east, the percentage of female workers in the east is much higher than that in the west. It is particularly true in the mountains and foothills indicating more involvement of female workers in different working activities presumably due to the presence of tribal population in this region.

Table 8
Percentage Distribution of Male and Female Workers in Total Working Population

	Sub-Division			
	West		*East*	
Regions	*Male*	*Female*	*Male*	*Female*
Mountains	76	24	65	35
Foothills	98	2	88	12
Plains	98	2	96	4

The distribution of workers to total working population in respect of certain activities has been shown in Table 9. It is observed that 70 to 80 per cent of the working population is engaged in four types of occupations which have been analysed here.

In general, cultivation is the major activity. In the western region, highest percentage of cultivators is found in mountains which are 69. In eastern part, the highest percentage of cultivators is found in plains. The next highest percentage of workers in the eastern region are engaged in livestock Forestry, etc. in the mountains and foothills, whereas, this position has been occupied in western region by the agricultural labourers.

From Table 9, following salient features are observed:

1. Cultivators decrease from mountains to plains through foothills in the west, whereas they decrease from mountains to foothills and again increase to plains in the east.

Table 9
Distribution of Workers to Total Working Population

	Regions					
	Mountains		*Foothills*		*Plains*	
	West	*East*	*West*	*East*	*West*	*East*
Cultivators	69	58	50	48	47	61
Agricultural Labourers	4	5	17	11	18	15
Live Stock Forestry etc.	3	12	1	19	1	2
Household Industry	3	1	4	1	4	2
Total	79	76	72	79	70	80

2. Cultivators are more in the mountains and foothills of western region than those of the eastern region, but the position is reversed in respect of the plains. It appears that cultivation is relatively easier and advantageous in mountains and foothills of the west. But possibly due to better rainfall and fertility of land in plains of eastern region, number of cultivators is much higher in the plains of the east than that in the west.
3. Agricultual labourers are more in foothills and plains of western region in comparison to the areas of the eastern region. This is possibly due to excess of landless population in the west.
4. Number of workers engaged in livestock, forestry, etc. is quite high in mountains and foothills of the east in comparison to the west. This again reveals the presence of tribal groups and more forest in the east.
5. In the western region more people are engaged in household industry in comparison to eastern region. It suggests a difference in culture between the two populations of the west and the east.
6. Gradual increase of agricultural labourers from mountains to plains through foothills in both the west and the east is observed.
7. Distribution of male and female workers within working groups in respect of four types of occupations is shown in Table 10. The most important feature is the

Table 10
Percentage Distribution of Male and Female Workers within Working Groups

	Regions											
	Mountains				*Foothills*				*Plains*			
	West		*East*		*West*		*East*		*West*		*East*	
Workers	*Male*	*Female*	*Male*	*Female*	*Male*	*Female*	*Male*	*Female*	*Male*	*Female*	*Male*	*Female*
Cultivators	68	32	65	35	99	1	98	2	99	7	99	1
Agricultural Labourers	84	16	57	43	98	2	92	8	97	3	94	6
Live Stock, Forestry etc.	87	13	69	31	97	3	56	44	94	6	80	20
Household Industry	89	11	77	23	94	6	83	17	95	5	75	25

involvement of more females in all the four fields of activity, in the east than in the west. Though the presence of female workers in the mountains of the west and the east are 32 and 35 per cent respectively, participation of female workers in cultivation in foothills and plains of both the regions is rather insignificant. It is also observed that participation of female workers in the working groups of livestock; forestry etc is the highest in foothills of the east (44 per cent). Agricultural labourers come out as in mountains of the eastern region. Number of female workers in household industry is also much higher in the east than in the west in all the areas, viz., mountains, foothills and plains. Within the western region, participation of female workers is more in mountains in all four types of activity in comparison to foothills and plains. But the involvement of more females in various activities over different geographical areas in the eastern region may be explained in the background of the presence of a number of tribal groups in this region.

Summary

The population density in each of the different geographical areas of the east is much less than that of the west. The increasing pattern of the population from mountains to plains through foothills is, however, conspicuous in both the regions.

Urban population increases from mountains to plains through foothills in the west, while the picture is reverse in the east.

Sex ratio in the eastern region is much higher than the western region.

Literacy rate of the total population and the male female break up of the literates are almost same in different geographical areas of both the west and the east.

Workers participations are more in the mountains than in the foothills and plains of both the regions. It is, however, more in the mountains of the east than in the mountains of the west.

Though the number of female workers declines considerably from mountains to foothills and plains in both the regions, the number of female workers is much higher in the east than that in the west, particularly in the mountains and the foothills.

Cultivation is the major activity of the working population. Number of cultivators is highest in the mountains of the west, whereas it is highest in the plains of the east. Number of agricultural labourer is more in the west than in the east. While more people of the west are engaged in household industry, the number of people engaged in livestock, forestry, etc is higher in the east. Number of agricultural labourer increases gradually from mountains to plains through foothills in both the regions.

In comparison to the western region, participation of female workers in various activities over different geographical areas is more in the eastern region. Number of female workers in cultivation in the foothills and plains of both the region is insignificant. Within the western region, the involvement of female workers is more in mountains in respect of all four types of activity than in the foothills and plains. While the number of female workers engaged in cultivation in the mountains is highest in the west, maximum number of females in the east are seen engaged in livestock, forestry, etc in the foothills areas.

On the whole, the difference is more between western and eastern regions than that within the region.

Acknowledgement

The author is indebted to Dr. S. Bose, Sr. Ecologist, Dr. P.C. Dutta and Dr. G.C. Ghose, Anthropologists, Sri V. Saha, Sr. Statistician and others of Anthropological Survey of India, for their active help and guidance in preparing this paper. He is also indebted to Sri S.K. Saha, Draftsman, An. S.I. for his invaluable help and co-operation and also indebted to Sri C. Ghose, Statistical Computer for his active co-operation. The author is especially thankful to Sri P.R. Das and his team of the Photography Section for preparing the Photo-slides. He is also thankful to Sri N.K. Nathaniel for typing the paper.

Reference

Census Report of India, 1971.

Series 1 - Part II - A(ii).

20 Women and Wealth – A View to Cultural Adaptation

Shibani Roy

The social Anthropologists are endowed with the expertise to examine socities, social structures and cultures which are viewed as operating functional wholes, thus maintaining the exclusiveness of each cultural type. In this paper I propose to reevaluate the three concepts of '*zar*', '*zan*' and'*zamin*' meaning wealth, woman and land respectively in the context of Asna Ashariyas of Uttar Pradesh, wherein the entire social processes of marriage, property and inheritance are based entirely on the phenomena of 'nasab' and 'hasab', meaning purity of blood and socio-religio-economic status. For long, the high incidence of consanguineous marriages in this group had been attributed to various social factors (Basu and Roy, 1972); however, this paper throws further light upon the prevalence of this age old custom as ancient as the Islam itself for the retention of the landed property within the '*Khandan*' due to the Koranic law of partible inheritance. The data for the present study had been collected during 1978 from the three villages of Uttar Pradesh namely, Mohan, Orai and Bilhaur. The case study of three Asna Ashariya families from the three respective villages reveal that the high incidence of consanguineous marriages as an important politico-economic strategem which has a high functional aspect and has been accepted as an adaptive measure to retain harmony in the'*zar*', '*zan*' and '*zamin*' aspect of the related *'khandans'*. 'The widely prevalent and popular proverb amongst the inhabitants of Uttar Pradesh is:

"Jhagre ki jad teen – zar, zan aur zamin" meaning "the three root causes of all conflicts are wealth, woman and land'. This is however based on facts. The Muslims have conveniently tamed all the three by culturally adapting some of the sanctioned rites and duties of Islam. Following is an account of that.

The Asna Ashariya of Uttar Pradesh is a closely cloistered group who separated from the first three Khalifas and established their allegiance with the fourth Khalifa, Ali, proclaiming him to be the rightful heir of Prophet. Their main concentration is in Iran and in India; they were patronized by the Nawab of Oudh and rulers of Hyderabad and Golconda. They differ from the Sunni Muslims in ritual practices and mode of prayer – the two groups retaining their antagonism till date. The earlier work on Muslim social struture reveals that neither caste model nor the class model can be exclusively used for studying the Muslim set up. Prior to discussing about this group, the definition of this population, its typology and characteristics should be clarified. Foremost I want to bring forth the concept of 'Ajlaf' and 'Ashraf' (Ansari, 1960). The Indian Muslims do not comply with this distinction which is purely conjectural terminology adapted by social anthropologists. Secondly 'biradari' (Alavi, 1972) does not fulfill all the features observed amongst the Muslims of the sample. Khandan is the term popularly used by the Muslim respondents. Their understanding of Khandan as used by Prophet, which can be defined as 'lineage of recognition' i.e. where the persons are traceable and recognized or a 'corporate group' (Weber, 1950: 41) ..... when it possesses any one of a certain number of characters, if its numbers, or its adult male members or considerable proportion of them, come together occasionally to carry out some collective action – for example, the performances of rites; if it has a chief or council who are regarded as acting as the representatives of the group as a whole; it is possesses or controls property which is collective, as when a clan or lineage is a land owning group". Added to this is another character it is obligatory for a man to marry a girl from his own *'Khandan'*, thus making the *'Khandan'* an absolutely self reliant and independent group.

Marriage according to Islam is merely a civil contract. The prohibitive categories include mothers, daughters, sisters and maternal and paternal aunts and daughters of sisters and brothers and foster sister to whom the mother had given suck. The last category is referred to as 'doodh ka bachaw, in which the entire sib group becomes prohibitive in case one of them had been given suck by ego's mother. The prescriptive type of marriages is restricted to ones lineage bilaterally. The first priority and preferences is given to the father's brother's daughter who is "bint-s-um" (first wife) or the paternal parallel cousin of the ego. The second preference is given to the paternal cross cousin or father's sister's daughter. The maternal cross cousin or the mother's brother's daughter is another popular type of preferential mate. Parallel cousin from the maternal side also come within the category of prescribed mates. Besides, ego can marry bilaterally parent's cousin at least once removed.

During my association with the Muslims of Uttar Pradesh nine 'Khandan' have been so far recongised amongst the Asna Ashariya these are:

(a) Fatimi

(b) Hussaini

(c) Hasani

(d) Zaidi

(e) Bagri

(f) Kazimi

(g) Rizvi

(h) Askari

(j) Naqvi

In the sample the Mohan case belongs to the Rizvi 'khandan'. Bilhaur case belong to the Askari 'khandan' and Orai sample is drawn from Naqvi 'khandan'.These 'khandans' are named after respective Imams Ali-Ibne-Musa-al-Raza, Hasan-al-Askari and Ali-al-Naqvi. Based on personal communication it has been affirmed that percentage of consanguineous marriages amongst these three groups is as follows:

Khandan	*Percentage of Consanguineous marriages*
Rizvi	88.66
Askari	70.37
Naqvi	79.57

The rest of the marriage alliances are between these 'khandans'. Thus inspite of high degree of urbanization the marriage distance of these 'khandans'are limited within the village and in case some of the 'gharanas' have settled in Lucknow or Kanpur, they at the most spread out in and around Lucknow and Kanpur, having the highest concentration of Asna Ashariya. Rizvis in the sample have their marriage concentration of Asna Ashariya. Rizvis in the sample have their marriage alliances within an area of 20 miles. The main marriage distance of Shias as calculated does not exceed beyond 44.2 miles. Thus the marriage distance varies from house next door to 44.2 miles. The later of late occurrence since they seek better job opportunities many young men shifted to the nearest towns that is Lucknow and Kanpur, their families also migrating in due course of time. Three sample villages are gradually turning to townships. However, they retain their agriculture base. The soil of this region being highly fertile, land is held as an important part of ones existence. Besides, this region is famous all over India for its cash crop Mango- the'*dessehri*' and'*langra*' varieties are grown only in this region. Ownership of the mango groves or '*bagh*' is one of the chief economic strongholds besides attaining a status symbol for the landed aristrocracy. The agricultural fields are especially known for their good yield of wheat, groundnut and cereals. Lately, the younger educated generations have added vegetables as cash crops to increase their income. Thus ownership and inheritance of land in the village is not only the means for livelihood but is his passport of '*izzat*', '*hasab*' and'*nasab*'.

As has been mentioned earlier the Koranic law endows the woman with the right over property as mother, daughter and wife. So far I had always viewed kinship as an important key for transmission of status and property from one generation to the next. But in the case of Muslims the close inbreeding of the 'khandans' establishes them as effective social groups which not only guards its property but zealously protects its women from being married outside the 'khandan' since, it would entail gradual dispersal of the landed property.The institution of 'purdah' facilitates to adequately segregate the women from the menfolk of the house. The typical layout of the Muslim house demarcated the'zanankhana' from the 'mardana' and even the brother and father announce their desire to enter the 'zanankhana' by coughing, tapping the walking stick or loudly calling out the name of the grand child playing in the inner precincts of the house. At present the houses of the cities retain the'khirki' that is short narrow windows leading from one house to the next, exclusively meant for the use of the woman. Since, this institution of 'purdah' has koranic saction hence it acted as the surest and safest way of protecting the women of the 'gharana' from the outside men. 'Gharana is a much smaller unit of 'khandan' and is comprised of father, and his married and unmarried children. Within the 'khandan' members the 'gharans' are referred by the name of the head of the family like 'Sharif Sahab ka gharana', 'Naqqan Miyan ka gharana' etc. Now a days the'gharanas' are more frequently found in cities and villages since, the households have split up into smaller units mainly migrating to economically profitable towns and cities. Added to this is the concept of 'nasab' or 'nasal' which emphasizes upon the purity of blood and its retention by close inbred marriage. Thus, in this bilateral setup where cross as well as parallel cousins is prescribed unions and the affinal relatives are always located within the consanguinies – the man and woman become the coparceners that are agnatic and uterine relatives are shareholders to the property. Many of the Africanists have elaborately dealt with the marriage of a patrilineal man with the matrilineal woman and the property distribution therein (Goody, 1969). However, the presence and prevalence of bilateral trend in the mode of inheritance is unique to the Muslims.

Karl Polanyi, an economic historian identified three modes for the allocation or movement of goods and services within a society (1959) which are reciprocity, redistribution and market exchange. In the Asna Ashariya families the daughters Koranic half shares are commonly assumed to have been made over by them to their brothers. Since, even if a dughter were to inherit land, she will have to turn it over either to her husband or brother for its management. In case, the man is from other 'khandan' he can always have a threat on the man saying that his sister wishes for her legal share. This would entail bad blood between the brother and sister initially induced by the sister's husband. Thus it is very vital and important for the man to maintain good relations with his sister and appease her so that she never comes up with her rightful claim (equal to one half the claim of her brother) upon the patrimony. Firstly this threat on the property is avoided by close marriages and the illustrative geneaology and the over all frequency of the consanguineous marriages duly substantiate the claim. Since the first cousins become affines or uterine claimants to the same property, they never pose the threat of dividing the ancestral property which remains a source of income for generations. Here, I would like to emphasize that in these societies rights in things are not held exclusively by individual as they tend to be in western societies, but rather by specified groups, as in this case it is based on kinship. Moreover the recently trend of the shift from the agrarian base to the white collared jobs in the neighbouring towns, for these city based nuclear families a sack of wheat, cereal and a tin of clarified butter jaggery and peanut at the end of the harvest season is sufficient to last them for a year. Thus the food supply being confirmed, by their monthly pay they indulge in other luxuries. The brother takes care of the farm land is neither questioned nor enquired about the year output of the farm, since it is he who supplies the yearly 'galla' (food grain) to the respective brothers settled in town. If he wishes so he can stop the supply of yearly food grain to the brothers by his clever manipulations showing low farm yield and debt. Hence, the man taking care of the farm land is left on his own, he supervises the farm work, and he maintains the ancestral house and gives shelter and food to the old issue less relatives. However, they never venture to sell any portion of the land. Thus inspite of the increase in the family size the ancestral property remains intact.

As regards the sisters every 'khandan' keeps a high amount of dower money or 'mehar' for their marriage. The amount varies from one and a quarter of rupee to 75000 rupees. However, this is simply symbolic and has to be paid to the woman in case of divorce. With divorce is attached a social stigma and coming across a divorce case is a rarity-rather this high amount is one of the main hurdls to a easy Islamic dirvoce. Besides, this high amount of 'mehar' also keeps the none 'khandan' suitors at bay since they feel this large sum of money is a great personal risk for a girl who is alien to him. On the other hand the first cousins never give a second thought to the 'mehar' money since; the family and the girl are familiar to them since childhood. Mostly these cousins are engaged right at the time of birth, which is referred to as 'thikre ki maang' (10.23% of the total number of marriages was betrothed by this rite). Moreover, the assumption that in societies where the girl is an asset or coparcener with her brothers, there the direct or indirect payment that is, bride wealth (in this case 'mehar' is the security money for divorce and should actually be paid at the time of the marriage) is always higher than the other societies. This is mainly to inhabit marriages with outsiders. Thus by close marriage and high amount of 'mehar' money the Asna Ashariya avoid the threat to their property.

Though sanctioned, in practice women never own any land. Since there is no custom of payment of dowry for the girl, the jewellery and clothes along with a few articles of use which a girl is given during her marriage are her own personal assets. However, the custom of 'mayke aana' of the daughter as long as she lives compensates for her unclaimed paternal property. Even after the death of that father the brother continues with the practice. This entails providing her with the two way rail fare for visiting the village along with her children. On her return she is given new sets of clothes and even her children are presented with new apparels. Till date some of the old woman claims that they never had purchased any clothes for themselves or their children from the Husbands money. Clothes throughout the year were provided by her natal relatives. Depending upon the financial circumstances the daughter sometimes refuses to accept clothes instead of demanding cash or something else in kind within the means of her parents. Thus the yearly 'mayke aana' literally meaning 'coming to mother' is actually a type of economic exchange in the form of presentations and fits in the category of "generalized (delayed) reciprocity" which entails "a predominantly one-way exchange". No return of gift of equal value is required to balance any particular gifts. Instead, the donor gains prestige and respect in return of generosity. There was no immediate return of anything of commensurate material value. In the long run however, things do balance out", (Vivelo, 1978, p.129) in this case in lieu of these yearly presentations the daughter forgoes for claim on the parental property. In some of the cases where it had been noted that the brother had sold out the ancestral property and gone abroad and settled, even in such instances it is obligatory for them to send some money to their living sisters. Thus inheritance in lieu of yearly presentations to the living daughters of the house brings a set of brothers closer and they re align themselves by cleverly arranging the matches of their children right at the time of the birth. Thus these marriages imbibe an element of soldiatory within the agnatic cluster which invariably turns out as the uterine cluster, thus aligning the near colltaral agnates non-agnatically. The 'corporate group' i.e. 'khandan' even after dispersal 'gharana' retains its feeling of a cloistered group where a system of co-operation as well as competition prevails.

The geneaology illustrated below is a typical one of the contemporary Asna Ashariya family. From the extended geneaology it is evident that each of the 'Khandan's' are interrelated through marriage alliance in the ascending generations. As 1 Askari married 2 Rizvi, in their following generations several Rizvi and Askari marriages were performed. Thus alliances between 3 and 4, 5 and 6, 7 and 8, 9 and 10, 11 and 12, do not necessarily depict consanguineous marriages primarily inter 'khandan'. But here it is the question of exchanged of 'zan' between two primary groups. Once the women have been exchanged between two 'khandan', the fear of the daughter claiming over the landed property of the father get nullified, since a counter claim can always be initiated from the other family. Thus in the third descending generation the two 'khandans' merge to a corporate unit having agnatic and uterine kins in the same generations. The Naqvis residents of Orai have greater intermarriages with the residents of Kanpur, and show less number of alliances with Rizvi and Askari in this particular family.

One Askari being afraid of the land grab movement divided his landed property amongst all his seven sons and daughters. The girls were also allotted large portions of agriuclture fields, however the claim of the ancestral house remaining with the sons. 13 Askari being the eldest child of one Askari was not only educated but was a woman who did not lack self awareness. Since, the respective lands were registered in their names, after her father's death she lost no time and took the management of the land in her own hand. For this she had to stay back in the village during the harvest season leaving behind her children. Since the dividend of this hardship was large she continued managing her own property till death, her brothers 5 Askari took over the management of her portion and give the money to the 13 Askari unmarried daughters (not mentioned in the geneology). Rizvi on evaluating this own property against that of his wife found that his wife's (5 Askaris) land was more profitable, he lost no time on converting his land at Mohan to cash and investing the same for bettering the farming conditions at Bilhaur. Seven Askari being 'economically well' gave over her portion of the land to brother 3 Askari, who still cotninue with the formality of the yearly presentations. 9 Askari 14 is lieu of yearly 'galla'. The last two sisters 15 and 11 have given the land to brother 14 Askari who carries out with the yearly hospitality for these two sisters. Thus in the entire geneaology comprised of basically three 'khandans' four prominent 'gharanas' are discerned today - which are referred to as 13 sahib ka gharana (Naqvi), 3 ka gharana (Askari), 14 ka gharana (Askari) and 16 ka gharana (Rizvi). Thus bringing to light the inter-relatedness of various 'khandans' amongst Ansa Ashariya.

Table 1 : An extended genealogy showing intra-and inter-khandan marriages.

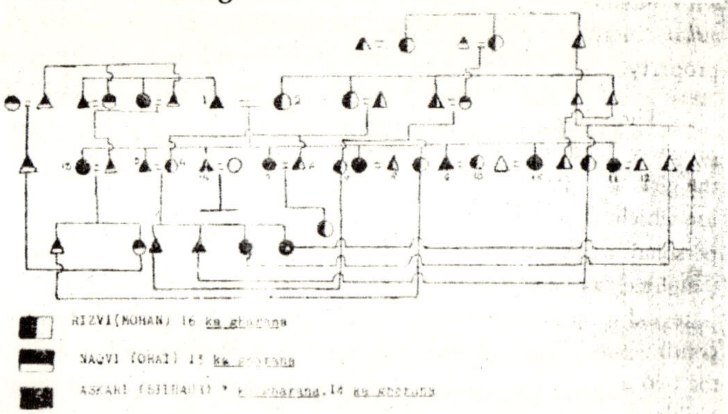

Through the Figure (1) I have tried to depict the city based 'gharanas which may link to the 'khandans' - to maintain their 'nasl', 'hasab' and inheritance and the solidarity of the 'khandan' forms the strong basis of sociopolitical status of the Asna Ashariya 'quam' in U.P. Thus, for the Asna Ashariya of these three villages 'zan' and 'zamin' are two things which maintain their 'nasab' and 'hasab' - the chastity of which had be their pride for centuries. For the same reason 'zan' and'zamin' form the two features for which quarrels and disputes ensue within the 'khandans'.

Thus by separating the world of women by keeping her in secluded protection they have been greatly successful in throwing the encroachment of suitors from other 'khandans'. 'Mehar' is the second factor which keeps away the alliances. However, the match making within the 'khandan' entails the basis of unity and independence of the 'khandan men at the cost of bearing the expenses of 'mayke aana' of the daughters.

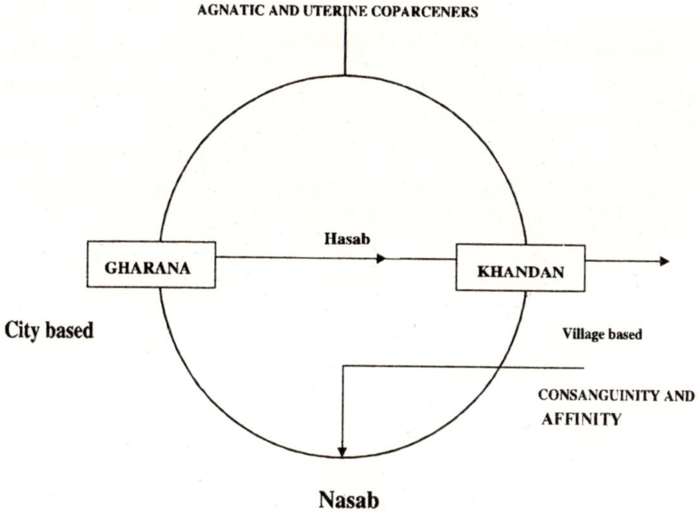

Figure 1

Here the agrarian based community of the Asna Ashariya have cleverly utilized the Islamic saction of cousin marriages for the utilitarian factor of retaining the land and have adopted a cultural trait of 'mayka aana' (since mothers house is closely inbred families is nothing exclusively but is the agnatic or corporate group i.e. 'khandan') and the yearly presentations ensuing from it. Thus in the Asna Ashariya culture, the 'purdah' system, 'thikre-ki-maang' and 'mayke aana' form the basic structure on which the Islamic tradition of partible inheritance is continued.

References

Alavi Hamza A. (1972), Kinship in West Punjab Villages. *Contributions to Indian Sociology New Series,* New Delhi. Vikasnub Have No. VI

Ansari Gaus, (1960), *Muslim Castes in Uttar Pradesh.* (A Study of Culture Contact). U.P. Lucknow, E.F.C.S.

Basu, A and Roy, S. (1972), Change in the Frequency of Consanguineous Marriages Among the Delhi Muslim after Partition. *Eastern Anthropologist,* XXV. I.

Goody (1869), *Comparative Studies in Kinship,* London, Routledge and Kegan Paul.

Karl, Polyani (1944), *The Great Transformation,* New York: Holt, Rinehart.

Vivelo (1978), *Cultural Anthropology Handbook,* Mc Graw Hill.

Webex, Max (1947), *The Theory of Social and Economic Organization* (Translated by A. M. Henderson and Talcoh. Parsons.) London, The Geepress of Glencoe Collies-Macmillan Ltd.

21 Ecology as Controlling Factor of Economy Village Type and Political Organisation in Arunachal Pradesh

Jayanta Sarkar

Arunachal Pradesh with its varied ecological settings is an ideal field for examining the nature-man relation. On the basis of human inhabited terrain, which covers approximately 80 percent of the geographical area this Union Territory can broadly be divided into three ecological settings namely, narrow valleys, broad valleys and plateau, and foot hills. The three ecological settings are inhabited by a population of 4,67,511 (Census, 1971). Narrow valleys in general are located within an altitude of 1800 mtrs to 3300 mtrs where the hills start from the river beds and the slope is extremely steep. The area is covered by temperate forest. Average altitude of broad valley ranges from 900 mtrs to 1800 mtrs and the slope of the hills is gentle and is covered by sub-tropical forest. The foot hills, is almost flat and have an average altitude of 120 mtrs to 900 mtrs, is covered by dense tropical semi-evergreen forest.

In course of different cultural anthropological field trips to Arunachal Pradesh, conducted in different phases from December 1972 to May 1977 a correlation between the nature of terrain and mode of production with certain level of technology, land ownership pattern, types of village and political organisation could be noticed. Table 1 shows the distribution of the tribes in three ecological settings and their mode of subsistence, type of village together with the level of political organisation as found.

Mode of Subsistence in Different Valleys

Agriculture in narrow valleys, as indicated in Table 1, is characterized by the predominance of shifting cultivation. The sandy and rocky river beds are not suitable for any type of cultivation. The inhabitants of these valleys, therefore, had to go to find suitable cultivable land on the slope or the hill tops. To the tribes of broad valleys where slope is gentle, shifting cultivation is also the main mode of subsistence. The mode of preparation of field is simple. The trees, plants, bushes, shrubs are cut down and left to dry. When dry, the fire is set to debri and are allowed to burn for a few days. The land is cleared alongwith unburnt plants and ash is spread all over. To the tribes of broad valleys where slope is gentle, shifting cultivation is also the main mode of subsistence. The cultivators aim at growing everything in the field at a time that are required for immediate consumption or use by the family. A field is generally cultivated for two to three years. In the first year a number of crops are grown while in the second and third year a simple crop, usually paddy is cultivated.

The implements used for shifting cultivation are very simple. For felling trees *dao* (Chopper) is used. Sowing is usually done by a pointed branch of tree using it as digging stick or with the help of the tip of *dao*. Harvesting is also done by the same *dao* when required.

Most of the tribes living in the foot hills have come down from the high hills and have been practicing both shifting and wet cultivation. Their original means of agriculture was shifting cultivation but after coming down at the foot hills they have taken to wet cultivation as well. The Khamti are the only tribe of the foot hills who are traditionally wet-plough cultivators. The implements and mode of preparation of field is not as simple as in case of shifting cultivation. As the technique of ploughing was not known to the other tribes of foot hills they brought hired labourer from the plains of Assam who plough the land, level it, make the arrangements of irrigation etc. Paddy

Table 1
Tribe, Mode of Subsistance, Village type and political organisation

Ecological Setting	*Tribe*	*Mode of Subsistance*	*Type of Village*	*Type of Political Organisation*
1. Narrow Valley	Nishi	Shifting cultivation	Small and scattered	Least developed
	Sulung	Hunting, gathering and	Small and scattered	Least developed
	Tagin	shifting cultivation	Small and scattered	Least developed
	Mara	Shifting cultivation	Small and scattered	Least developed
	Hill Miri	Shifting cultivation, trade	Small and scattered	Least developed
		Shifting cultivation		
2. (a)BroadValley	Wancho	Shifting cultivation	Large and compact	Well Developed
	Nocte	Shifting cultivation, trade	Large and compact	Well Developed
	Tangsa	Shifting cultivation	Medium and compact	Well Developed
	Sherdukpen	Shifting, wet cultivation	Medium and compact	Well Developed
	Monpa	Shifting, wet cultivation	Medium and compact	Well Developed
(b) Plateau	Apatani	Terrace cultivation	Very Large and compact	Well Developed
3. Foot hills	Khamti	Wet cultivation, trade	Large and compact	Well Developed
	Padam	Shifting, wet cultivation	Large and compact	Well Developed
	Singpoh	Shifting, wet cultivation	Large and compact	Well Developed

Note: Information on Nocte, Monpa, Sherdukpen and Apatani have been collected from published works.

is the main crop grown in the land though now-a-days mustard is also produced for selling in markets.

Availability of very limited amount of cultivable land might have influenced the land ownership pattern in the narrow and broad valleys. The villages in narrow valleys are in most cases inhabited by consanguineally related families and the land in such cases is owned by village/clan. If the settlement history of such a village is taken it would reveal that the common ancestors of the present inhabitants of the village first cleared the unclaimed surrounding jungle on the hill top and owned it individually. In course of time the land thus cleared by the ancestors, passed to their descendants who cultivate a portion of the same land separately. As all of them share the same land, originally cleared by their ancestors, it ultimately becomes the land of the clan/village. Thus, the land in the narrow valleys becomes the property of the clan inhabiting the village rather than of a particular household as immovable property is not immediately divided even after the death of the common ancestor. However, a family maintains a loose control over that plots of land which it first clears for *jhum* and reserves its claim to revert to its cultivation after the *jhum* cycle. The cultivable land of the clan/village in narrow valley distributed in different hill tops are usually cultivated one after another leaving one land fallow for a period of 10 to 15 years. Then a *jhum* field is cleared at a considerable distance the land owner for his convenience shift his hut nearer to the agricultural land along with his family members making the villages in narrow valleys unstable. But the distribution pattern of the *jhum* field on different hill tops near the original village restricts any haphazard movement of the families within certain limited areas. (Sarkar, 1976).

The land ownership pattern among the permanent cultivators of the plateau and foot hills differs from those who live in the narrow valleys and practise shifting cultivation. Land ownership pattern of the Apatanis can be divided into three categories; privately owned land, clan land and common land. The irrigated rice-land is privately owned. Apart from the agricultural land, house site is also owned by the individual who normally lies in the village quarter inhabited by other members of his clan (Haimen dorf, 1962). Among the Khamtis, in principle, land is owned by the village chief. But once a land is cleared by an individual for permanent cultivation it becomes his private property.

Since clearing of jhum field is a labourious job, it is very difficult for the land owner to complete the work with the help of his family members only. Therefore, he seeks the help of his kin and friends of the village. The agricultural activities in narrow and broad valleys are thus completed mainly through mutual cooperation. The concept of hired labour is totally absent among them. In all the cases the persons who extend help in clearing agricultural land give importance to the enjoyment than to the work. Their work is compensated by rice beer and/or meal offered by the land owner for the cooperation extended by the kin/friends. Everyone gets rice beer and/or meal as per their consumption capacity irrespective of their input of work. The labour is put by the persons as a social obligation rather than any contract. On the other hand, except the Khamti, the other tribes of foot hills who have adopted wet cultivation mainly depend for the agricultural activities on the hired labourers. Since the technique of ploughing is alien to them they engage hired labourer from the plains who, if they so desire, can get their labour charge in kind. The well to do Khamti also engages the non-Khamti for preparation of agricultural land for which they are paid both in kind and cash depending upon the contract between them. Thus a section of absentee land lord has emerged among the permanent cultivators of foot hills.

Ecology and Village Settings

The size of villages and their settings in the three ecological zones can directly be related with the nature of terrain and availability of cultivable land there in.Table-1 indicates that the villages located in the narrow valley are small and scattered. The agricultural land in these valleys, as already mentioned are distributed on different hill top and slopes. The number of cultivable plots on the hill top is limited. The land owner faces great difficulties to take proper care of the crops if he does not stay near the agricultural field. That is why in the narrow valleys we find very small villages either on the hill top or on the slope. The villages on an average have 3 to 4 houses, having 15 to 20 families, sometimes even 5 to 6 related families having in a big house form a village. The table shows that in broad valleys and plateau no single type of village is pre-dominating. As the cultivable land of Apatani is located within the walking distance is a vast flat land they do not face any problem to pay visit to their agricultural land regularly as in case of the settled agriculturist groups of plains. On account of their permanent terrace cultivation they have established permanent and very big compact villages having 150 to even 500 households. The average size of the villages of Wancho and Nocte of broad valleys ranges from 100 to 200 households. While the favourable ecology and mode of subsistence can directly be made responsible for establishment of large size of the Apatani villages, it is the cultural heritage of Wancho and Nocte, namely, the institution of head hunting, which compelled them to establish such villages. (Sarkar, 1976).

The Tangsas of Nampong area in Tirap district, though practising shifting cultivation, have comparatively larger villages with 25 to 30 households, in average. In their broad valley it is not difficult for the land owner to pay constant visit to his agricultural land. The problem of taking care is further solved by establishing field house near the land where almost all the family members stay during agricultural activities. In the foot hills, as has been indicated in Table 1, the tribes have large and compact villages which are normally located near the bank of rivers. In average such villages have 60 to 100 households. As in the foot hills sufficient cultivable land is available within the walking distance of villages and the communication is comparatively better than the hill dwellers, the villagers do not feel to establish their houses in scattered way as the tribes of narrow valleys do (Sarkar, 1977).

Beside the mode of production with different levels of technology the three ecological settings have a stricking correlation with the different types of political organisation. Table 1 shows that the tribes living in narrow valleys have least developed political organisation while those inhabiting in other two ecological settings have comparatively developed and well developed political organisation. This can directly be related to the population size of the villages which in-turn can be attributed to the nature of terrain as has already been mentioned. The Kaman Mishmi, Tagin, Mara, Nishi and Bangni living in small villages in narrow valleys can be considered as more weak in political organisation. An old man of the village, who is respected by the villagers due to his personal influence or ability to negotiate with the super natural power, is generally approached to settle down the disputes. The most important agents of settling down the disputes are the messangers or intermediaries. They go to and fro in the interest of peace and compromise. Oaths in front of the village elders are taken and there are ordeals to test a man's innocence or guilt. This simple system is mainly based on belief and faiths. As in the narrow valleys, the villages are small and in most cases the villages are inhabited by related families they do not face serious problem in convincing the person involved in any dispute to arrive at a solution. But the tribes of foot hills and broad valleys practising settled agriculture and living in large and compact villages have well developed political organisation. The Mukehup of Khamti, Kebang of Padam, Wanchu-Wancha of Wancho, Ngothun of nocte, Builang of Apatani have a number of officials with specific function to perform (Sarkar, 1978). They are taken as representative of the different clan/hamlets of the village after a regular interval. The verdict given by such a council is considered final. Since the large and compact villages are populated by more than one clan the possibility of occurrence of disputes is more and solution of such disputes through negotiation by a single person is comparatively difficult. So for dealing with disputes they take at least one member from each clan and form a council so that the decision taken by the council becomes acceptable to the persons involved in disputes and thus ultimately emerges out well developed form of political organisation.

Summing Up

The foregoing discussion brings into light that the tribes living in different valleys in Arunachal Pradesh have been maintaining a balance with the respective ecological settings. With the change in nature of terrain from narrow valleys to foot hills main mode of subsistence varies from shifting cultivation to wet-terraced and wet-plough cultivation, which brings also a variation in the level of technology from simple to more eleborate form. The more elaborate form of alien technology, necessary for wet-plough cultivation, brought in the non-tribal hired labourer removing the age old system of mutual cooperative agricultural activities through the kins and members of the village. The land ownership pattern varies from a loose control of the village to individual ownership with the changes in mode of production, which again is directly conditioned to the various ecological settings.

The terrain has directly influenced the type and size of the villages, which in turn has influenced the extent of development of political organisation. The scattered location of the land and villages in difficult terrain of narrow valleys, where even to keep a proper watch to the field is extremely difficult because of the communication problem, perhaps provide a possible explanation for the least importance of the village community. Elsewhere Elwin (1959 : 22) remarked that most obvious features of the Mishmi life, like Dafla life which distinguishes it from that of most of the other tribes in NEFA, is the unimportance of village community. Villages sometimes have only one house and others consist of scattered buildings as much as a half-mile away from each other. The real social unit is thus the house. Such a situation also disfavoured the formation of any developed form of political organisation in narrow valleys.

On account of the inadequate agricultural return from the shifting cultivation and the production of immediate consumption oriented crops idea of accumulation of wealth in the narrow valleys is not prominent. But to the tribes of plateau and specially of foot hills, like the Khamti and Adi, comparatively better agricultural return, supplemented by their earning through market oriented production, in the land and also the exploitation of timber from the surrounding forest has favoured the emergence of a richer section leading to the formation of a dichotomous economic division within the respective tribal societies.

References

Barthakur, J. K. (1971), *Census of India,* General Population Table, Arunachal Pradesh. Part 11A. Series No. 24.

Elwin Varrier (1959), *Philosophy for NEFA,* Shillong.

Haimendorf, V. Furer (1965), *Democracy in NEFA,* Shillong.

Haimendorf, V. Furer (1962), *The Apatanis and their Neighbours,* London.

Sarkar, J.K. (1976), Ecology, Economy and Ethnic Conciousness; (Unpublished Paper Presented in a Seminar on Border Area Study Held at Calcutta).

Sarkar, J. K. (1977), An Observation on Some Economic Aspect of the Tribes of Arunachal Pradesh. (unpublished paper presented in a Seminar on Tribal Economy in Calcutta).

Sarkar, J. K. (1978), Terrain, Village Types and Traditional Political Organizations Among the Tribes of Arunachal Pradesh. (unpublished).

22

Social Hierarchy and Eco Zones: An Emerging Concept in Manipur Valley

R. K. SAHA

Both physical environment and the society changes through time. The rate of change, however, varies. Comparatively physical environment changes slowly whereas the human society changes rapidly. Here, in case of Manipur valley, the ecology of Manipur valley changed a little during the historical periods that were taken in the formation of a political state and the development of a social hierarchy amongst different ethnic groups living in the valley. In the physical environment the change was the only reduction of the quantity of some mineral resources whereas in the human society a stateless non-hierarchic society has been changed into a state based hierarchic society. From this point of view for the purpose of analysis here in this article I presume that physical environment is stable through time and the social environment changes through time. Human society changes because the persons living in the society always face to make choices between several alternatives, and they deal with the arbitrariness of personal ambitions and charms. The analysis of the interplay between these two, the physical environment and the social environment is the aim of this article.

In this article I shall deal with three variables, namely, (a) physical environment in which the variations of resources and the means of production in different eco zones including levels of subsistence will be dealt with; (b) political environment, i.e., political history in which I shall deal with the historical process how the Meitei state has been formed in Manipur valley; and (c) human environment which analyse how a non-hierarchic egalitarian society has been changed in historical process into a hierarchic feudal like society. In dealing with these three variables I shall examine: (1) what part is played by ecology itself in the process of formation of a hierarchic society; (2) the part played by personal ambitions and choices in utilizing the physical environment to fulfil the goal, and (3) how far ideas from outside have been incorporated in dealing with both physical and human environment.

Physical Environment

Manipur, a north eastern frontier state of India covers an area of 22,356 square km of which one tenth (about 1,843 square km) is the central valley and the rest nine tenth (about 20,513 square km) are the hilly areas which surrounded the valley. On the hills, there are 29 tribal groups belonging to Naga and Kuki stock. In the valley there are six ethnic groups, namely, Meitei, Loi/Chakpa, Yaithibi, Brahman, Bishnupriya and the Pangan (i.e., Muslim). The density of population in the valley is about 380 per square km (statistical handbook of Manipur, 1972).

The hills surrounding the valley vary in height. The highest altitude is in the north-east where peaks rise above 8000 ft. above the sea level. The valley is situated at an average of 2500-3000 ft above the sea level. The southern part of the valley is comparatively lower resulting into marshes. There are a number of lakes in this part of the valley. The important lakes are Ikok, Waithou and Logtak.

The valley of Manipur itself has different ecological conditions. The Principle Rivers of the valley, namely, Imphal, Iril, Thoubal, Nambol and Nambul, have their sources in the hills. The first three rivers, Imphal, Iril and Thoubal rise is the hills to the north and flows down to the south but do not fall into the Logtak Lake. The Iril joins the Imphal at Lilong bazaar (11 km from Imphal on the Indo Burma road) and their combined flow meets the Thoubal at a point near Mayang Imphal (24 km south-east of Imphal). The Nambol and the Nambul rise from the west and the North West and falls into the Logtak Lake. Their overflow results in one stream known as kartak. This kartak joins the flow of Imphal-Iril-Thoubal to form one river called Imphal or *turel achouba* (the big river) and flows past shugnu and finally to chindwin. Though these rivers are insignificant in size at the source they carry a large amount of water with rapid current during the rains. In rainy season, the water of all these rivers irrigates the land situated on the northern part of the valley and thus makes it the most fertile area. The excess water of this part of the valley flows down to the marshy areas in the south. The water accumulates in the marshy areas in the southern part of the valley. This area is often inundated by flood water and thereby the average production of this land is less than that of the northern areas. Besides these principle rivers, there are a few small streams, e.g., Ablok is a small stream which passes through the northern part of the valley.

On the basis of types of land, water resources, and cultivation, the valley may be divided into three eco zones - zone A, B and C. Zone A, that is, the "northern fertile plain" is situated in the northern part of the valley. The land of this zone, *fourel lou* (the most fertile land) (Table 1) is irrigated by the water from rivers and the small streams which, carry in rainy season, and is made fertile to considerable depth and is enriched constantly by, the silt deposits brought down by the rivers and small streams. As the excess water is flows down to the south in rapid speed there is comparatively least fear of damaging the crop by flood water. Paddy is the only product which too is surplus in this zone. Zone B, that is, the "marshy low land", is situated in the southern part of the valley. The land of this zone is mostly the *taothabi* and the *Patlou* type of land (low and mostly situated beside lakes but less fertile). There are also *foural lou* comparatively less in quantity to that of the *taothabi lou* and *Pat lou* wherever available. All the villages of this zone do not posses this type of land. Although people call it *foural lou* it is comparatively inferior to the quality of *fourel lou* of zone A.

Table 1
Possession of Arable Land in Three Villages

Name of the Village	*Situation in eco-zone*	*Possession of Land with percentage*							
		Fourel	%	*Patlou/ Tabthablou*	%	*Angoufoulou*	%	*Chinglou*	%
Lairenkabi	ZoneA	158.1	100	-	-	-	-	-	-
Nachou	Zone B	407.0	37.9	521.8	48.6	145.2	13.5	-	-
Thoubal Khunou	Zone C	93.5	28.9	76.1	24.2	-	-	143	45.8

**The land measurement presented here is calculated in acre*

Besides, there are a few *angonfou* type of land (foothill areas which are less fertile). As *patilou* and *taothabillou* are very often inundated by flood water and the production of the *angonfou lou* and *fourel lou* of this zone is poor, the people who live in these areas do not depend on agriculture and also pursue other occupations based on natural resources. For instance, the Muslims occupying the river banks grow vegetables, the people of the village Ithing and Thanga fish in the logtak lake, Ngaikhong Khunou make *loo* (fishing basket), and the Toubul weave *laa* and *inn* (fishing nets). About a century ago, when raw materials were available, the people of Ningel were involved in salt making, the Shugnu prepared lime and the Kakching collected iron from iron ore dust from the river bed. The people of Palel were famous for making plough shares. Now-a-days, because of shortage of raw mterial these people have taken to agriculture. As a precautionary measure to avert flood they are now constructing dams in different lake areas. One such dam has been constructed in Waithou lake near thoubal, close to the village Thoubal Khunou. The government has accepted a plan to irrigate the *augonfou lou*. The Logtak project is still under construction. In these ways people of this zone are trying to control the nature in their own favour. Zone C that is, the "peripheral zone" where the foot hill meets the valley. The land of this zone is mostly the *chinglou* type of land, i.e., hilly areas. They also possess *angonfou lou* and *fourel lou* of the same type of zone B and a few *pat lou*. The people of this zone depend on both the valley and hill products. As for example, the people of Thoubal Khunou practice agriculture in the *Pat lou* and cultivate pineapple on the hills. As the products are not sufficient to survive, the people of this zone are engaged in different activities too. The Andro Loi who practise agriculture in their small area of valley land available to them, produce charcoal from the forest woods. Besides, the people of this zone depend on certain other occupations which are suited to them on the basis of the availability of natural resources. For example, the Phayeng Loi and the Andro Loi practise liquor distillation, swine rearing, and poultry farming. Both the fuel and the raw material is plenty for distilling liquor.

It is, however, reported that the Phayeng Loi had to give up distillation since 1974 because the police did not allow them to distil liquor. As the situation of the phayeng Loi is favourable, sericulture has been accepted by them as their traditional occupation. As the clay of the surrounding area is favourable for pot making the Andro loi and the Sekmai Loi accepted pottery as their occupation. In these ways the people of this zone are doing maximum use of nature for their subsistence and existence.

Political Environment

Although kingship in Manipur valley has now been abolished we can get an idea of the structure of the Meitei kingship system from the sketchy description of the British authors (Brown, 1975; Dun, 1975; Hodson, 1975), from the records of the manuscripts possessed by the Pandits (Singh, 1969), and from the works of the Indian historians (Singh, 1965; Roy, 1973) and also talking to the surviving people who worked in the palace during the period of last king. It is understood that the political structure was a hierarchic structure of different categories of ranks of people. The king was at the top of this structure. He was the supreme authority in all respects. The king paid much regard to the advice of the palace Pandits in every activity. There were many departments in the palace each of which dealt with a specific job. And there were many offices under one department each of which was vested with specific responsibility. There were people who supervised the works of these departments and offices. All these people including the Pandits performed non-labourious prestigious services and enjoyed some privileges. For example, they enjoyed a fixed quantity of tax free land. Some of these officers were even entitled to *loi-ill*, *yum-tinuaba* and *pothang*, i.e., personal servants. The rank of these people of this category in the political structure was just below the king. In the next category there were the people who gave *lalun* service, i.e., to give essential service to the king ten days in every forty days by rotation. In this system persons belonging between the age of sixteen and sixty were soliders in war period and their service were civil in peace period. Those who performed *lalu* were entitled to cultivate one pari of land (2.5 acre) for their support subject to the payment of tax in kind (Brown, 1975: 85). In the last category of rank there were people who performed dishonourable services, i.e., *loipot* services. It includes paying tribute to the king in cash or in kind and performing heavy duties what they were asked to do. They were allowed to exploit less and least fertile land only.

This political structure in terms of hierarchy of ranks has been formed in historical process. As there is no proper historical data, this historical process can not be understood by historical facts. Let me here emphasise that what follows is a historical çonstruct developed through the study of genealogy, historical and social remnants, stories, narrations and statements of different categories of informants etc.

Although at present the lineage members are so widely distributed in the valley and there are almost all the 7 clan (viz. Ningthouja, Angom, Luwang, Khuman, mairang, Khabanganba and Chenglei) members in a village of was not the situation in the past from the comparative analysis of the rituals such as ancestral worship (Apokpa khurum jabal), festival (Laiharaoba), and the social structure, it is understood that a clan was originated at a particular time, day, month and place. The pandit also explains that originally the member of the clan inhabited in this place of origin. As a result of that a single village was populated by members of a single clan only. This was the state of complete equalitarian tribal society. As the clan is an exogamous unit, each of these social groups distributed in different villages had to look for marriageable girls from groups other than their own. This, however, was not an easy task. Fights used to break out between two groups in the matter of marriage by elopement. At this juncture the aspiring chiefs (Ningthous) framed rules that all the able bodied persons should act as soliders to organize inter-clan fights for getting girls in marriage. This created a problem that during war all the able bodied persons could do no other work except fight. So the chiefs felt the need for accumulating food. This arose the need and desire for grabbing more land under control, which again became another source for fights amongst different clan members. Every clan chief wanted to be more powerful both in military vigour and in economy because they felt that they could not fight if they were not economically sound. In this process of accumulation of power, the Ningthouja (the then Meitei clan) became most powerful. In small or large the Meitei fought with the other clans in different centuries till they could manage to merge all the other clans under their sovereignty and taking their clan name the ethnic name Meitei was given to all the superstructure of kingship. The Ningthouja chief when became the ruler of the Meitei state was at first designated as Lainingthou. Later on it was changed to Maharaja in the Sakabda 1646, i.e. in the year 1724-25 (Singh, 1969; Singh and Singh, 1967). Kangla is the place of origin of the Ningthonia clan. The land surrounding Kangla was most fertile. So they were in most favourable condition to win over others. The literati rationalize the supremacy of the Meitei, by explaining that the Meitei chief is the first man in the genealogical frame.

Human Element

The pattern of population in the valley villages is uniethnic. And the present day situation of the villages in the valley shows that the Loi/Chakpa and the Yaithibi villages are in zone C. The Bishnupriya and the low status Meitei villages are in Zone B and the high status Meitei villages in Zone A. The two exogenous groups, namely, the Brahman and the Pangan (Muslim) do not follow this pattern of distribution. As expert agriculturist and horticulturist the Pangan live along the banks of the rivers while normally there is one Brahman family in a small Meitei village, and more than one Brahman family are found in big Bishnupriya villages.

If we go back into the historical past, this was not the situation. This is an end result of a process. The end result can only be understood if followed through the historical process, which again let me emphasize, is a construct based on anthropological methods as mentioned above and not based on historical facts.

Originally there were 7 Meitei clans and, to the Meitei, two more clans for the Loi/Chakpa distributed in different parts of the valley. To the Loi/Chakpa once they occupied areas in Zone A. But the Ningthauja defeated them and drove them to the foothill areas. Since then, as a defeated group, the Loi/Chakpa villages are in the foothill areas. It is agreed by all that the outcaste people, Yaithibi, once belonged to the Meitei society. They were excommunicated by the king. Meiteis who became Yaithibi (Yai = luck, thiba = bad) were punished either on real cause or on allegations falsely imposed on them by some jealous persons. It is stated that they either married their near relatives of the most forbidden category or they had illicit relations with the queens. The people undergoing punishment for crimes, the people captured in war, the people whom the king did not like for various reasons were all forced to settle in marshy low land and were forced to accept occupations such as salt making, lime making, and collection of iron from iron ore dust etc. which the high status Meitei did not like to perform. The Kuki who came down to the valley and have now merged with the low status Meitei were allowed to settle in the villages known as sepoy villages as police force of the king. Some of the people coming from the east and the west (Nongpokharam and Nongchupharam) were also settled in this region with the permission of the ruler. The people who were, later on, subdued by the king were also forced to settle in this region. All these people are considered as low status Meitei. It is stated that the Bishnupriya were brought by the Meitei king and were allotted their settlement villages in this zone B. The Pangan are the war captives. As they taught the Meitei the method of paddy transplantation they were allowed by the king to settle on the banks of the rivers so that they would produce vegetables. The king being Meitei permitted his people, i.e., the Meitei to settle in zone A. After the acceptance of vaishnavism in eighteenth century the king brought the Brahmin from different parts of India and allowed them to settle in Meitei and Bishnupriya villages to perform Vaishnava rituals and to teach them the vaishnava way of life. The king also imposed restrictions on the Bishnupriya and the Loi/Chakpa to establish new villages. As a result the growth of population was accommodated in the same old villages. The average village population of a Bishnupriya or Loi/Chakpa villages increased then that of the Meitei (Table 2).

Table 2
Village Population*

Ethnic Groups	*No. of villages considered*	*Total Population*	*Average Population*
Meitei	4	1540	385
Bishnupriya	7	20392	2913
Loi/Chakpa	6	6396	1066
Yaithebi	2	488	244

Notes : Data are based on 1961 Census.The selection of villages made as follows;The four Meitei villages which were visited by the author are considered here.Though the Bishnupriya live in eight villages, one of which is a new settlement and as such have not appeared in 1961 Census.Though the Loi/Chakpa live in eight villages, two of their settlements are not completely Loi/Chakpa settlement, but composite market areas, So these two settlements are not considered here.The Yathibi are, living in two villages. A few of them are living in another area which has not been considered here, because their number is very small.

A village in Manipur valley is inhabited by different Lineage members virtually belonging to a single ethnic group. In their day-to-day interaction in a uni-ethnic village the villagers are guided by tribe-like egalitarian principle. But the villagers are also aware of the presence of other ethnic groups living in different ecological zones of the valley and refer to them in terms of a "notion" of hierarchic relationship. Though at present this notion of hierarchic relationship has no functional implications it is a hang over in the memory of the people of a once functional hierarchy.

During the period of kingship the rank in the political structure which was based on the differential distribution of services and benefits were related with the status in social hierarchy. The king was at the top of this hierarchy. And those who gave prestigious non-manual service i.e. aristocrats had the higher status than those who gave manual services. In this last group also those who gave essential services, i.e. "commoners" had the higher status than those who gave dishonourable services i.e., "the degraded". These services were institutionalized as Famdon (prestigious posts), Lalup (essential services) and Loipot (menial services). Though this hierarchy was not functional in the sense that there was no inter-group service relationship it was functional in the sense that the different status groups had the service relationship through the parameter of kingship. The king played key role in the formation and function of this hierarchy. The three departments, namely, the administrative, judicial courts and the religious courts worked in unison in internal and external organization of the state based hierarchic system. The judicial courts made some people outcaste, deployed some people to marshy low land and even degraded some others. The administrative units forced someone to accept particular occupation in the marshy low land (zone B) areas. Based on such incidents the Pandits grouped some lineages together and put them at a particular structural distance (Evans Pitchard, 1940). As per example, the royal connection is significant in grouping all the lineages belonging to aristocratic section including the royal lineages into a single ascending point for the purpose of considering structural distance. Similarly the ascending points of the common Meitei lineages, the degraded Meitei lineages and the Yaithibi lineages calculated and thereby comparative structural distances of these groups of lineages from the king are made. The three distances, namely, the structural distance, the hierarchical distance, and the service distance correlated and coincided with the political rank to form a well organized state based hierarchy in Manipur Valley. Lastly, after the acceptance of vaishnavism, when the king came in contact with the neighbouring states he brought the Brahmin as priestly group who introduced intelligently the Hindu value of purity and pollution along with vaishanvism. There was an implicit and explicit pressure from the king behind the acceptance of vaishnavism. Those who would accept vaishnavism were considered higher in status than those who would not accept. It, however, could not organize the ethnic group after the model of Hinduized state related to the caste system. Rather it strengthened the existing socio-political hierarchy.

At present the people rationalize their notion of hierarchy in terms of their experience in historical past. According to them the highest status position is given to those who were favoured by the king through holding honourable posts in the palace in judical, administrative and military services and having enjoyed the privilege of marrying the daughters of royal lineages and getting the royal permission to occupy the most fertile land in the northern fertile plain and are also not formerly forced and punished by the king, have no assigned or derogatory occupation and are believed to have accepted vaishnavism since its introduction in Manipur. The middle status is given to those who were not favoured by the king in any way and were formerly forced to follow a particular occupation (not derogatory), live in allotted residential locations in marshy low land and are believed to have brought under control by subjugation and isolation as well as accepted vaishnavism at a later period. The lowest status is given to those who were formerly punished by imprisonment or exile, have assigned derogatory occupations and did not accept vaishnavism during the period of kingship. The analysis of these rationals too, indicates that the king's ambition and choice played significant role in changing in egalitarian tribal society into a state based hierarchic society.

Discussion and Conclusion

A concept of hierarchy of social groups has been developed and has been functionally incorporated followed through the contours of kingship in Manipur valley as contribution of three variables, namely: ecology, ambitions and choices of persons, and ideas from outside. Of these three variables the contributions of ecology and ideas from outside is limited whereas personal ambitions and choices played major role in exploiting ecology and ideas from outside to change the stateless egalitarian society into a Hierarchic feudallike society. Environment provided certain facilities in terms of surplus generation, capital formation to those who lived in Zone A and imposed certain limitations in terms of subsistence to those who lived in Zone B and C. As a result of surplus production, life became comparatively easy to those people of Zone A and whereas from the point of view of subsistence life became comparatively hard to those of the zone B and C. These basic variations have been utilized by ambitious people and dealt with it accordingly to their choices. Surplus in products relieved the ambitious people of thinking for subsistence. Instead they could put their mind to mobilize the whole labour force in formation of power. Thus to fulfil his personal ambition of becoming most powerful, the Ningthouja clan chief utilized his choices of defeating others and organizing and reorganizing the settlement in favour of creating variations from point of subsistence and surplus and thereby centralizing power and capital in his own hand. In securing his position he utilized the sentiment of the people and like the laity had much faith on the literatcy and made use of the genealogical principle and thereby the structural distance with the help of these Pandits. Seeking for power was the basis for social choice and the society changed because there were choices to deal with (Leach, 1954).

To sum up, nature contributed variations in terms of subsistence and surplus generations. Having a lesson from the nature itself persons working through their ambitions and choices utilized these variations in formation of power, capital and ultimately a social hierarchy enacted through the distribution of benefits and services. Idea from outside could not change what has been formed rather it was utilized by the ambitious to strengthen the already formed social hierarchy. Ultimately change has been brought by personal ambitions and choices through utilization of ecology.

Notes

The article is based on the fieldwork done by the author as a member of the Anthroplogical Survey of India in Manipur valley during the period 1970-1974.

The structural distance is the structural relationship between the last living persons in the line of descent and the first person in the ascending line.

References

Brown, R. 1975 (1874), *Statistical Account of Manipur*. Delhi: Sanskuran Prakashak

Department of Statistics (1972), *Statistical Handbook of Manipur*. Imphal: Government of Manipur.

Dun, Captain, S.W. (1986) 1975, *Gazetter of Manipur*. Delhi: Vivek Publishing House.

Evans-Pritchard, E.E. (1940), *The Nuer*. London: Oxford University Press.

Hodson, T.C. (1908), 1975. *The Meltheis*. London: David Nutt.

Leach, E. R. (1954), *Political Systems of Highland Burma*. London: G. Bell and Sons. Ltd.

Roy, Jyotirmoy (1973), *History of Manipur*. Calcutta: East Light Book House.

Singh, Jhalajit, R. K. (1965), *A Short History of Manipur (From 33 A.D. to the Present Time)*. Imphal: The O.K. Store.

Singh, Ningthou Khongjam Khelchandra (1969), *Ariwa Manipuri Sahityagee Itihas* (In Manipuri). Imphal: Churachand Printing Work.

Singh, Late L.I. and N.K. Singh, Editors (1967), *Cheithtarol Kumbaba* (In Manipuri). Imphal : Manipuri Sahitya Parishad.

23 Occupational Adaptation among the Semsa and the Langia Saora

SANCHITA GHATAK

Occupational adaptation is influenced by its geographical setting or environment, physical and cultural. Physical environment includes climate, soil, slope, altitude, natural vegetation, etc. and cultural environment deals with people and their culture. The environment affects the ways in which men lead their lives. In this paper, an attempt has been made to show the effect of the environment, both physical and social, upon the occupational adaptation of the people. Two ethnic groups from two states namely, Assam and Orissa have been selected for this purpose. Field work was done in 1977-78 in Orissa and 1979 in Assam under projects taken up by the Anthroplogical Survey of India, Calcutta.

Saoras, one of the 62 tribes of Orissa had a population 3,42,757 in 1971 i.e. 6.76% of the total tribal population in orissa. They are distributed in 13 districts, but their maximum concentration was noticed in Ganjam district which accounts for 1,19,262 persons in 1971, that is, 34.8% of the total Saora population in Orissa. So from Ganjam district, Talasing, a Langia Saora (a Section of Saora) village, was selected for study. The total tribal population in Assam in 1971 was 19,19,947 (including Mizoram) with 23 tribes. Of this figure, the Disasa Kachari population is 39,344 in Assam, i.e. a mere 2.20% to the total tribal population of the State. The Semsa forms one of the sections of the Disasa. For the present study Semkhor village of North Cachar Hills was selected as they are found only in that village.

In the respective areas, the tribes mainly live in deep forests hilly tracts having steep slope, high rainfall, inaccessibility and low population density. The above factors and other local conditions favour the practice of shifting cultivation. As such the two villages, Talasing (Orissa) and Semkhor (Assam) constitute the field units of our study. Physically both the villages are located in the hilly areas. Semkher village lies in the high hill region of the Barail range. Barail range forms the water divide of the area. The maximum height is 1800 metre whereas the minimum height dips to 550 metre. Except near the riverbed the slope is steep (35^0 average slope). The main river of the village is the Langting, a tributary of the river Diying. It originates from Nairacula hills of Barail range. The Langting river with its tributary flows through the village. In the south, the Jenam River flows with its tributary, the Bailekdisa. Both the Jenam and the Langting rivers are perennial. The soil of this area is hill soil having shallow depth.

Talasing village lies in the Eastern ghat range of the Deccan area. Here maximum height is 900 metre whereas minimum height is 450 metre. Average slope is 25^0. Soil pattern is red laterite. Northern Tropical Semi-evergreen forests are found in this village. Table 1 presents salient physical features of the villages understudy.

Table 1
Physical Attributes of the Study Villages

Name of the village	*Total area (in ha.)*	*Altitude (in mtr. Approx.)*	*Average slope (in degree approx.)*	*Soil (General)*	*Natural vegetation*	*Density of population per sq. km.*
Talasing	103.46	900 max. 450 min.	25	Red Coarse laterite	Northern tropical semi-evergreen	16
Semkhor	406.02	1800 max. 550 min.	35^0	Hill Soil	Northern tropical evergreen	30

According to the situations of the two villages people of these areas adopt different occupations. Agriculture is the main occupation of the people of both the villages. Beside this they also depend on food gathering, hunting, daily labour, livestock, household industry and trade, barter.

Table 2
Familywise Distribution of Occupation

Types of Primary Occupation	*Talasing (Orissa Village)*	*Percentage of Families*
Semkhor (Assam Village)		
Only cultivation	34.3	41.9
Cultivation and labour	62.5	8.7
Cultivation and household industry	0.0	30.8
Cultivation and trade	0.0	9.9
None of the above item but purely on collecting and gathering stage.	3.2	8.7

Familywise occupational distribution of the two villages represent variation. In Talasing, majority of population (62.5%) are engaged in'cultivation and labour'. In this village, virgin forest land has been almost exhausted. Miles after miles bald hillocks are a common feature here. Though the people of the area are engaged in shifting cultivation, the land is not able to meet total food requirements of the village for the whole year. The total annual agricultural production of the village can meet the villagers need for 224 days only of the year. This is because of high population in comparison to the available cultivating land in the village. Moreover, the gap for regeneration of forest growth in shifting cultivation cycle has considerably decreased. Therefore, to secure required food for the remaining period of the year, the people took to other means of earning such as the daily labour work, or some other works.

In this area, the period of regeneration of forest growth in the cycle of shifting cultivation is short (6-7 years) which consequently affect the production rate (average rate is 5-10 kgm. production from 1 kgm. seed of paddy and 4-5 kgm production from 1 kgm seed of millets). The rate of production is also decreasing due to the decreasing fertility of land. So along with cultivation, the people are engaged in other occupations. They are mainly engaged in daily labour. They work as daily labour or 'cooli' in the neighbouring villages. Those who do not have land take part in such work throughout the year, others do this sort of work during the lean season of agriculture.

The Langia Saoras are well acquainted with wage labour in which they are involved as they are very much in demand by the surrounding communities having excess production. Usually these tribals are at bare subsistence level as grow food for themselves.But the surrounding caste groups often grow more or surplus production, with a profit motive also. Since they want to obtain maximum production from land, they invest capital and also hire labour from the Langia Saora. The Langia Saoras themselves produce much lesser quantity than their requirement from their own land.

For procurement of the balance food they have no other avenues, but readily available occupation of wage labour which they grab. Among various occupations, in terms of frequency, the second major occupation is cultivation (34.3%) in this village.

Table 3
Agricultural Land and Ecological Factors

Village	*Types of land*	*Actual area (acre)*	*Area in % to total geographical area*	*Average slope (degree)*	*Average altitude (mtrs.)*
Talasing	Bagada	20.37	19.69	25	650-9006
	Padara	1.38	1.33	17-20	00-650
	Billow	4.60	4.44	17-15	500-650

From Table 3 it is seen that Bagada (Shifting cultivation land) is more (20%) than Padara (semi-terraced land) and Billow (terraced land). Only 1.33% of the total geographical area of village Talasing is utilized as Padara land. Due to the scarcity of water, terraced cultivation cannot be properly done here. It is in the process of terrace construction. Here in a single plot particular crop is cultivated such as Biri (pulse), Kulutha (pulse), Mandia (ragi) etc. The land is dependent only on rain water. The production rate therefore, is very low (in 1 kg seeds only 4-5 kg production). The Billow lands are terraced lands developed near the water courses. They are constructed right up to the beds of the hill streams. Only paddy of local variety is cultivated there. Cowdung is used by the villagers as manure.

In Talasing, Bagada (shifting cultivation) is the primary occupation of the villagers (see Table 2). Bagada is cultivated for 2-3 years and then left fallow for 6-7 years, for regeneration of forest growth. There they produce many varieties of crops, such as, Kamburung (Small millet) Burian (millet), Saremoi (Beans), Kurui (Small millet), Sitri (ragi), Kandrung (Pulse), Ganga (Jobstear), Sa (finger millet), Ragu or Kandula (red grams) etc. Only 3.2% of the village families indulge in food gathering and collecting. They have no land, and many are unable to plough due to old age.

The situation in Semkhor village is somewhat different. Here, shifting cultivation is the primary occupation (42.9%). Total cultivated land during 1979 was 621.50 acre. The villagers have two categories of cultivated land e.g. (1) Jhum and (2) Paniketi, Paniketi is permanent land for cultivation. It is generally situated by the side of the river. Only paddy is cultivated in this field. Nineteen percent of the total cultivable land of the village is under this category. This type of cultivation started here only ten years ago. In this type of cultivation they generally use crude implements and method also. For this the production rate is not more. Production is same as Jhum field. Semsa people prefer Jhum cultivation to Paniketi. Eighty one percent of land is under Jhum cultivation. Usually they cultivate the land for one year but in some cases it extends upto 2 years also. After that the land is kept fallow for regeneration of forest growth for 6-8 years. The Semsas grow paddy, cotton and sesame in separate plots. With local hill paddy they mix the seeds of maize, sweet grourd, country bean, brinjal, chilli, arhar (pigoonea) lady's finger, mustered etc. and broadcast them in the same field.

The other important occupations in Semkhor are household industries like weaving and basket making. Crop produced in this village is not sufficient. So the other types of occupation like weaving, basket making supplement their income. Here the situation is somewhat different from the Saora area. The Semsas are surrounded by tribal communities like Naga, Kuki, Hmar and Dimasa Kucharies. Usually the tribal people grow food for themselves only. So they do not have any surplus. As the Semsa do not shift from there village, pressure of population on land is gradually increasing. Now, only cultivation cannot sustain the population. So they adopted other types of economy which are suitable in this environment. The Semsa women weave clothes and men do busketry. The women folk are known to be good weavers of cotton and endi-cloths, usually for their consumption. The weaving is generally done in the primitive looms with cotton raised in their fields and subsequently spun in a wheel. They also raise endi silk. They dye their own yarns in fast colour prepared out of raw indigo and other herbs available in the vicinity. But they do not sell clothes. It is because of two reasons (1) the peoples of communities who purchase handloom products are Nagas and Dimasas. In Dimasa culture women do not wear cloths woven by other women. So market of clothes among the Dimasa is nil. Again Naga community may purchase clothes from Semsa but they prefer to wear their particular design. The Semsa can weave only their own traditional design in their look which Nagas do not prefer. So they have no market for clothes among the Naga also. (2) Production of cotton in Semsa village is poor and the quality of the cotton is short staple. They have no such capital to invest money in this household industry for raw materials. Naturally for these reasons they have not adopted weaving economy.

The next household industry is basketry. For basketry raw material is bamboo which is readily available here. Due to conducive environmental condition, the bamboo grows here, in abundance. Heavy rainfall in this region favours bamboo's growth. Natural vegetation of this area is dominantly bamboo and grass. Of the two, bamboo based craft has developed here and large part of their material culture is supported by bamboo.

In the past Semsas were not taken to basketry as a household industry. At that time those were prepared for own use. But now-a-days it became their economy. It is because of (1) Bamboos are aboundant here. (2) It is usuable and durable also. With wood or other metals it is not possible to make things which are made of bamboos. So no alternative is there. (3) It is also fitting with their technology. It is known to them from long time. (4) So naturally, already, they have skill in this industry.

From bamboo they produce different kinds of basketry for which they have ready market also. The Dimasa of the valley often buy baskets from the Semsa though the Dimasa also prepare their own baskets. But they are mostly busy with cultivation, for which they cannot devote much time in basket making. All the containers of this area are made by bamboo. Even they prepare their rice specially "biran" rice in the bamboo. They carry water by "difyeng" which is made of bamboo. From roof of the house up to the plaftform of the house is made of bamboo. They prefer to take bamboo shoots also. So bamboo culture is very much familiar to them. For these reasons they have adopted to this type of occupation.

Other two occupations are trade and labour. Trade means they purchase paddy from the valley and turn it into rice and sell these in the high altitude market, especially to surrounding Nagas where paddy is less produced. Usually females, those who have less land, are doing this type of job. A few numbers of labours is present here. Usually they work in the agricultural field in their respective village and get food for lunch (except rice) and 'Ju' (local drinks) for three times from the owners of the land. At the end of the day's work they get 4 kg of paddy.

Thus from the above discussion, we may note the following:

1. Both the community groups of the tribes are having cultivation as their primary occupation.
2. While choosing the side occupation, the Langia Saora accept the daily labourer work, but the Semsa engages themselves in household industry of bamboo products.
3. In their occupational adaptation of the secondary occupation cultural environement rather than physical environment is influencing factor. The Langia Saoras

are surrounded by caste groups practising a wage labour economy. Inspite of physical resources available, the Langia Saoras have some cultural difficulties in weaving clothes or making bamboo products as an occupational job.

4. But the Semsa is living in a purely tribal area. Among the tribes the practice of wage labour economy is not prominent. Only for cultural reasons the Semsa has accepted weaving of cloths for themselves and making bamboo products as their secondary occupational job.

Notes

Data on the Semsa were collected under the official project: *Socio Cultural adaptation in a Shifting cultivation village* supervised by Dr. (Mrs.) Dipali Danda. The field work was conducted in the year 1979.

Data for Langia Saoras were collected under the official project: *"Shifting Cultivation in India"*, supervised by Dr. S. Bose. The field work was conducted during the year 1977-78.

References

Danda, Dipali, G. (1978), *Among the Dimasa of Assam*. New Delhi, Stertling Publishers (Pvt.) Ldd.

Forde, C. Daryll (1970), *Habitat, Economy and Soceity: A Geographical Introduction to Ethnology*. London: Methuen.

Herskovits, M. J. (1955), *Cultural Anthropology*.

Mason, O.T. (1895), *Origin of Invension: A Study of Industry Among Primitive Peoples*.

Census of India, 1961, 1971.

Part-6

Environmental Perspectives: Multi-disciplinary Approach

24 Environmental Perspectives in Psychology

S. C. Panchbhai

Reviewing the 'long past but a short history' of Psychology, one gets the impression that a good number of its stalwarts have taken two somewhat extreme positions on emphasizing the biogenetic nature of man, and the other placing emphasis on the nature of environment in which he lived. While through the perspective of the former position human nature was seen as universal and having unity, the latter position developed a frame for highlighting its relativity and diversity. Tracing the origin and development of these two positions or views, one can clearly mark the influence of other disciplines on Psychology : the former view greatly influenced by Philosophy, Biology and other natural sciences, and the latter by social sciences like Anthropology, Sociology and Human Geography. However, lest an impression should be created to the contrary, one needs to add here that these positions though apparently poles apart, were in no way contradictory and rather proved complementary for developing a third perspective through which human nature was explained as interaction between the self and the outer world.

Before discussing the different approaches that have been adopted for understanding human nature and behaviour, let us briefly examine the concept of environment and other related concepts which found currency in psychological litrature in course of its development. The two lexical meanings of environment are: (a) the complex of climatic, edaphic, and biotic factors that act upon an organism or an ecological community and ultimately determine its form and survival; (b) the aggregate of social and cultural conditions that influence the life of an individual or community (Webster's Dictionary). These two dictionary meanings have clearly covered two types of environment: the physical/biotic, and social/cultural. The former type may be conceived as purely the objective reality surrounding an individual and community, while the latter may be seen as representing partly objective (as in material culture) and partly subjective (as in abstract culture). What has not been covered by these meanings is that aspect of environment which may be called symbolic and which is of primary importance in understanding human behaviour.

Though the physical objects in one's environment have more or less enduring properties, the way they are perceived by the individuals depend much on the individual's state of mind, needs, cultural meanings, etc. associated with the objects. In other words the physical world is not perceived as a photostat or a carbon copy of the physical reality. It is rather a selected and recongnised subjective version of the reality that makes sense of the perceiver. We generally perceive the objects in the concept of their utility and meaning which decide our behaviour towards them. It is in this sense that the "meanings are primarily a property of behaviour and only secondarily a property of objects" (Saibutani 1961). This explains why the same physical world may present different realities to different people or why similar ecologies may sustain different cultures allowing different types of expressions for satisfying similar biological needs or drives.

In other words, it may be said that only that aspect of physical environment which is perceived by an individual or community constitutes the symbolic environment which largely controls one's behaviour in respect to the objective world. The term 'subjective culture' which Triandis (1972) defines as "a cultural group's characteristic ways of perceiving the man made part of the environment" partly covers this concept. Moreover, as we do not live in the world of immediate sensory impressions and as our effective environment has spatial and temporal extensions (Shibutani, 1961), even beyond the unseen future, an undersanding in our effective/symbolic environment is essential for explaining our behaviour in any given context.

The fact that, the effective environment may differ according to the person, place and time and that it is not less important than the individual under study, came to be realized gradually since the turn of this century. With this realization Psychology as the science of mental life became the science of behaviour in which there was hardly any place for introspective methodology and more important place for observation and experimentation. Freud's Psychoanalysis (though basically an extension of the biogenetic thinking) and Watson's Behaviourism seem to have stimulated a new area of research in which environmental factors received more and more attention. One of the major postulates of the Freudian theory was that in a normal person the ego constantly tries to keep a balance between *Id* (biological drives) and the reality (environment) and that abnormal behaviour is the result of the ego's failure to maintain this balance. Watson's position was that of an environmentalist's which held that the innate/genetic propensities could largely be overridden by learning/environment. Through subsequent developments in Psychology the neo-Freudians took note of the sociocultural reality more seriously than Freud and the radical Behaviourists, more than Watson, reached the extreme end of environmentalism by doing away with the mediating role of the organism as intervening variable between a stimulus and a response.

New Concepts

Many scholars taking a clue from these movements developed new concepts for explaining man-environment interaction. Murray's 'press', Thoma's 'situation', Lewin's 'field', and Dewey and Bentley's 'transactionism' (giving rise to 'feedback' theory) are some of the examples of this new awareness.

Murray's contribution (1938) is of particular relevance in this sphere.He elaborated the concepts of 'press' (environment) and 'need' (drive) through his Thematic Apperception Test (TAT) which is considered a landmark in psychological testing and is widely used even today. He postulated 29 'needs' and 27 'presses' within the analytical frame of his test. Any behaviour according to him was a combination of 'need-press' combination called 'thema' (a single creature-environment interaction).

With the new awareness about the role of environment, it began to be accepted generally "that there is no autonomous life of a person, not even a conceptual life of a person, except in endless reciprocity, give and take, mutual exchange, dyadic communication with his surroundings. And that each individual is endowed with a personal inner world as well as with the objectively observed interacting world in which he is embeded" (Murphy 1968 : 32).This development according to Murphy was the most promising of the multidisciplinary conceptions of personality. Through this development it also became imperative in almost any explanation of behaviour that not only one has to take into account the inner world of the individual and his surrounding outer world but also their interaction in the context of time and space. And, to achieve this aim neither the Behaviourists' environmentalism nor the early evolutionists' instinctivism, but an eclectic approach - sometime combining the both, could provide effective conceptual and methodological tools.

The interactionists' movement received a particular impetus after the fifties when more and more researches with environmental/ecological perspectives appeared in the field of Psychology, Antrhopology and Sociology. There developed a new multidisciplinary 'social systems approach' which emphasized that culture, environment and behaviour are linked in multi-dimensional cause effect bonds and changes in one effect the other (Altman and Chemers 1980). A few more concepts like Barker's 'behaviourial ecology', Clark's 'pertextuality' (person in context) and Hall's 'proxemics' were added to the vocabulary of this new orientation during this phase.

Culture and Personality

It may be mentioned here that the interdisciplinary field of culture and personality or Psychological Anthropology had incorporated this orientation earlier through the influence of neo-Freudian Psychology. It had accepted the suggestion that "personality is the product of the interaction of the biogenetic nature of the human individual ('instinct') and the often incompatible demands of cultural life ('civilization') (Johnson, 1978: 119). During its earlier phase in particular the neo-Freudian model which suited Kroeber's superorganic view of culture proved its handy conceptual tool. Kardiner and Linton's work in this sense is considered 'culture-deterministic' as against Fredian 'biodeterministic', as it emphasized the importance of primary institutions (child rearing practices, etc.) in shaping basic personality which through projective systems developed secondary institutions (religious beliefs, etc.) in a society (see Johnson, 1978). Kluckhohn (1953) giving due importance to ecology, also tried to present a model in which cultures could primarily be understood in terms of their relation to nature: whether they were subjected by or dominating over or part of (equal to) nature.

As Psychology had established itself in Anthropology through the advances in the interdisciplinary field, so had culture in Psychology - developing a new sub-discipline of Cross-cultural Psychology. These developments stimulated more and more interaction among allied disciplines - involving other bio-social sciences, in which ecology, both as a variable of study and as a discipline, had a crucial role to play. Our subsequent discussion will be confined to a few significant studies which illustrate various dimensions of research with this perspective in the field of Psychology.

Psychological studies taking note of the environmental influences on animal or human subjects may broadly be divided into two categories: (1) the studies in comparative or Animal Psychology, and Developmental Psychology, and (2) the studies in Personality and Cross-cultural Psychology. Historically the former preceeded the latter. While in the former category of researches environment only meant physical or at best socio-economic reality, in the latter category it meant also culture. While the former had significant impact of Biology, Primatology and Ethology, the latter received main impetus from the allied social sciences like Anthropology, Sociology, and Human Ecology.

Studies I: Comparative/Developmental

Let us begin with a few brief illustrations that fall under the Comparative and Development Psychology. These researches had a direct bearing of Darwin's evolutionary model in Biology and were, in most cases, directed to resolve nature-nurture controversy. Perhaps the first glimpse of a systematic enquiry in this field was available in *Heredity Genius* of Francis Galton in 1869, just after ten years of Darwin's *Origin of Species*. Though he established the hereditary factor by showing that the relatives of the eminent men were in greater proportion eminant (Vale, 1980), he did not rule out the possibility of family environment in such cases. Herbert Spencer, applying the evolutionary laws of nature to society, introduced the philosophy of 'social Darwinism' to show how society like an organism adjusts itself to change through various stages of disequilibrium and harmony. Subsequently, the new generation of researchers began to emphasize that as a biological man has many non-biological-social, cultural, psychological, characteristics and environments, their influences on him must have to be taken into account for a better understanding of the 'social animal'.

The extreme form of concern for the 'reality exterior to individual' is manifested through the environmetnalism of Behaviourists mentioned ealier. Though the other more balanced views were not less appealing to the contemporary scientific community, Behaviourism had a special appeal as it tried to promise almost a natural science methodology and status for Psychology. The position of this school of thought is perhaps best illustrated by the following oft-quoted passage from Watson (1930 : 104) : "Give me a dozen healthy infants, well-formed and my own specified world to bring them up in and I'll guarantee to take any one at random and train him to become any type of specialist I might select –doctor, lawyer, artist, merchant-chief and yes even beggar-man and thief, regardless of his talents, penchants, tendencies, ambitions, vocations, and race of his ancestors".

Many studies in mental illness, social pathology and Developmental Psychology had predominantly an environmental orientation after the forties. Etiologies of schizophrenia and some other mental disorders, psychopaths and deviants were explained with the help of the organic and environmental theories suggesting that the genetic potentialities could be aggravated by a long contact with a precipitating environment.

The effect of various forms of depriving environment (physical, social, cultural or psychological) on children had also been a major area of interest for Developmental and Educational Psychology for the last four decades. Many experiments showed that deprivation of children due to parental separation, large size of family (related to poverty, bad housing/hygienic conditions, poor educational facilities) resulted in emotional imbalance and intellectual impairment (see Mangan, 1975). The children deprived of maternal care or rose in foster homes/institutions showed sense of insecurity, anxiety and less scholastic achievement in general. All such findings pointed out to the important role that environment played in shaping human personality.

Some parallel studies during this period were also taking similar shapes in animal laboratories. One of the important animal studies that may be mentioned here in some detail was the ten-year long research on rats conducted by the University of California (see Mangan, 1975). Rats controlled for strain, sex, age, etc. were divided into three groups : the rats in the first group kept separated in impoverished environment (isolated cages), those in the second put together in an enriched environment (a big cage having some colourful mazes) and those in the third, in a standard (in-between) environment for about one hundred days. The result showed that compared to the other two groups, the rats in the second group had significant weight gain in the context – maximum in the visual area which had received maximum stimulation. Further experiments proved that it was possible to affect any chosen area of brain under specific conditions and that learning ability could be controlled under these experiments. A few other experiments on emotional and social deprivation with monkeys and fish as subjects also corroborated the expectations that both phsycial and psychological growths are affected adversely by severe isolation and positively by enriched environment.

Studies II: Cross-Cultural

We may now extend our discussion to the second category of environmental researches that relate to the fields of personality and cross-cultural psychology. As mentioned earlier, these studies were greatly influenced, and at times formed part of, culture-personality researches in Anthropology. They represented in a real sense an ecological orientation by which ecology was related to social structure, economy, social character, world-view and culture as a whole.

One can trace the beginning of cross-cultural studies in this area of interest at the turn of this century. River' Torres Straits Expedition in 1901 by showing for the first time that the natives were less prone to the Muller-Lyer illusion and more susceptible to the Horizontal-Vertical illusion, pointed out the influence of ecology on human perception. Subsequent studies in this line also proved that the people reared in more man-made environment (e.g. carpentered, rectangular shaped houses, etc.) were more susceptible to these illusions than those dwelling in more natural environment (e.g., round houses, etc.). Similar experiments on the plains-dwellers and the tree-dwellers also pointed to the fact that human perception cannot be understood merely as a biological phenomenon but also have some ecological/environmental component.

Perhaps the most significant and systematic contributions in this area have come from Whitings (Whiting and Whiting, 1975) and Berry (1979) and their colleagues. The Whiting model explains the interrelatedness of different factors thus : the environment (ecology) and history (migration/settlement) of a people interact with each other to determine their maintenance system (subsistence pattern, etc) which in turn influences the child-rearing practices of that population; these practices largely mould the infant's innate needs/drives which result in the learned behaviour/values of the adults and consequently, give rise to the 'projective-expressive system' (religion, art, etc.) of a community. The Whiting model also relates (with higher probability) the 'sociable-intimate' behaviour of children to nuclear families, loose residence rules, low event husband-wife aggression, and close father-child relation suggesting thereby that the opposite factors are correlated with the 'authoritarian-aggressive' type of behaviours. Some other researches have also tried to show that socio economic background is related to social character which develops certain kind of ideology and values, and the latter in turn sustain/modify the social character which again interacts with the socio-economic milieu.

Berry, employing some psychological tests among many technically and ecologically different communities, showed how some psychological faculties got adapted to the needs of ecology, culture and biology. The following chart taken from one of his latest works (Berry, 1979) is self-explanatory.

Antecedent variables to psychological differentiation: ecological, cultural and biological adaptations.

	Prediction of psychological differentiation	
	High	*Low*
Ecological adaptations	Hunting, gathering	Agriculture
Subsistence pattern	Nomadic	Sedentary
Settlement pattern	Low	High
Population density		
Cultural adaptations		
Role diversity	Low	High
Stratification	Low	High
Socialization emphasis	Assertion	Compliance
Biological adaptations		
Protein intake	High	Low
Hormone balance	Balanced	Imbalanced
Genetic selection	Fo differentiation	Against differentiation

Along with some other psychological tools, he administered the 'embeded figure' test to see which of his subjects were 'field-dependent' and which 'field-independent'. He related this faculty of psychological differentiation to their 'cognitive style'. He found that the 'embedded figures' are generally more easily located (perceived) by the nomadic hunting/gathering communities which have less stratified roles, assertion rather than compliance in socialization, high protein intake, etc (see chart). Thus such communities, he concluded, were 'field-independent'. This phenomenon he explained primarily in term of adjustment to ecology. In the case of sedentary agricultural societies, he felt, there was no compulsion of ecology to develop this faculty. He also showed that this faculty is developed to a high degree by acculturation through education, wage-employement and urbanization.

Though Berry is not explicit on this point, his generalizations about acculturation seem to be applicable only in the case of communities whose recent past was nomadic (with hunting/ gathering economy) but which are at present acculturated. It cannot be said why, when sedentary peasant communities are also acculturated, the acculturating agents (education, etc.) in their case are not effective in developing this faculty in them. We are not definite whether apart from ecology; ethnicity or culture also could have a role to play. Some more elaborate research design with controlled variables if applied on a single ethnic group having diffeent segments at different stages of acculturation may perhaps give a better explanation to such question.

References

Altman, I and M.M. Chemers (1980), Cultural Aspects of Environment-behaviour Relationships. In H.C. Triandis and R.W. Brislin (Eds.) *Handbook of Cross-cultural Psychology – Social Psychology,* Vol. 5. London: Allyn and Bacon Inc. pp. 335-393.

Berry, J.W. (1979), Culture and Congnitive Style. In A.J. Marsella et al (Eds) *Perspectives on Cross-cultural Psychology.* New York : Academic Press. Pp.117-135.

Johnson, A.W. (1978), *Quantification in Cultural Anthropology – An Introduction to Research Design.* California: Stanford University Press.

Kluckhohn, F.R. (1953), Dominant and Variant Value Orientations. In C. Kluckhohn et al. (Eds) *Personality in Nature, Society and Culture.* New York: Knopt.

Mangan, G.L. (Ed.) (1975), *Psychological Deprivation in Childhood.* New York: John Wiley & Sons.

Murphy, G. (1968), Psychological Views of Personality and Contiributions to its Study. In E. Norbeck et al (Eds) *The study of Personality – An Interdisciplinary Appraisal.* New York : Holt, Rinehart & Winston, Inc.

Murray, H.A. (1938), *Explorations in Personality.* New York : Oxford University Press.

Shibustani, T. (1961), *Society and Personality – An Interactionist Approach to Social Psychology.* N.J.: Prentice Hall Inc.

Triandis, H.C. (1972), *The Analysis of Subjetive Culture.* New York: Wiley.

Vale, J.R. (1980), *Genes Environment and Behaviour – An Interactionist Approach.* New York: Harper & Row, Publishers.

Watson, J.B. (1930), *Behaviourism.* Chicago: University of Chicago Press.

Whiting, B. & J.W.M. Whiting (1975), *Children of Six Cultures: A Psycho-cultural Analysis.* Cambridge Mass: Harvard University Press.

25 The Aspect of the Museum in Environmental Prespective

T. K. GHOSH

Museum is a storehouse of articles produced by man in his environment. Environment of man forces him to improve himself certain need necessitated objects. Some of them may be to satisfy his basic wants, e.g., utensils to cook his meals, clothes for protection against the vagaries of nature etc. Others may arise out of his desire to satisfy his aesthetic tastes e.g., objects of body decoration etc. A collection of all these objects to preserve man's culture that was and that is – this is the basic function of an Anthropological Museum. For man's wants and desires are under a continuous process of change. New environmental developments give rise to new wants and desires. This may result in a gross revolution of all the material objects under use by him or a modification of artifacts already in use with him to give effect to the changes circumventing him.

What an Anthropological Museum proposes to display is man in his environment. His capacity to withstand heat, cold, noise, sound, rain, storm, violence, other vagaries of nature and natural growth is materialized in the matter that he produces or devices to counter the effect of their several impacts. These are amply displayed in his house types, the clothes he wears, the shades he implements, the weaponry he improvises to make himself secure against dangers and perils that may befall him otherwise. To preserve these developmental activities and their outputs is the object of museums.

Coming to modern times, a museum is a collection joint to expose the dangers and hazards of modern developments also. Modern day problems include transport explosion, communication explosion, population explosion, development explosion, industries explosion, etc. All these severally have their effects and impacts on human lives in their respective capacities. These could well be illustrated and meaning fully presented in a museum for man's furtherance and future strategy.

Some of these items e.g., pollution, must necessarily be ingrained in man so as to educate him sufficiently to counter its effect, e.g., against deadly gases which adversely affect man and his habitat. The various types of the problems will have to be effectively displayed, so that human development, growth and sustenance or subsistence may attain a scientific model. Such imparting of knowledge to the public is only possible through a well kept, well devised, well organized and well informed museum which can thus educate so that the ecological balance may not be so disturbed as to reproduce disastrous consequences, but may keep a certain amount of equilibrium towards progress. All these, will, however, have to be shown in their regional variations, so that a systematic accommodation can be effected and afforded.

A physical Anthropological display of man's past will also have to be entailed in a presentation of plaster casts. In such a display, a sequence will have to be followed. This sequence should be based on the evolutionary ladder. Reconstructed skulls could also be placed in this sequence. But they must be done with justification. Variations must also be shown and this will impart more information. This representation is necessary for educating man about his environmental past and his inevitable future. That will make possible for him to realize the importance of being what he is, which is essential for his reproductive capacity.

The specimens collected and displayed in a museum, must first be located to the culture context. Identification follows and this includes the functional value of the objects. This functional value should not only be related to the past, but also in the present context, and its feasibility in the future development of the culture, taking into account the accumulation of change, how best it could be suited to it or can be re-oriented. Sometimes, quite functional objects may be discarded in the process of or to accommodate change, just for the sake of change, without realizing the adverse consequences that may follow. The job of the museum should be to highlight the effective functional value, taking into account also the possibilities of innovation, should that be required in the changed circumstances, in the context of the change process, rather than discard it altogether just for the sake of change and replace it by something less functional in the context of the culture and environment. The function of the Museum should be to present to the public in its proper perspective the benefits of retention of cultural objects and values which are likely to be lost in the process of change leading to blind imitation. Preservation of a culture is a must, for the benefit of manking, so that the future build up may be based on what there is already which had been developed, taking into account the environmental factor. For instance, wooden houses are aptly suited for cold regions rather than stone or brick buildings, which seem to have become the fashion of the day in certain areas, without taking into account the adverse effects of them. The motive here should be to highlight the benefits of wooden structure, which man had devised taking the environment into question. Here, what could be done is to present how best wooden houses could be innovated to suit the changing conditions, requirements and tastes, and live up to the demands of time. Similarly, the benefits of the respective food habits, garments etc. in respective environments should be dealt into at length to highlight their feasibility in the respective areas and climate. Tradition should not be lost to modernity. Tradition can even be preserved in or suited to modern conditions. Handicrafts, folk arts etc. can yet be re-oriented to survive under and be suited to modernity. Herein lies the importance of museums, wherein they could be preserved, properly focused and preserved against decay. This holds true even of household articles and decorative pieces and every aspect of human culture and development. These can easily be blended to suit modern developments rather than totally be forgotten or discarded. And, many may be the aspects of old, which, if yet practised, may result in prosperity in the climate concerned and if discarded may spell doom. One has to dwell into the fact, how much and to what extent modern development may prove to be a boon in any particular environment and to what extent preservation of the tradition may prove to be a blessing rather than blind imitation or development which may produce negative effects.

In bringing home to the general public the impact of such a museum display, the utility value and purpose of the specimens in question, in context of the environment concerned, will have to be expressed through an analytical display of the objects, so that the mode and nature of any particular community in a particular ecological set-up could be represented with a clear conception. To this end, even sketches could serve the purpose and these can as well enhance, along with the display, the presentation which they can supplement. An aesthetic display could make any point all the more attractive and effective. In depicting any theme, and realizing the objective, integration of culture in the region should be stressed in relation to itself and its surrounding and to the wider concept of the country, rather than the symbiotic relationship.

Objects collected in the field are the material symbols in the cultural life of the people. Their implications will have to be known to save it from being a curious object. Objected, such as these arise curiosity as to who prepares, how, the ceremonial aspect, material exchange (barter system or monetary payment), symbiotic relationship in relationship to objects, also the entire transaction process, functional value, thing of manufacture what it consists of there must all be recorded for completing the picture.

Utility, value and the purpose will have to be expressed through the objects, so that the mode and nature of the community in question could be displayed through the objects and one could visualize a clear conception. Furthermore, the realism of the object must be presented.

Cultural artifacts also tend to depict the degree of progress, a culture to which they belong has made. They also tend to display the type of environment in which they have been fostered. Hence, a study of the nature of the environment and the effects it produces own schemes of development which can increase the tempo of development with effective results in the specified climate. New discoveries and inventions can be built upon and devised from a minute study of these. We also owe a duty to posterity; and from such a preservation and presentation, posterity will be well versed in their tradition and beliefs nurtured in a particular environment or surrounding and accordingly reflect their sentiments and feelings for any future development which would and could be perfectly congenial to the environment concerned, rather than prove to be counter productive, due to a misadventure in a mistaken surrounding.

Further more, such display would also broaden the outlook of the viewer and tend to increase his knowledge of man and his environment. This would inculcate an amount of tolerance and respect for man and his output. In different environments man tend to vary in order to satisfy the needs or demands of his surrounding environment and thus is produced the variety. Yet the basic unity of man is thereby amply displayed, for certain things are common to man even though the environment differs. Each culture is relative to its surrounding and man has to lean to respect each and every one, so that he may also, in his turn, be respected in his own peculiar and particular set up. This is also one of the many aspects of Museum display when it focuses the objects in their environmental perspectives.

Coming to know of certain common aspects would procreate in us a feeling of fraternity. This broadened outlook would enable us to know the differences or the variance, if it can profitably be fitted or accommodated in the culture contact, as to enhance or improve it. It would then educate us the fact that we have to adjust differently in different environments and this results in variations.

Our general aim is to bring to light the complex cultures that surround us so that a general appreciation follows. This propagation and preservation is required so as to enable a continuity of any culture and enrichment of others. This would also help break the messmaric spell of blind imitation. Environment produces the necessities to meet the exigencies in the environment concerned and blind imitation may bring in its wake more harm than good. A Museum can best portray the sound logic of any environment biased and based cultural development, which conforms judiciously to the environment pattern.

For this reason, in any effective materialization of environmental anthropology, recourse has to be taken to anthropological museums and their effective presentation. For, in here one can obtain all at one place, and at a glance, a systematic presentation. A comparative analysis is available to the public and this will enable the viewer to formulate and evolve a definite strategy for their own benefit. Reconciliation can be made in here, from a study of what we have already, our developing need in the environment concerned and the technique to be adopted to realize our purpose.

In this context, the creative force must not be measured against blind innovation or inventiveness, but we must find out the most suitable and effective formulae by fusing tradition with invention and innovation for realizing our purpose. Museums can thus act as propaganda centers and enthuse as exploring spirit.

26 Ethnographic Museum in Environmental Framework

A. K. Das

The ethnographic materials of a museum are not a collection of disparate parts of a given culture. In fact the cultural materials as a whole are supposed to reveal the particular eco-cultural situation in which an ethnic group's life is lived. Researches conducted by many ethnographers have shown that through particular aspects of material culture or technology one can look deep into a society, its behaviour, economic order, and even the religious norms. Thus, the ethnographic materials when presented as exhibits in a museum gallery should convey certain amount of information relating to the socio-cultural background. Unfortunately, as has been frequently noticed, the cultural materials as soon as they find place in a museum gallery, tend to loose their very character and significance.

A collection of objects of ethnographic importance are normally organized under a conventional display-system to represent a particular facet of a culture. In such a system it is desirable that the objects collectively depict a general picture of the environment to which they were once intimately connected. To conceive and visualize a system of this nature one has to overcome a number of technical limitations such as the spatial limitation for organisation of the showcases or an improvised gallery.

In many ethnographic museums, the materials on display give some idea about the nature and function of the objects without any environmental context. There is considerable difference in viewing an object in its natural setting on one hand and the artificial environment of the gallery on the other. The spatial limitation of the showcase is an obstacle in environmental approach in presenting ethnographic materials. Sometimes the exhibit design is found to be unusually elaborated which overshadows the objects on display.

Breaking the Spatial Limitations

The primary objective of an ethnographical display is to communicate to the visitors the complete story of a group of people. The museum not only endeavours to give an idea about social environment of the people but also their physical environment which is responsible for the shaping and reshaping of the culture. Some of the ethnographer-designers have experimented in the past to recreate a part of the physical environment within the spatial limitation of the showcase (diorama). This system appears to be effective for a limited period and purpose. There is, however, every chance for it to be considered as a stereotyped presentation with the passage of time. As an example one may conveniently refer to the Anthropological Gallery of the Indian Museum, Calcutta, in this context. In contrast to the above, the feasibility of breaking the showcase and placing the object directly before the visitors in a natural environment has been experimented in India very recently[2].

In most cases it is not feasible to project the complete story of the man in a single exhibit-design. This story is diverse and multi-faceted, and evens a modest projection requiring skill and money. This is not possible for the ethnographical museums which are normally small in size and regional in nature. We may take here the example of the museums of the various tribal research institutes or the Zonal Anthropological Museum (ZAM) of the Anthropological Survey of India. As a matter of fact all these museums either portray the life and culture of the small ethnic groups (tribes) or peasant communities of a particular region.

Micro Themes

The story of these small communities is the story of the mankind in a nutshell. His birth, stages of his growth, his struggle for existence, his customs and aesthetics, his world view, his decadence and death, are the various stages in the chain of human life cycle. Visualization of this whole gamut of life processes inside the four walls of the museum gallery is a great challenge to the modern museum technique. The three dimensional museum materials are only keys to the story - they serve as connecting link. The gap in the story is generally filled up by supplementary audio-visual aids. Many of our smaller regional museums are not in a position to install the modern audio-visual equipment due either to lack of funds or to inadequate space or manpower. The method, which seems feasible for the smaller museums, has been experimented in India in recent years. It is a technique of dividing the whole story into several segments and turning them into a number of micro-themes. In fact it is easier to go into details in such a micro-theme representation particularly in ethnographic museum.

One of the finest examples of a micro-theme display designed by a non-anthropologist[3] and organized by the Crafts Museum in 1978 in their newly constructed building in the Pragati Maidan, New Delhi, may be referred to in this context. This particular exhibition, entitled *Aidti*, has been committed to the child life and their immediate world as seen by them. The entire materials have been collected with great care and selection from the rural and tribal areas. The designer has given due thought to the problem of time and space. It is noteworthy that the required balance between the time and the space has successfully been attained. The display begins with the birth of a child depicted symbolically without any touch of eroticism.

The story gradually proceeds through various stages as the child grows till he attains the age for adventure into the world which lies outside his home. I do not visualise any better example of mico-theme than *Aditi*. It covers the first five years of the total span of a man's life. A child is born, he/she sucks his/her mother's breast, he/she plays, eats, drinks, sleeps, and reacts to the immediate environment with his/her own fantasy. Thus he/she is subjected to early socialization. This is the gist of the theme woven through a very short time span, and within the spatial limitation of a small village hamlet. Here the whole exhibit design has been moulded through the time-span dimension. With the integration of these two vital factors in the display formulations, the designer got ample scope for intensive coverage of minute details.

Environmental Approach

One of the significant points of this particular exposition is the re-creation of the original environmental background. The designer has achieved a considerable amount of success, probably, due to his long and intimate association with the life of the peasantry. As soon as the visitor enters the gallery through broad entrance - he suddenly encounters an atmosphere of rural environment and folk-life.The immediate impression is created by the Madhubani paintings reproduced in cardboard cut-out. All the exhibits along with other corollary items are combined together to reproduce the folk life in its totality. Modern display equipment and the conventional visual media have entirely been replaced by the traditional materials. Even the background colour, floor-covering etc. which are normally overlooked in museum display, have given a careful rustic touch. On the whole the total effect of this exhibit design is an antithesis of the modern audio-visual technique.

In this context another novel experiment in the recreation of environment may be cited. The organisation and development of the "village-complex" under the auspices of the Crafts Museum, New Delhi, has opened a new vista for the ethnographic museums[2]. The main feature of this open air display lies in breaking the spatial limitation of the gallery in general and showcases in particular. The entire display had been envisioned through the perspective of environment, which rendered the whole exposition free, open and without any artificial barrier. As a result the exhibit design becomes self-explanatory and the audio-visual aids non-functional. The display equipment is natural and purely traditional. A mud wall, a thatched roof, bamboo-mattings, wooden-pillars, a stone-platform, etc. have carefully been used to achieve the required balance between the objects on display and the environmental condition.

This is the first successful open-air display in India. It is, however, reproduced in a miniature scale. A far bigger project of open-air exposition, which will not only cover the habitation pattern but also the economic activities and religion of the tribes and peasants, has been taken up by the Government[4].

Composite Display System

The display of the ethnographical materials in smaller regional museum in a more effective way has been experimented by the Anthropological Survey of India since 1976. This new method may be called as "composite display system", which is a combination of the environmental and the conventional method of presentation.

This system has to be evolved in view of functional importance of certain categories of ethnographic materials. It is obviously not possible to render a meaningful display for all types of ethnographic objects in an environmental system. Manikins, dioramas and other visual media have an equal share in this integrated approach. Objects connected with habitation pattern, minor economic activities and sacred complexes may be successfully exhibited in an environmental unit. Smaller and more delicate objects such as items of dress and ornaments, apparels, objects of art etc. naturally require more secure condition while on display. And hence its display in conventional showcase or display panels is inevitable. Along with these a few open display units may also be devised for these categories of objects which might not be possible to accommodate inside the showcases. The Central Museum of Anthropology, Anthropological Survey of India, Calcutta, opened recently, has combined all these systems together in an effort to experiment effectiveness of the multi-media exhibit design for ethnographical materials[5].

Summary

It is an established fact that a given ethnographical collection has an intimate connection with a given natural setting. This setting is entirely different from the artificial environment of a museum gallery. The difference between the original environment and the new environment of the gallery sometimes leads to the misinterpretation of facts. And hence it has been established that at least a part of the natural setting is to be recreated in a gallery of ethnographic objects. The recreation of the environment should be strictly conditioned as per the normal requirement of conservation and security measures of the museum concerned. The open-air environmental display can be maintained by a museum of considerable standing having huge funds, substantial manpower and other resources. The security obviously poses a big problem for this type of display. Naturally there must be constant guard against the vandalism - which is very common and acute in some parts of our country. And then there also remains a constant threat of fire-hazzard and natural calamities. On the whole the open air display is highly expensive in so far as the regular maintenance is concerned.

The composite display system, on the other hand is more feasible for smaller regional or state level museums. It is comparatively less expensive and the recurring expenditure is minimal and normally does not go beyond the modest annual budget of average museum. And hence, this system should earn more appreciation from the ethnographic museums.

Notes & References

1. Majumdar, D.N., and Madan, T. N. (1956), *An Introduction to Social Anthropology*. Lucknow: Asia Publishing House.
2. All India Handicrafts Board, New Delhi 1977. Village Complex (Brochure)
3. Shri Rahiv Sethi, A Free Lance Designer of Delhi.
4. Anthropological Survey of India, Calcutta 1977. Plan outline of the National Museum of Man.
5. Anthropological Survey of India, Calcutta 1981. Central Museum of Anthropology (Brochure).

27 Environment, Symbols and Performing Arts: A Case Study of Jharkhand Cultural Region

Pashupati Prasad Mahato

"Enviroment" in its specialized usage, holds the phrase 'environmental determinism', which expresses the position that the natural environment of a culture not only sets the cultural stage but also determines the action that takes place on this stage. Natural setting of life and social setting of life are the interaction between ways of life of a people and the scene in which these ways are brought into being and are continued from generation to generation. Natural setting of human existence comprises the physical feature of the region inhabited by people, its natural resources actually or potentially available to the inhabitants, its climate, altitude and other geographical features to which they have adapted themselves. Culture includes the material objects of human manufacture, technique, social orientation, world view, performing arts etc. which are the conditioning factors underlying human interaction. Environment is the aggregate of all the external condition and influence affecting the life and development of an organism. A student of culture may be strongly against environmental determinism, because many forces play on in any culture. But here in my paper environment is definitely determinism but never to be deterministic.

The environment provides men with the raw stuff of experience and the habitat is an integral and constant element in this environment, must thus never be lost sight of. The possible variation is greater in art or religion or in agriculture etc. The symbolism of decorative art may draw on the habitat, the gods are customarily related in someways to the forces of nature, stories about animals rarely refer to creatures found outside the habitat of the tellers. It may be analogous, it may influence natural settings. All groups who have built irrigation system have changed the physical structure of their habitat thus extending its potentialities. Thus it can be said, "The more adequate the technology of a people, the less direct will be the demands made by the habitat on them" (Harskovits 1958).

The anthropological contribution to the understanding of symbolism is unique. The anthropological approach to understand symbolism is comparative, observationalist, functionalist, relatively neutralist. It links the occurrence and interpretations of symbolism to social structure and social events in specific conditions. The anthropologists observed what symbols people actually use, what they have said about these things, the situation in which the symbols emerge and the reaction to them.They also equip themselves to explain the meanings of symbolism in the cultures they have studied. This helps them to understand the processes of social life.

The anthropological approach provides a systematic description and analysis of such a symbolic act in its verbal, non-verbal communication in the context of social matrix of kinship, modes of bodily decoration, authority and power in secular and sacred terms. Some of the anthropologists like Firth (1973), finds in working out their position on symbolism a means of examining and stating, perhaps resolving some of their individual views about the nature and determinants of human social relationships and activities. According to Firth (Op.cit.) a symbol is a device for enabling us to make abstraction" but "with the same end in view - a symbol has instrumental value", as instrument of expression, communication, knowledge and control. The most obvious field of symbolic study was primitive art by Franz Boas (1927) and decorative symbolism of Arapaho by Kroeber (1901). The great success of anthropologists is in breaching the wall of secrecy and to judge from the internal evidence of classic studies like Malinowsky's Argonants of the Western pacific (1922) and Evans-Prichard Witch-craft, orcles and Magic among Azande (1937). Durkheim was concerned primarily with the symbolism of groups, as an abstract excerise of interpretation; Freud was concerned primarily with symbolism of individuals. Radcliffe-Brown (1922) discussed questions about processes of symbolic thought of Andamanese myths in terms of expression of interest and relationships of importance to the society.

Ritual in its cultural context is a pattern of symbols. It recalls and present in symbol, form the underlying order that is supposed to guide the members of the community in their social activities. Tikopia ritual acts as symbols for social order according to Firth. The Nuer ideas, as considered by Evans-Prichard are a relation of spirit to person.

Performance of ritual or songs and dance are symbolic mode of communication of saying something. Levi-Strauss, who has contributed much to our understanding of meta-linguistics mode of communication, constantly refers to the structural similarity between myth and music. Here Levi-Strauss is simply making the point that the senders and receivers of messages which are contained in cultural communication are very often the same people. The music as a whole is divided into 'movement' which is related to each other by aesthetic rather than manifest association. Theme elements from one movement are likely to appear in direct or transpired form in another. For musically sensitive listener, each phrase, each movement, and the symphony as a whole, form a system of inter-connected unities. The whole performance may take an hour but the message is transmitted as if everything happened simultaneously (Leach - 1976).

With the above background of 'Environment' and symbols, I shall try to understand the most integrative ritual of *Gajan* and connected performing art *Chow* of Purulia in West Bengal and Mayurbhanja in Orissa. The whole area may be termed as Jharkhand cultural region. The field study was carried out in village Murguma in 1973, 1975 and in Purulia and in village Chitorda in Mayurbhanja, Orissa in 1976, 1977 and 1979. In both the villages tribes like Mura (Munda), Bhumij and Kurmi-Mahatos are numerically dominant. Both the villages are multi-ethnic.

Chow is the ritual dance of Siva-Gajan and it continues to be performed from Chaitra Sanskanti to Rohini, the most auspicious day for the agriculturists. On that day, the peasants prefer sowing of seedlings. Every village has got a fixed date for the performance of Siva-Gajan in the Jharkhand cultural region. Dr. Ashutosh Bhattacharya assessed that "Chhow" dance is the ritual dance of the 'Sun-God'; Sun-God may be synonymous to Swijahi-Puja or Dharam diety which is the supreme God of the Mahatos, Bhumij, Oraons, Mundas and Santhals of Jharkhand. It is totally different from the God Siva, Gajan and Chow is only related with Siva God. On the other hand Dharam puja or worship of Dharam diety is associated with the social structure of the different ethnic groups of the region (Mahato, 1981). The clan and lineage members of a particular ethnic group only participate in the feast.

While giving the detail ethnographic account of chow dance, Mahato (op. cit) observed that chow dance consists of six folk dance forms of the region namely Dhanr Nach, Natua Nach, Jawa or Karam Nach, Majhi Nach, Kirtan Nach, Nachni Nach with perfect blending of regional tune 'Jhumur' with Bhadria rong with musical accompanyment of Dhol, Dumsa and Sahnai.

The major ethnic groups namely Kurmi-Mahato, Bhumij, Bouri, Dom, Hari, Rajowar, Deswali, Turi, Ghasi, Munda, Santhals, Bathudi, Bhuiya of the region participate in the chow dance. They are sons of the soil. No high castes or class people of the region participate in the dance. All the performing artists of the region, in the light of stratification of Jati-varna model are lower castes. But they are born and brought up in such an ecological and cultural background that they developed a peculiar tune of their own which is known as Jhumur. The Jhumur tune along with chow dance and other cultural markers with tonal quality and dance quality represent the collective wisdom and collective excellence of the creativity of the entire people of the region.

The Gajan festival rituals signify some of their outward activities like dandi Nach of the Bhogtas or devotees. Symbolically according to them pale is phallic and Dandi represent the phallic symbol. The Laya or priest also dances with them with Kamana-Ghat or pitches of desire. Carrying pat or patri or a flat wooden piece with nails signify a woman, pouring of water on the head of the Patri locally known as seem-jal. Symbolically means water discharge from the penis, while moving door to door with patri the women folk, mostly wives of the devotees collect the water and drink it for early conceivement. Some of the members of village Murguma and Chitore were of the opinion that Danda is symbolized here as Lord Siva and Patri or Pat as mother goddess of fertility. The performances of Niva-Pat is Agun-Pat or Manda-pat (walking over fire) and Bhogta-Gura (tied in a rope two iron hooks penetrated on the shoulder's skin of devotee), are associated with controlling of desire of sex and discharge.

As soon as Danda Nach or Gajan Nach is over in Chiterda in Mayurbhanja and Murguma in Purulia, the author founds that the rythemic furry of chow dance started. The symbol or gaits locally known as Bhaba of this performing art are taken from man-nature man to man and production relationship. The performing artists have already in their mind the regional folk tune Jhumur. Ethnomusicologist Binapani Mahanta and Girish Mahanta (1978) said Jharkhand may be termed as Jhumur Desh or the country of Jhumur.

The structural relation of Chow dance may be classified as follows (Mahato, 1981).

(a) The daily routine of the work and play of the Jharkhand boys.

(b) Casual work done physically by them.

(c) Their material craft.

(d) Movement of the animals, birds and snakes.

Purulia Chow is the mask dance based on Puranik stories or stories from Epics. For all the epic heroes, Gods and Demons male or female there are fixed masks with costumes. The permanent Bhab of Bir-rash (mood of warriors), Lasya (mood of sex appeal) and Tandava (mood of destruction) are fixed in the mask. In Purulia only male dancers participate. But in Mayurbhanja Chow has got no mask. Their facial Bhab or mood is clearly seen in relation to Birrash, Tandava or Lasya mood. Every story of the dance has got a Chhak or structure and every chhak consists of Deg or stepping and Chal or Chali or movement. According to Padmshri Gambir Singh Mura, the Chhak is the Chow dance. In between the frequent movement there is Ura-Malat or keeping the balance of the body, for the performance of Ulfa or vault. The knee bending or Hatu-Gara or Torso-movement they have taken from snake without moving the legs. The Bahi-Malka or Bhuja-Hilla or the movement of the muscles of the hand and Buk-Hilla or Chati-Malka, the movement of the muscles of the breast takes place. They have taken it from peacock dance. Eri-Ghura or toe movement is necessary for the rapid jumping, this gait the dancers have taken from deer.

While staging the fight, the strategies of buffalo and tiger are taken in very well manner. The monkey movement in Chow is very common. The 'Bhanj-utta' is the gait to lift the heavy material from the earth. So while lifting bow and arrow or Gada (a metal weapon), the body movement here blended in Chow. The buffallos fight and their itching of soil is well reflected in the dance specially in the Ganeser Danta Bhanga Pala or drama by the epic hero Parasuram.

In the Chow dance, the dancers the musicians and the audience are from the same cultural background sometimes same ethnic group. Without understanding their ecological setting and cultural participation Chow symbolism will be just abstract.

After the dance was over, I often asked them, after a few days of the festival, about the present context of the dance and different Chhak or drama of the dance. And it was observed that some people though do not yet understand the total magnitude of modern days political participation and political fight, they always compare with the episode of Mahiravan Badh or killing of demon Mahiravan by God Ramchandra or killing of Abhi-Mannyu by Saptarathi or seven warrior etc. with present national, regional or even village level violence and politics.

References

Firth, Raymond (1973), *Symbols, Public and Private,* George Allen and Unwin Ltd. London

Leach Edmund (1976), *Culture and Communication*.Cambridge University, London.

Mahato, P.P. (1981), The Continuum of a Performing Art form of Jharkhand Region, Chho dance of Purulia. *Folklore,* March, Vol. 22, No. 3.

28 Palaeo-environments of Sivaliks and Prospects of Finding Plio-pleistocene Hominids

A. R. Sankhyan

Sivalik hills of the Indian sub-continent have since been known for very rich fossil assemblages of vertebrate fauna, and especially drawn world wide attention for the fossil remains of the earliest hominoid ancestors of man and apes. The Sivaliks of Potwar region of Pakistan (Pilbeam et al. 1977 a & b 1980), Ramnagar (J&K) and Haritalyanagar (H.P.) (Chopra 1978) and recently Nainital in Uttar Pradesh (Sahni, *et. al.* 1980) have yielded the bulk of hominoid fossils from Indian sub-continent. The Sivalik hominoids are now well recognized by the taxa- *Dryopithecus sivapithecus, Ramapithecus, Gigantopithecus* and *Pliopithecus* and demonstrate that the Sivaliks had been a major center for the adaptive radiation of the Mio-pliocene primates during Chinji-Nagri times about 13 to 8 million years ago.

Among the known hominoid fossil taxa from Sivaliks, Africa, Europe and recently, from Turkey (Andrews and Tobien, 1977), Ramapithecus, is most likely the earliest hominoid candidate for human ancestry and ranges in time from about 15 Myr in Turkey and 14 Myr in Africa to 13-8.5 Myr in Indian sub-continent. Recently Greenfield (1979) has however, considered the entire Ramapithecus fossils to be included under four species of genus Sivapithecus, of which three species, *S. indicus, S. Sivalensis* and *S. brevirostris* represent the Asian, and *S. africanus* the African Ramapithecine material.

Accordingly, the adaptive syndrome for the evolution of Pleistocene bipedal African hominid *Australopithecus* which is known to have eventually evolved to *Homo* in Africanl ands lies in the species of *Sivapithecus*. The hominid Sivapithecines (or Ramapithecines) beyond 8 Myr as well as *Australopithecus* and *Homo* are not so known from the Sivalik rocks, and thereby represent the great palaeoanthropological hiatus commonly known as the "Missing Link". Besides these, the physical relics of the Quaternary Man (known from numerous stone tool kits) are also not known from Indian sub-continent. All this has greatly baffled the students of human evolution and led to various conjectures on the fate of the Sivalik hominoids during Plio-plestocene and the Quaternary tool making man in Indian sub-continent. It is often believed that the hominoid/hominids migrated or became extinct or were replaced by the cerecopithecoid monkeys during plio-pleistocene in the sub-Himalayas. It is also suggested that perhaps conditions were not favourable for the preservation of hominoid/hominid fossils in the Sivaliks during plio-pleistocene.

In view of much confusion and differences of opinions on the issue of "Missing link" in India a critical re-appraisal of the various view points is desired. As such, a reconstruction of the broad spectrum of the palaeo-environments during the sedimentation of the Sivalik series is attempted in order to evaluate the various hypothesis and prospects for future palaeoanthropologlical studies in the Sivalik hills.

Fossil fauna are great markers of the geological time and environments of the ancient times and a change in fauna denotes temporal and environmental change. The fossil faunal successions therefore, indicate palaeo-ecological, palaeo-geographical and palaeo-climatic variation at various time periods. The rich vertibrate fossil assemblages of the Sivaliks may be usefully employed for understanding palaeoenvironments during the sedimentation of these hills.

The Sivaliks rocks have been deposited during a vast span of about 14 million years between middle Miocene to middle Pleistocene. These rocks are grouped under three divisions and seven major formations or stages (Pilgrim, 1913) viz., (i) Lower

Sivaliks (Kamlial and Chinji Formation), (ii) Middle Sivaliks (Nagri and Dhok Pathan Formation) and (iii) Upper Sivaliks (Tatrot, Pinjor and Boulder conglomerate Formation). The Lower Sivalik rocks were formed during middle to upper Miocene (about 14-12 Myr) and the Middle Sivaliks during late Miocene to Middle Pliocene (about 12-4 Myr), whereas, Upper Sivaliks deposited in late Pliocene to middle Pleistocene (about 4-1 Myr.) times.

Fossil fauna from the Lower Sivaliks are more readily recovered from the Chinji Formation which is well exposed in the Potwar, Ramanagar (J&K) and to some extent in the Nainital (U.P.) areas. The lower Sivalik vertebrates are characterized by very primitive forms of mammal with the abundance of carnivores (*Dissopsalis, Amphicyon, Sansanosmilus, Vishuictis, Vishnufelis, Hyaeneluros, Sivalictis martes, Eomellvora, Crocuta* etc.) anthrocotheres (*Anthracotherium*), large-sized tragulids (*Dorcatherium* and *Dorcabuna*), very primitive suids (*Listriodon, Palaeochoerus, Condhyus, Propotamochoers,* Tetraconodon etc.) primitive proboscideans (*Deinotherium*), graffids (*Giraffokeryx*) and rhinocerotids (*Gaindatherium, Chillotherium* and *Aceratherium*). Bovids are few in number and only very primitive types of *Gazella* and *Tragocerus* are present. Hominoid Primates are recovered in large number like Dryopithecus, Bivapithecus and Ramapithecus. Reptilian (*Crocodylus* and *Trionyx*) and fish fauna are in abundance. The preponderance of forest-loving vertebrates speaks of very densely forested biotype with warm and humid climate and low relief like that of the tropical rain forests. Tattersall (1969) suggested a similar palaeoecology and Nandi (1975), on the basis of microflora, suggested that tropical to sub-tropical humid climate existed during the sedimentation of the Lower Sivaliks.

Middle Sivalik vertebrates especially the mammals are considerably different and more evolved than that of the underlying Chinjis; they however, also differ in frequency of certain types and addition of new forms within the two stages of the Middle Sivaliks. The Nagri formation has yielded a great bulk of the mammalian fauna which constitute both primitive and evolved types with the prepnderance of new carnivores

(*Sivanasua, Sivaonyx, Enhydriodon, Viverra, Crocuta, Lycyaena, Ictitherium, Megantereon, Vinayakia* etc.), great diversity of suids (*Tetraconodon, Lophochoerus, propotamochoerus, Dicoryphochoerus, Conohyus, Hyppohyus, Sus*, etc.), several species of *Rhizomyoides, Mastomys, Sivacauthion, Saymys* and *Kanisayamys* rodents and several Hominoid (*Dryopithecus,Sivapithecus, Ramapithecus, Gigantopithecus* and *Pliopithecus*) and prosimian primates (*Indraloris*, and recently recovered treeshrew, *Palaeotupaia* (Chopra and Visishat, 1979). Small anthracotheres and tragulids are also readily recovered and two types of giraffids *Giraffokeryx* and *Hydaspithorium* and some more bovids (*Gazella, Pachyportax, Selenoportax, Tragocarus*, etc.) existed during Nagri times. The equid (*Hipparion*) made the first appearance in the lower Nagris and occurs quite frequently throughout the Nagri horizon. Reptilian fauna also occur but less frequently than as in Chinji. The author has also recovered gastropod (molluscs) shell and several opercula from Nagri horizon of Haritalyangar.

The fossil vertebrates, especially the mammals also reveal the preponderance of forested canopies but a considerable increase of the grassland stretches with relatively less humid climate. Tattersall (1969) and Prasad (1971) observed a mixed forests and savannah palaeoecology of the Nagri, interspersed with broad streams.Simons and Pilbeam (1972) said that climate during Nagri times was of intermediate type between Chinjis and Dhok Pathans.

The later part of the Middle Sivaliks (Dhok Pathan Formation) has yielded rather more evolved and large sized mammals with the dominance of equids (*Hipparion*), bovids (*Gazella, Boselaphus, Pachyportax, Proamphibos, Selenoportax, Tragocenus, and Taurotragus* etc.) large giraffide (*Vishnutherium* and *Hydaspitherium*) rhinocerotids (*Rhinoceros*) and prob oscideans (*Stegodon, Stegolophodon, Pentalophodon, Trilophodon* and *Tetralophodon*). Carnivores are rather fewer and are of only more evolved type (*Promellivora, Mellivorodon, Felis, Alleuropis* and *Paramachaerodus*). The only homonoid *Gigantopithecus* is known from east of Haritalyan agar area. Reptilian fossils (*Corcodilus* and *Trioenyx*) are also frequently found. The author has recovered some pelecypod (Mollusca) shalls from the Dhok

Pathan beds east of Haritalyangar and also observed at some places lignite coalveins.

The Dhok Pathan fauna speak of tremendous increase in open-country grass land and wood-land habitat with shallow streams and marshy basins and prevalence of dry and relatively cold conditions, during middle Pliocene. The forested ecozones had considerably decreased and reduced to patches. Simons and Pilbeam (1972) and Sahni and Mitra (1980) also noted a marked increase in steppe grass-lands and open country habitat with cold climate during Dhok Pathans. Lakhanpal (1978) on the basis of floral evidence showed an increase in aridity during middle Miocene to late Pliocene. However, Sivaliks showed varied sedimentary history in different sectors during Pliocene as observed in Western, Northern, north-eastern and eastern parts (Prasad, 1972; Tandon, 1972; Biswas 1963 and Biswas, 1965). Sahni and Mitra (1980) have also observed different climatic pictures ranging from tropical marshy to tropical humid and tropical dry on the basis of different micro flora during Pliocene phase.

The late Pliocene Sivaliks is denoted by theTatrot Formation, which has yielded relatively very few fossils and accordingly many palaeontologists have regarded the Tatrot as a transitory stage between the Pliocene Dhok Pathan and Pleistocene Pinjor. The Tatrot fauna are also of the intermediate type. Some Pliocene forms terminated in tatrots, viz., *Hipparion, Propotamochoerus, Potamochoerus, Pachyportax, Proamplibos, Selenoportax* and *Paramachoerodus*, whereas, other Pleistocene mammals made appearances, such as *Protashyoryetes, Nosikia, Camelus, Hyosus, Hippopotamus, Hexaprotodon, Corsus, Sivatherium, Hemibos, Sivatragus, Hyderpicobus* and *Sivaeobus*. No primate fossils are as yet known from the Tatrot Formation. The fauna suggest palaeoecology not much different from the underlying Dhok Pathans and mezic to xeric conditions.

The end of the Pliocene epoch in the Indian sub-continent was marked by growing continentality and shrinking of the Sindhu and the Bangla seas caused by the rise of the Himalayas from about 400 metres to 1,500 metres height and the onset of very cold conditions (Sahni and Mitra, 1980). The Lower

Pleistocene Sivalik deposits are extensively exposed around Pinjor-Chandigarh area and accordingly named as Pinjor Formation. These rocks are highly fossiliforous and contain modern types of mammalian fauna like European Villafranchian.The Fauna is characterized by the abundance of large mammals several elephants (*Elephas, Archidiskodon, Hypselephas, Platelephas, Stegodon*), giraffes (*Giraffa, Sivatherium*), diverse forms of cattle, antelopes, sheep and goats (*Bison, Bos, Hemibos, Leptobos, Platybos, Bubalus cobus, Hippotragus Capra, Bucapra, Sivaonyx* etc.), dears (*Cervus*, hippopotamuses (*Hippopotamus* and *Hexaprotodon*), rhinocerotids (*Rhinoceros* and *Coelodonta*), horses (*Eques*), camels (*Camelus*), pigs (*Sus, Hyposus, Hyppohys* etc.) and carnivores (*Felis, Sivafelis, Panthra, Hyaenictis, Crocuta, Canis, Agriot crium Lutra Mellivora* etc.), a few rodents (*Rhizomyoides* and *Hystrix*). Large reptiles (*Gavialis, Crocodylus* and *Trionyx*) are also recovered in considerable numbers. No hominoid primate but some cercopithecoid monkeys - *Papio, Semnipithecus, Procynocephalus* and a pongid - *Simia* are recovered from the Pinjor beds. The fauna indicates vast stretches of open country steppe grasslands and woodlands with very limited forests and very dry and cold climate.

The end of the Sivalik series is represented by deposits of huge boulders, cobbles, pebbles and conglomerates overlain on the Pinjor beds known as Boulder conglomerate formation. These huge bouldus of the rudaceous rocks were deposited by very turbulent rivers and sliding glaciers coming from the rising slopes of the Himalayas during middle Pleistocene. Boulder conglomerates are practically barren of fossils. This stage denotes a very cold phase which is largely responsible for mass extinction and migration of the fauna.

Thus we see that the Sivaliks had experienced a history of varied environmental phases ranging from warm-humid tropical forests in Miocene to relatively dry mixed forests and steppes in Pliocene and dry cold steppes terminating in glaciation in Pleistocene. The primate fossil evidence revealed that the earliest hominoid were highly diversified in the warm tropics of Miocene to early Pliocene with an apparant absence in Pliocene. The cercopithecoid monkeys made their presence at the end of the Pliocene in the dry and cold sleppes, in the sub-Himalayan region. Why hominoids/hominids are lacking in the mid to late Pliocene as well as Lower Pleistocene Sivalik deposits? Whether the hominoids/hominids had migrated elsewhere or were displaced and replaced by cerecopathecoids or conditions were not congenial for the preservation of their remains? Or the unrecovery of the hominoid/hominid primates from Plio-Pleistocene Sivalik deposits is just due to change? The various possibilities may now be discussed in view of the mammalian fossil evidence and the palaeoenvironments of the Sivaliks just reconstructed.

Many authors have believed that migration is largely responsible for the palaeoanthropological hiatus. Geologists (Sexena, 1975) have greatly emphasized tectonic earth movements of the Himalayan orogeny owing to changes in earth's magnetic poles bringing about mass catastrophy of life around last 3-4 million years. The abundant fossil remains of various kinds of vertebrates from all Sivalik horizons except from the Boulder conglomerate stage, however, suggest that environments were considerably stable and favourable, and major catastrophic changes occurred in middle Pleistocene which have much affected the quaternary Man and fauna, but obviously not the hominids during Pliocene and lower Pleistocene.

The migration and extinction of the warm tropical forest loving Miocene hominoids is just possible when the environments turned out to be dry and cold savannahs at the end of the Pliocene.The palaeoecology during Pliocene in the sub-Himalayas was however, rather mainly of the mixed sub-tropics and steppes and quite reasonably suitable for small sized semi-arboreal and large sized terrestrial hominids. Such palaeoecology was rather adaptively significant for a gradual transformation of the arboreal hominids, to terrestrial bipeds. As such, evolved hominids are very likely to have existed in the sub-Himalayas during Pliocene. Their lack in fossil records seems to be unreal and possibly due to low population/ densities of the hominids, suggested by Boaz (1979) and to their patchy distributions.

A peculiar phenomenon is displayed by the anthropoid fossil records. The hominoids had an adaptive radiation during Miocene times where cercopithecoid monkeys are not found and the latter radiated quite late in Plio-Pleistocene times when hominoids are apparently absent. (Kay, 1977) opined that corcopithecines of the present day, mirror the extant apes in adaptive zones, diet and diversity as if the cercopithecoid monkeys replaced the apes in the middle to late Miocene times. However, this situation does not comply with the fossil evidence from Sivaliks, because, so far both the hominoids as well as monkeys are unknown from the mid to late Pliocene of the Sivaliks. Moreover, the evolved terrestrial hominoids or hominids perhaps could have not been displaced and replaced by the monkeys in Pliocene.

Conditions for preservation of the skeletons of animals at a given time almost equally affect all, though smaller and gracile animals are not better preserved as the larger and robust ones. Nevertheless, conditions prior to and post fossilization, such as scavenging, transportation, drying, wetting, weathering etc. quite often destroy the unburied parts. The arboreal communities, like primates, rather rarely become part of the accumulating sediments also because the dry debris of the forest floors considerably destroy the dead animal by chemical processes. The primates especially the hominoids or hominids vested with higher capabilities, intelligence and some kind of social and cultural behaviour have lesser chances of becoming victims of the predators and natural calamities and this factor also adds to their rarity in fossil records. The Plio-Pleistocene hominids, as suggested earlier, were reduced in numbers and had pocketed distributions, which further minimizes the chances of their discovery in Sivalik rocks.

On the basis of mammalian adaptive syndrome, Geist (1979) stated that the primitive and small bodied mammals occupy the warm humid tropical forests whereas the larger and evolved forms are adapted to varied extreme climates, xeric or arutic, and open habitats. He applied the same analogy to our prehuman ancestors and said that the adaptive sydrome of the earliest hominids lived in the warm tropics and eventually evolved to the large-sized terrestrial bipedal hominids adapted in the extreme steppe climates. A similar situation may be noted from the mammalian evidences of the Sivalik series and the environmental shifts from warm forests (Miocene) to open mixed forests and grasslands (Pliocene) and dry-cold steppes in Pleistocene. As such evolved terrestrial hominids have very likely existed in the sub-Himalayan region during Pliocene to early Pleistocene times.

In view of the preceding discussion, our knowledge of the existence of the quaternary Man in sub-Himalayas as known from numerous stone tool-kits, discovered at various places in the Sivaliks, and fossil evidences of the earliest hominoids and hominids from the Mio-Pliocene Sivalik beds, there is a strong possibility that the pro-tool making hominid precursors of the Mid-Pleistocene tool maker had also survived in the sub-Himalayas and evolved to tool making man. The recovery of various sequences of the Stone-age cultural traditions of the Early Man from various glacial and integlacial deposits during Mid-Pleistocene to Holocene times in the sub-Himalayan region speak of an endemic nature of Pleistocene man in Sivaliks. The very hostile palaeogeomorphology of the Sivaliks terrain disturbed by a series of tectonic upheavals with an extremely cold climate in the region, would have avoided the penetrance of palaeolithic man into that region as an immigrant from elsewhere. The rapidly changing palaeoecology of the Sivaliks during Plio-Pleistocene times rather expedite the rapid behavioural, physiological, morphological and genetical transformation of the early hominids into Man.

Although, the physical type of the Palaeolithic man is as yet unknown in Indian sub-continent and has also frustrated the recent attempts of Kenedy (1977) to seek for this in the Pleistocene Holocene caves, yet its possibility cannot be ruled out. Saxena (1975), however, considered the possibility as remote and suggested the higher inner reaches of the Himalayas to look for early man. But, it is rather very strange to expect man to have climbed to higher snow-clad peaks of the Himalayas to face more difficult cold climate and informidable terrain.

Researches if directed to certain areas in the Sivaliks as being palaeogeogrpahically suitable for establishing open-air-camps by the palaeolithic hunting and gathering man, such as, beds of the small antecedent channels or choe terraces (Mukherjee 1975), gentle Sivalik slopes, cup shaped basins and the hiding rock-shelters in the vicinity of the antecedent water reservoirs may very likely to be rewarding.

References

Andrew, Peter and H. Tobien (1977), New Miocene Locality in Turkey with Evidence on the Origin of Ramapithecus and Sivapithecus. *Nature,* 268 : 699-701.

Biswas, B. (1963), Results of Exploration for Petroleum in the Western Part of the Bengal Basin, India. *Proc. Symp., Dev. Pet.Res. 2nd ECAEE Min. Res. Dev. Ser.* 18(1) : 241-250 (cited from Sahni and Mitra 1980).

Biswas, S. K. (1965), A New Classification of the Tertiary Rocks of Kutch, Western India. *Bull. Geol. Min. Met. Soc.* India 35(1) : 1-6, (cited from Sahni and Mitra 1980).

Boaz, Neol T. (1979), Early Hominid Population Densities: New Estimates. *Science,* 206: 592-595.

Chopra, S.R.K. (1978), New Fossil Evidence on the Evolution of Hominoidea in the Sivaliks and its Bearing on the Problem of the Evolution of Early Man in India. *J. Human Evolution,* 7(1): 3-9.

Chopra, S.R.K. and R.N.Vasisthat (1979), Sivalik Fossil Tree Shrew from Haritalyangar, India. *Nature,* 281 : 214-215.

Geist, Alerius (1978), *Life Strategies, Human Evolution, Environmental Design : Towards a Biological Theory of Health,* New York, Heidelberg, Berlin, Springer–Verlig.

Greenfield, Leonard Owen (1979), On the Adaptive Pattern of 'Ramapithecus'. *Am. J. Phys. Anthrop.,* 50 : 527-630.

Kay, R.F. (1977), Diets of Early Miocene African Hominoids, *Nature,* 268 : 628-630.

Kennedy, K.A.R. (1977), Fossil Man in India: The "Missing Link" in our Knowledge of Human Evolution in Asia. *The National Speleological Society Bulletin,* 39(9) : 99-103.

Lakhanpal, R. N. (1970), Tertiary Floras of India and their Bearing on the Historical Geology of the Region. *Taxon*, 19(5) :675-694 (cited from Sahni and Mitra 1980).

Mukherjee, A.B. (1975), The Early Man's habitat in the Sivalik Hills : Some statements on the geomorphological setting. *In Early Man in North West India* (ed. Chopra, S.R.K.) Bombay Allied Publishers. Pp. 98-106.

Nandi, B. (1975), Palynostratigraphy of the Sivalik Group of Punjab. *Himal. Geol.* 5 : 411-424.

Pilbeam, D.; J. Barry; G.Meyer; Shah; I.S.M.; M.L.H. Pickford; W.W. Bishop, H. Thomas and L.L. Jacobs (1977), Geology and Palaeontology of Neogene Strata of Pakistan. *Nature*, 270 : 684-689.

Pilbeam, D.; G. Meyer; M.D.Rose; M.H.L. Pickford. C. Badgley; A.K. Behrensmeyer and S.M. Saha (1977), New hominoid primates from the Sivalik of Pakistan and their bearing on hominoid evolution. *Nature* 270 : 689-695.

Pilbeam, D.; M.D. Rose, G. Badgley and B. Lipschutz (1980), Miocene Hominoids from Pakistan. *Postilla*. 181: 1-94.

Pilgrim, G.E. (1913), Correlation of the Sivaliks with the mammal horizons of Europe. *Rec. Geol. Surv. India*, 43 : 364-374.

Prasad, K.N. (1971), Ecology of the Fossil Hominoidea from the Sivaliks of India. *Nature* 232 : 413-414.

Prasad, K.N. (1972), Observation on the Sivalik system of India. *Rec. Geol. Surv. India*. 49(2) : 17-26.

Sahni, A. and H.C. Mitra (1980), Neogene palaeobiogeography of the Indian subcontinent with special reference to fossil vertebrates. Palaeogeography, Palaeo-climatology, *Palaeoecology*, 31 : 39-62.

Sahni, A.; B.N. Tiwari and K. Kumar (1980), A report of the occurrence of Ramapithecus punjabicus (Hominoidea) from the Uttar Pradesh Sivaliks. Abst. Proc. XI *Himal. Geol. Seminar* (Nov. 24-26, 1980) Wadia Institute of Himalayan Geology, Dehradun, India.

Saxena, M.N. (1975), The Himalayan uplift, antecedent drainage and the Elusive Fossil Man in North Western India (Memiograph). Seminar on Early Man in North Western India, Punjab University, Chandigarh, Dec. 23-24, 1975.

Simons, E.L. and D. Pilbeam (1972), "Hominoid Palaeoprimatology" in the functional and evolutionary. Biology of primates, pp. 36-70. (cited from Sahni and Mitra 1980).

Tandon, S.K. (1972), Mechanical analysis of Middle Sivalik sandstones from Ramnagar, Nainital district, Kumaun Himalayan. *J. Geol. Sec.* India 13(1): 57-58.

Tattersall, I. (1969), More on the ecology of the North Indian Ramapithecus. *Nature* 224: 821-822.

Index

F

T

U

V